Chula Vista Public Library
Chula Vista, CA 91910

W9-AMB-099

"A fun, user-friendly handbook for wannabe filmmakers with big visions but few funds."
— *Publishers Weekly*

"We never put out an actual textbook for the Corman School of Filmmaking, but if we did, it would be *Fast, Cheap and Under Control*."
— Roger Corman, Producer, New Horizons

"This book proves again and again the best lesson that Orson Welles taught me: 'The enemy of art is the absence of limitations.'"
— Henry Jaglom, director (*Hollywood Dreams, Going Shopping, Festival in Cannes, Deja Vu*)

"This book is as good as film school, and a lot less expensive. It is required reading in Tromaville!"
— Lloyd Kaufman, President of Troma Entertainment, creator of *The Toxic Avenger*

"There's something to be learned from every film in here — even those you might hate — and that's no small feat. By turns illuminating, hilarious, insightful, instructive and, oh yes, a little bit terrifying, *Fast Cheap and Under Control* should be must reading for anyone who is serious about making the best sort of film — a picture driven not by money but by passion, ingenuity and an original idea."
— Mark Gill, President, Warner Independent Pictures

"Just when you thought the low-budget film topic had been strip-mined to death, John Gaspard and his merry crew of subjects hit a whole new mother lode. His book spans the years, but in an intelligently structured way, and avoids whitewashing."
— John Pierson, author of *Spike, Mike, Slackers, & Dykes: A Guided Tour Across a Decade of American Independent Cinema* and star of *Reel Paradise*

"If this book doesn't get you making movies enthusiastically, on your own terms with your own low-budget inventions, nothing will!"
— Rick Schmidt, filmmaker/author of *Feature Filmmaking at Used-Car Prices*, *Extreme DV*, and *MovieMaker* columnist *Extreme Indie*

"I wish I'd read this book before I made *Re-Animator*."
— Stuart Gordon, director, *Re-Animator*

"A richly-detailed, highly readable and inspiring book jam-packed with information that will keep low-budget independent filmmakers from making costly mistakes. Filled with a ton-full (not a spoonful) of fascinating, insightful interviews, with a you-can-do-it approach."
— Dr. Linda Seger, script consultant, author, *Making a Good Script Great*

Chula Vista Public Library
Chula Vista, CA 91910

"Filmmakers have always been devising new and creative ways to get their films made. Gaspard puts many of these stories in wonderful context that not only provides for entertaining reading, but gives the emerging filmmaker a valuable reference to live by. An insightful and enlightening read that reaffirms the old saying, 'Where there's a will, there's a way.'"
— Daniel Myrick, co-director, *The Blair Witch Project*

"An invaluable guide to maneuvering though the obstacles of storytelling for the next wave of filmmakers."
— Griffin Dunne, director/producer/actor

"An entertaining and very informative read. It's just the ticket for beginning filmmakers, demonstrating how cleverness can count more than money in film-making."
— John Badham, director, *Saturday Night Fever, Wargames, Dracula, Isn't It Shocking*

"A perfect companion for the aspiring filmmaker, filled with filmmaking anecdotes by some of the most respected independent filmmakers around. Reading this book is like having a conversation with your favorite directors, with first-hand, practical examples of what it takes to be a filmmaker."
— Josef Steiff, author, *The Complete Idiot's Guide to Independent Filmmaking*

"John Gaspard has brought it all together, extracting lessons learned the hard way by successful indie filmmakers. *Fast, Cheap and Under Control* is an indispensable manual for those about to go into the trenches. It tells you most of what you need to know to succeed in the very risky business of putting your vision on tape or film. Write a good script, read this book, add guts and stir... and you'll be halfway there. (The other half will be in the hands of the 'film gods.')"
— William Bayer, author, *Breaking Through, Selling Out, Dropping Dead and Other Notes on Filmmaking*

"Indie filmmakers at all levels would benefit greatly by reading this incredible collection of filmmaker war stories. Part history, part instructional guide, part confessional, this is a must read for indie film fanatics."
— Chris Gore

"John's book is a valuable contribution to the growing legions of would-bes, wannabes, and should-bes of low-cost filmmaking. It teaches the best way, through example and anecdote, and is at once funny, wise, instructive and insightful. If anyone wants to turn a movie dream into a movie reality, this is one hell of a good place to start."
— Tom Pope, screenwriter, *Hammett, Lords of Discipline*; author, *Good Scripts, Bad Scripts: Learning the Craft of Screenwriting Through 25 of the Best and Worst Films in History*

"Don't even think about making a film until you have read this book!"
— William Martell, screenwriter of 18 films, *www.scriptsecrets.net*

"This book is a fascinating look at the practical, behind-the-scenes knowledge required in the making of low-budget films; but most important, it's an inspiration for filmmakers and filmmakers-to-be to continue the struggle to achieve their dreams."
— Mark Borchardt, *American Movie: The Making of Northwestern*

"*Fast, Cheap and Under Control* is not only a wonderfully written presentation of the essential rules for making low-budget films; it's also a book filled with riveting stories of how a wildly diverse group of filmmakers, with very little money and an abundance of passion, determination and courage, got their movies on the screen."
— Michael Hauge, Hollywood script consultant and author of *Writing Screenplays That Sell*

"Every year I see hundreds of films that make mistakes that could have been avoided if the filmmaker had only read this book."
— Hopwood DePree, co-founder, Waterfront Film Festival

"Before you even think about picking up a camera, pick up this book. Better to know the pitfalls than fall into them yourself."
— Sheryl Mousley, curator of film/video, Walker Art Center

"In *Fast, Cheap and Under Control*, John Gaspard provides a guided tour through the jungle of low-budget filmmaking, helping the reader see where avoidable mistakes are lurking in the tall grass, and helping them evade the myriad whirlpools and eddies that can destroy budgets. It's full of first-hand perspectives and on-point case studies that illuminate a mystical process and make it seem almost logical. Almost. Any budget-conscious filmmaker would be well advised to read this very valuable book."
— Thomas F. Lieberman, executive producer, *Sweet Land*

"The only thing more fun than being on one of John Gaspard's indie film sets is reading one of John Gaspard's indie filmmaking books. *Fast, Cheap and Under Control*, his best to date, contains anecdotes from indies that are fonts of information, equal parts funny, frightening and fascinating. I will read this book during preproduction of every film I ever make from now on. Indispensable."
— Patrick Coyle, writer/director, *Detective Fiction*

"*Fast, Cheap and Under Control* is a worthy addition to MWP's invaluable line of how-to guides for the independent filmmaker. Author Gaspard's assemblage of successful filmmaking talent and the lessons they share will save you time, money and headaches."
— Barbara Peterson, editor and publisher of *The Thunder Child: The Journal of Science Fiction* web magazine, non-fiction book reviewer for Associated Content

"Part reference book, part how-to guide, Mr. Gaspard's book gets to the heart of independent guerilla film-making. It has something for everyone — from the casual film fan to the next great film director. An amazing book and an amazing look into the world of low-budget filmmaking. If you have camera in hand, read this book first. It will save you a lot of time, energy and heart-ache."
   — Matthew Terry, screenwriter/teacher, Seattle Central Community College, columnist for *Hollywoodlitsales.com*

"A testament to the innovation of the independent spirit, *Fast, Cheap and Under Control* inspires new adaptation and creation in the low-budget world by using historical examples to allow us to learn from the successes of the past while avoiding their mistakes. By tapping into the heritage of filmmaking, John Gaspard reminds current no-budget filmmakers that they are not alone and encourages newcomers to make the leap and tell their stories!"
   — Jeremy Hanke, editor, *Microfilmmaker* Magazine (*microfilmmaker.com*)

"Tells one great story after another, all focused on noted directors' unique ways of coping with small budgets and lack of experience. The emphasis on prepro-duction is superb; so too is the encouragement to use available resources and make the film you can and must make. I love the readability (I couldn't stop), the sense and clarity of suggestions. I also applaud tying the practical advice to specific and diverse films. The breadth and depth give *Fast, Cheap and Under Control* a usefulness well beyond the entertainment value of reading the case studies."
   — Diane Carson, Ph.D., Editorial VP of University Film & Video Association

FAST
CHEAP
AND UNDER
CONTROL

LESSONS LEARNED FROM THE GREATEST LOW-BUDGET MOVIES OF ALL TIME

JOHN GASPARD

MICHAEL WIESE PRODUCTIONS

...ed by Michael Wiese Productions
...Ventura Boulevard
...21
...ty, CA 91604
(818) 379-8799, (818) 986-3408 (FAX).
mw@mwp.com
www.mwp.com

Cover design by MWP
Interior design by William Morosi
Copyedited by Paul Norlen
Printed by McNaughton & Gunn

Manufactured in the United States of America
Copyright 2006 John Gaspard
All rights reserved. No part of this book may be reproduced in any form or by any means without permission in writing from the author, except for the inclusion of brief quotations in a review.

Library of Congress Cataloging-in-Publication Data

Gaspard, John, 1958-
  Fast, cheap, and under control : lessons from the greatest low-budget movies / John Gaspard.
     p. cm.
  Includes bibliographical references.
  ISBN 1-932907-15-7
  1. Motion pictures--Production and direction. 2. Low budget motion pictures. I. Title.
  PN1995.9.P7G374 2006
  791.4302'3--dc22
                                        2006003504

CHULA VISTA PUBLIC LIBRARY

3 3650 01722 91

For my lovely wife, Amy,
who watched all the movies,
loved most of them,
and made the entire process not only possible,
but also a pleasure.

CONTENTS

ACKNOWLEDGMENTS

First, thanks to Errol Morris, whose great documentary, *Fast, Cheap & Out of Control*, inspired this book's bastardized title. If I ever do a book on the lessons you can learn from the greatest documentaries of all time, his work will rank up there with the best of the best of the best.

I'd also like to express my thanks to the many directors, producers, writers, actors and crew people who graciously spoke with me about their low-budget films and the lessons they took away from them:

Stefan Avalos, Michael Bleiden, L.M. Kit Carson, Roger Corman, Alan Cumming, Greg Cummins, Mark Decena, Griffin Dunne, Edie Falco, Jon Favreau, Jonathan Gordon, William Greaves, Rance Howard, Henry Jaglom, John Jenkins, Chris Kentis, Laura Kirk, Adam LeFevre, Jim McBride, Eric Mendelsohn, Nancy Morgan, David Burton Morris, Daniel Myrick, Tom Noonan, Dan O'Bannon, Bob Odenkirk, Steven Soderbergh, Barbara Steele, Lance Weiler, and Gary Winick.

And special thanks to their assistants, receptionists, secretaries, agents, publicists, handlers and managers who scheduled the interviews and made them happen.

Dale Newton, Daniel Berks, David Garfield, Tom Lieberman, John Jansen and Matthew G. Anderson would be surprised if I didn't acknowledge their contributions to this book. No surprises here — thanks, guys!

And finally, thanks to Amelia Oriani, for her patient and thorough copy-editing and proofreading.

INTRODUCTION

*"Those who cannot remember the past are condemned to repeat it ...
This is the condition of children and barbarians, in which instinct has
learned nothing from experience."*
                                    George Santayana
                                    The Life of Reason, Volume 1, 1905

Don't take this wrong, but our friend Mr. Santayana could have been
referring to many independent filmmakers when he penned those famous
words.

Over the years I've come to believe that some independent filmmakers
are, on occasion, a bit *too* independent for their own good.

They insist upon taking what they believe to be the road less traveled,
when a quick glance down at all the footprints surrounding them would
reveal that many others have hiked that same path and made all the
same errors they're about to make — and a few more to boot.

Now, I don't want to start this off with a rant. I'm all for artistic
expression and singularity of vision. I just don't see a need for every
generation of filmmakers to re-invent the wheel, when the previous
generations did a fine job on the wheel and came up with the pulley
and lever in the bargain.

Other filmmakers — with as little money, as little time, and just as many
pressures as you'll be facing — have achieved remarkable feats in the
low-budget arena. They overcame the same problems you'll be facing,
and some that you could never have imagined.

The filmmakers profiled in this book learned from their experiences,
and there's no reason why you shouldn't benefit from their education.

That's the purpose of this book.

Each of the thirty-three movies highlighted here offer a handful of lessons, ranging from nuts-and-bolts concerns to larger issues of methodology and philosophy.

Some of the films and the filmmakers are household names. Others may be unfamiliar to you. But they all overcame the odds, got their vision on film or tape, and learned some important lessons in the process.

"There's not a day that goes by when I'm working on a film that I don't draw upon something I learned making my first one, Grand Theft Auto.*"*

Ron Howard

That statement from Ron Howard, made almost in passing on the commentary track of the *Grand Theft Auto* DVD, was the starting point for this book.

It got me to thinking, if someone as successful as Ron Howard learned lessons on his low-buck Corman classic that he's still using today, what other lessons are just waiting to be unearthed from similar small-budget gems?

As it turns out, quite a few.

There's considerable wisdom to be found in these pages, and I can say that without blushing, because very little of it is mine.

The lessons you're about to learn come from the mouths of the filmmakers themselves. Some lessons might seem obvious to you. Others may set off a series of light bulbs over your head, in a sort of domino effect as you connect their problem with your problem and suddenly realize a solution you hadn't considered.

You may find some lessons that simply don't apply in your universe. And other lessons that flat-out contradict each other. Such is the pluralistic nature of filmmaking.

In the end, however, most film productions are more alike than they are different and I think you'll be surprised by what you can take away from these low-budget classics.

The process of re-watching these movies, chatting with many of the filmmakers, and assembling these varied thoughts has certainly re-energized my interest in the world of low-budget production.

And having the rare opportunity to talk, one-on-one, with some of my filmmaking heroes was certainly a highlight of the process.

For example, nothing beats the experience of calling Roger Corman's company, saying I was calling for a scheduled interview with Mr. Corman, and then hearing the words, "Call me Roger. What can I do for you?"

Or chatting by phone with Henry Jaglom as he drove through snarled Los Angeles traffic ... or with Alan Cumming as he walked his dog through the noisy streets of Manhattan ... or with Edie Falco as she spoke softly, trying to get her new baby to fall asleep during the interview.

In those instances when I couldn't get on a filmmaker's schedule, I've gathered their thoughts from other extant sources, cutting and pasting the best of the best. And, rather than overload the book with footnotes, I've assembled all the sources in the Notes section in the back for easy reference.

Feel free to be as non-linear as you like in reading this book. You can read from the beginning ... or start with the movies you already know ... or dive into a movie you've never heard about.

Whether you read in a linear or non-linear fashion, you'll find that a handful of lessons are repeated throughout the book, a few with dogged consistency. These repetitions are intentional, as I found that many filmmakers learned the same lesson for different reasons.

For example, the reason Henry Jaglom follows the "Family and Friends Plan" is worlds away from why Darren Aronofsky subscribes to that notion. And the lessons learned about endings (All's Well That Ends Well) by the filmmakers of *Clerks* and *The Last Broadcast* are as different as ... well, as different as *Clerks* and *The Last Broadcast*.

So, if you want to compare how different filmmakers solved the same problem, refer to Chapter Eight (The Lessons Redux), which cross-indexes all the lessons.

I've had nothing but fun putting all this information together and I know my next movie will be better for all the ideas I've had the opportunity to sift through within these pages. I hope you find it beneficial as well.

Now, stop reading this fluff and get to the meat!

Chapter One

CORMAN & COMPANY

No one in Hollywood has launched bigger directing careers on smaller budgets than Roger Corman. In addition to the directors profiled in this chapter (Coppola, Bogdanovich, Demme and Howard), Corman can also lay claim to providing solid starts for the likes of Martin Scorsese, James Cameron, Joe Dante, Paul Bartel, John Sayles and others.

Most only worked with Corman once or twice. "You work with Roger until he can't afford you anymore," Sayles explained.

Be that as it may, Corman practiced what he preached. The low-budget techniques he insisted his directors follow were all based on his own experience behind the camera, and he has generously provided those lessons to several generations of filmmakers.

THE LITTLE
SHOP OF HORRORS

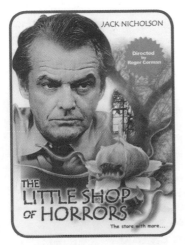

There are very few people in the movie business who are, quite literally, legendary.

Know this: Roger Corman is legendary.

Consider the following small sampling of Corman stories that have been told and re-told over the years:

• His first movie as producer, *The Monster from the Ocean Floor*, cost $12,000 in cash, and went on to make a profit of $100,000. It was shot in six days. The original title for the film was *It Stalked the Ocean Floor*, but "the title was changed," Corman said, "because the distributors felt it was too cerebral."

• For another early film, *Five Guns West*, he devised a story about five men whose job it was to head West, but they had to avoid being spotted by the Indians along the way. This story structure allowed Corman to buy stock shots of Indians riding past, which he then intercut with shots of his actors watching them, providing more production value (but not a lot more cost) for his small-budget western.

• Corman is known for always carrying an airline pilot's handbook, so he can check weather patterns and determine if a location is a good bet for a rain-free shoot. He offered weather advice to Francis Ford Coppola before that director started shooting *Apocalypse Now* in the Philippines. Coppola ignored the advice and his movie was shut down by a brutal rainy season.

• For his movie *Atlas*, which he shot in Greece, Corman paid for five hundred soldiers but only fifty showed up. Undaunted, he altered his big battle scene and re-staged it as a hand-to-hand battle, allowing him to shoot tight shots and disguise his lack of extras.

He then added some dialogue for the military leader, who declared that his theory of warfare was that a small band of efficient, dedicated, highly trained warriors could defeat any sized army. In his autobiography, Corman referred to this speech as his theory of filmmaking.

• He achieved his personal best number of camera set-ups — seventy-seven — in one day on the film *The Viking Women and the Sea Serpent*. Shots were set up so quickly that, according to actress Abby Dalton, "one of the Viking girls in the background raced through a shot with her sunglasses on. No one even noticed."

Fast. Cheap. And *mostly* under control.

Roger Corman knows how to make a movie for a buck, and he has passed that knowledge on to several generations of filmmakers, while at the same time helping some of the biggest Hollywood directors begin their careers.

"I think it's a worthwhile thing to help a young person of some talent get his start in films," Corman said. "It's enjoyable and stimulating, and I generally have made money at it."

One of the greatest examples of the Corman filmmaking philosophy at work is his film *The Little Shop of Horrors*. It was shot over two days (under the working title, *The Passionate People Eater*), using existing sets, followed by a couple nights of second unit photography.

The Little Shop of Horrors, the story of florist Seymour Krelboin and his man-eating plant, Audrey Junior, is an early black comedy most notable for a way-over-the-top performance by Jack Nicholson as a far-too-willing dental patient.

The story was later adapted as an off-Broadway musical and then a movie musical; however, lyricist Howard Ashman wisely changed the plant's name to Audrey Two, recognizing that there are actually very few interesting words that rhyme with "junior." He did give it a shot, though, in one song rhyming "junior" with "petunia." You see what he was up against.

"It was done partially as an experiment," Corman said of *Little Shop*. "It succeeded, and then I went back to a normal style of shooting, because you really can do better work with a little more time.

"I sacrificed too much by shooting that fast," Corman admitted. "For instance, I was using two cameras simultaneously, photographing from two different angles. If two people were talking, I'd have a close-up on one person and a close-up on the other."

In order to get coverage from two cameras simultaneously, Corman was forced to employ a bland lighting style, a compromise he doesn't recommend.

"Because it was a comedy-horror film, you could use flat lighting," he said, "but the lighting clearly suffered. In any other type of film, the bad lighting would have hurt the film."

Despite the fact that *The Little Shop of Horrors* was something of an anomaly for Corman, it does provide a number of key lessons — one of which was that Corman would never again shoot a movie that quickly.

"I did it almost as a joke," he said, "simply to see if I could do it. When I finished, Bob Towne, who is a good friend of mine, said, 'You should remember, Roger, making films is not like a track meet. It's not how fast you go.' And I said, 'You're right, Bob. I'll never make a two-day picture again.'"

REHEARSE

How much value does Roger Corman place on rehearsing? Consider the following statement about preproduction on *The Little Shop of Horrors*:

"You can hire an actor by the day or by the week," Corman explained. "But hiring an actor by the day is more expensive, so I hired all of the actors for one week, and we rehearsed Monday-Tuesday-Wednesday, and then shot Thursday-Friday."

Let's do the math. He is paying the actors for five days' work, yet he puts them in front of the camera for only two of those days, opting to use the majority of his time to rehearse.

Clearly, Corman found value in rehearsing. In fact, rehearsing is just the beginning of his preparation process, all designed to keep things moving while saving money.

BE PREPARED

If Roger Corman has a mantra, it's "Be Prepared."

"I'm a strong believer in preproduction and preparation," he said. "I want to be able to come onto the set and shoot.

"Ideally, everything is worked out in advance. Practically, it never quite works that way. You always are faced with new problems, or maybe you get a better idea. But at least you have your framework before you shoot.

"On a ten-day shoot, or a twenty-day shoot," he continued, "you don't have time to create from scratch on the set. As a matter of fact, I don't think you should do that anyway.

"My number one rule is to work with your actors in advance, so you and the actors are agreed on at least the broad outline of the performance. Then to have sketched out, if not all of your shots, most of your shots, so you have a shot plan in advance."

Despite his seeming fanaticism about preparation, Corman is the first one to advocate changing your plans if a better idea arises.

"Be flexible," he advised. "Even though you've done all your preparation, don't stick absolutely to the preparation if it doesn't seem to be working. Know that you've got the preparation, but situations change, so be prepared to change with the situations."

In short, strike a balance between having a plan and recognizing when circumstances suggest that the plan should be altered.

"I'm a believer in both instinct and preparation," Corman explained. "I think you have to go in prepared and then you have to be able to throw away your preparation, if something better occurs.

"But if you go in just with the vague hope that something brilliant will happen on the spot, you could be in a lot of trouble."

BUT WE'RE JUST A STUDENT FILM, OFFICER

There's a tendency among independent filmmakers to try to make their productions seem bigger than they actually are, such as printing up fancy letterhead and trying to look like a mini-major.

Corman advocates heading in the exact opposite direction: Think (and look) small. His reasoning?

"If you're young and starting, you get a tremendous amount of help," he said. "I was still claiming to be a student filmmaker ten years after I was making films. Don't bypass that; don't get into the trap of trying to say, 'If I pretend I'm from Metro, I'll be accepted better.' Go the other way and say, 'I've got a little amount of money, and I'm trying to get started.' In general, people will be glad to help you."

Although he did use the student film excuse for years, time (and graying hair) eventually required him to provide a new version of the story. "When I was young, I said we were all students, and we were able to get by with it. A little later, as I got older, I said I was the teacher and everyone else was the student."

KEEP MOVING

If time is money, and Corman's goal is to save as much money as possible, you'd think that he'd want to save as much time as possible. And you'd be right.

That's why he advocates keeping things moving on the set — really moving. Hopping, actually. As soon as you're happy with a take, move to the next set-up. And then the next. And the next. And the next. And don't dawdle between any of these steps.

"You waste a lot of time after you get a shot, where you're congratulating everybody, discussing the shot, and so forth," he said. "And that shot is already yesterday's news. You've got it.

"So what I do is I say, 'Cut, print, thank you.' Then maybe one sentence saying how good it was to the actors. And then, 'The next shot is over here.' And we're on to the next shot."

WRITE TO YOUR RESOURCES

The final lesson from *The Little Shop of Horrors* is one of scale, of understanding — and exploiting — the resources you have on hand. Or, to paraphrase *Dirty Harry*, a filmmaker's gotta know his limitations.

One of the key reasons *Little Shop* works as well as it does is that it was designed for the budget Corman had. He didn't overreach with his expectations, and at the same time he made sure that all the money (what there was of it) made it to the screen.

"I've been quoted as saying 'Make the most of what you've got,'" he said, "which I would translate as 'Use what you have around you.'"

"I've found from experience that working with low budgets, you're better off taking the elements at hand to make the best low-budget film you can, rather than taking your money and trying to pretend to make a big-budget film.

"I think you're more likely to fail doing that and I think you have a greater chance of success if you recognize the limitations of your budget, your schedule and so forth, and try to work within those limitations.

"I feel that any script can be made for any budget," he continued, "but the result will be somewhat different. You can make *Doctor Zhivago* in six days for fifty thousand dollars, but it's going to look somewhat different. I feel you're better not to try to make a spectacle on a low budget. You're better trying to work in depth on a subject that lends itself to your budget."

In short, be realistic about what you can achieve, and then put all your efforts into doing the best job possible. And realize that many of the limitations you may face have been faced, and overcome, by Corman.

"I'd like to have unlimited time, unlimited budget," he admitted, "but it has not worked out that way. So there's no point in fighting the fact that you've got three weeks to make a picture, and there's no point in spending half of three weeks bemoaning the fact that you've only got three weeks.

"You simply go out and do your best shot in three weeks."

DEMENTIA 13

||||||||||||||||||||||||||||||||||||||||||||||||||||||||||||||||||||||||||||||||||||||

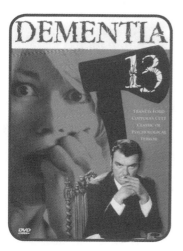

"You're stepping off a cliff when you start to make a film."

Francis Ford Coppola

Given the impressive list of filmmakers who got their start with Roger Corman, it's clear that the man has an eye for talent. And, when it came to Francis Ford Coppola, Corman got an eyeful.

"Francis came to me as a film editor out of UCLA film school and then advanced rapidly," Corman recalled. "He is one of the most brilliant all-around filmmakers I have ever met. When I say all-around, I mean that not only can he write and direct, but he can also edit, function as cameraman, and do almost every job connected with filmmaking."

The first assignment Corman gave Coppola was hardly auspicious. "I had bought the American rights to two Russian science fiction films," Corman said, "which had wonderful special effects, but they were filled with outrageous anti-American propaganda. And so I hired Francis to re-edit those films, and delete the anti-American propaganda.

"And then he went along and worked with me on several films as my assistant, particularly on a Grand Prix Formula One race car picture called *The Young Racers*, in which we traveled from track to track."

In order to make that traveling throughout Europe and England possible, Coppola turned his inventive mind to a prototype of a design he would employ through much of his career — the mobile studio.

"Francis and our key grip built racks and various compartments into a Volkswagen microbus," Corman explained, "so that the microbus was actually a traveling small studio. We used that, with a crew of six or seven professionals, and then we would hire local people.

"When the picture was finished, I had to go back to do a picture in the United States, but it occurred to me we had efficiently functioning crew and everything in the microbus, so we could stay and do another picture."

That was when Coppola stepped forward with a bright idea.

MAKE YOUR OWN OPPORTUNITIES

"The secret of all my getting things off the ground is that I've always taken big chances," Coppola said. "We were in Ireland with a movie crew that was just begging to be utilized. While the other guys my age were all pleading, 'Roger, let me make a film,' I simply sat down and wrote a script."

At the same time, Coppola also connected with an English producer, told him the script idea and sold him the rights to the as-yet-unmade film.

"Essentially, I sold the English rights for a movie which did not exist," recalled Coppola. "And with the $20,000 he paid me and the $20,000 Roger put up, I was able to direct my first feature film — based on a script it had taken me three nights to write."

Corman was impressed, as much with the script as with the chutzpah of the would-be filmmaker himself.

"He came up with a very interesting idea for *Dementia 13*," Corman recalled. "It was a very interesting psychological suspense story. We took one idea from Hitchcock, which was that the leading lady would die early in the film, just as she did in *Psycho*. I always thought that was great, because nobody ever expects the leading lady to die halfway through the film!"

Utilizing a few cast members from *The Young Racers* and a studio provided for free by his English backer, Coppola shot the film in nine days, with the addition of some pick-up shots that he grabbed later in Los Angeles' Griffith Park, which stood in for the picturesque Irish countryside.

The result is an interesting, if oblique, film that benefits from a cast that is stronger than the script. *Dementia 13* is probably best known today as the movie in *American Graffiti* that the kids are watching at the drive-in, which is fitting, as it never strives to be anything more than a scary popcorn picture.

"The film was meant to be an exploitation film, a *Psycho*-type film," Coppola explained. "*Psycho* was a big hit and William Castle had just made *Homicidal* and Roger always makes pictures that are like other pictures. So it was meant to be a horror film with a lot of people getting killed with axes and so forth."

Despite its exploitive beginnings, Coppola looks back fondly on his first feature. "I think it showed promise," he said. "It was imaginative. It wasn't totally cliché after cliché. Very beautiful visuals. In many ways, it had some of the nicest visuals I've ever done."

Coppola acknowledged that the film got made due to his willingness to do *whatever* was necessary to break into directing — a willingness that he finds lacking in many of today's would-be directors.

"I meet a lot of young filmmakers, because I'm interested in them," he said. "And they're all very lazy. They come and they want you to pay them to write the scripts. The first job I did for Roger I was paid $250 and I worked six months for that $250. No one's willing to do that anymore. I would have done anything. That's the difference.

"Roger was always straight with you," Coppola continued. "He never gave you any false hope. He was always very precise about what you were going to get and do. It was a fabulous opportunity for someone like me — it was better than money."

TARGETS

||||||||||||||||||||||||||||||||||||||||||||||||||||||||||||||||||||||||||||||||||||||

Roger Corman doesn't like to waste anything. So when he discovered that a famous horror actor owed him a couple days' work, he wasn't about to let that opportunity slip away.

Enter Peter Bogdanovich.

Like Francis Ford Coppola, Bogdanovich got his start in filmmaking by working as an assistant to Corman, who recognized talent when he saw it.

"Peter had a great knowledge of film," Corman recalled. "He had written some added scenes for me on previous pictures, and directed some second unit, so I was aware of his ability as a second unit director and his ability as a writer. I had the feeling that he had talent."

Corman trusted that feeling and gave Bogdanovich a typically Corman-esque assignment:

"As a result of various complications in a contract," Corman explained, "Boris Karloff owed me several days' work.

"I said, 'Here's the problem: The picture must star Boris Karloff, but he can only work for these days.' And Peter came up with the idea of Boris as an actor doing a traditional horror film, and in that way we could take some footage out of some of the horror films that Boris had done for me before, and also cut away and tell a parallel story."

That parallel story involves a young man who calmly shoots his family and then heads to a drive-in and starts picking off patrons.

The two storylines converge when Karloff arrives at the drive-in for the premiere of his new movie (which, in the funhouse-mirror world of *Targets*, was directed by a character played by director Peter Bogdanovich).

Corman was thrilled with the results of Bogdanovich's work, calling it "one of the best debut films of any of the directors I've worked with."

Critics weren't quite as effusive, with Roger Ebert opining, "*Targets* isn't a very good film, but it is an interesting one."

The truth, as is often the case, lies somewhere in between. However, Bogdanovich's debut provides a number of sharp lessons on how to make a movie for not much money.

SOUND THINKING

Bogdanovich had to move fast to get all the sequences that he and his then-wife, Polly Platt (with some additional, uncredited work by director Sam Fuller) had put in their script. And one of the ways that he kept moving was shooting without sound whenever possible.

Long sections of the film — in particular, a lengthy sequence atop a large gas storage tank, which the sniper climbs on to terrorize freeway drivers below — were shot silent, with all the sound added in postproduction. Although this made editing the film more complicated, it was far cheaper than the time it would have taken to get great images and great sound on location.

The terrific sound editing on these sequences was done by Verna Fields, who went on to edit Bogdanovich's *What's Up, Doc?* and another little movie called *Jaws*, among others.

Corman agreed with Bogdanovich's solution. "The one thing you can't replace is the image," Corman said. "So if you have a sound problem that is going to hold you up in any way, I very often will shoot knowing I will work with the sound later, because the sound you can create away from the set. You can't create the image for the film anywhere but on the set."

LONG TAKES

Bogdanovich is a big fan of long, continuous takes (check out *Paper Moon* to see some of his most virtuoso extended shots).

While long takes can be fun, it's a dangerous habit to get into in the low-budget world. They can burn up a lot of time (and film) and often leave you with very few editing options. Such was the case with one long take in *Targets*.

The scene, which runs five minutes, follows our young sniper during a typical evening at home. His parents are watching TV, his wife is getting ready for work. He follows her from the TV room to the bedroom, then back to the TV room. After saying good night to his parents as they head off to bed, he continues to watch TV, then goes to bed himself.

When it came time to put the shot into the movie, it was just too long, with no obvious way to make it shorter. Then Bogdanovich realized that the actor playing the sniper was sitting relatively still during the last 40 seconds of the take, while he sat alone watching TV before getting up and leaving the room.

Bogdanovich was able to do a jump cut on the motionless actor, taking 30 seconds out of the shot and getting to the end of the scene faster.

When asked about this sequence and long takes in general, Corman was philosophical. "It goes a little bit against my rules," he admitted, "but on the other hand, all rules are made to be broken.

"I do like to get coverage," he continued, "to get as many shots as possible. Yet, at the same time, when you're on a very tight schedule, sometimes you have to sacrifice coverage. And when you do that, sometimes you can make a virtue out of necessity."

EXPLOIT THE UNIQUE

Bogdanovich recognized that he had a rare opportunity with Karloff, who was one of the most recognizable and beloved horror stars of that or any other generation.

To that end, he created many opportunities for Karloff to tweak his film persona in the movie (such as having the actor be startled by his own image in a mirror).

But his best use of Karloff's unique talents was in a short scene where the aging actor tells a scary story to some visitors. Bogdanovich had recently seen Karloff's rendition of Dr. Seuss' *How the Grinch Stole Christmas*, and realized that Karloff's storytelling style could be put to use in *Targets* as well.

The story he recounts, from W. Somerset Maugham's 1933 play, *Sheppey*, is a chilling tale, made all the more so by Karloff's unique style of delivery:

There was a merchant in Bagdad who sent his servant to market to buy provisions.

In a little while the servant came back, white and trembling and said, "Master, just now when I was in the marketplace I was jostled by a woman in the crowd and when I turned I saw it was Death that jostled me. She looked at me and made a threatening gesture; now, lend me your horse, and I will ride away from this city and avoid my fate. I will go to Samarra and there death will not find me."

The merchant lent him his horse, and the servant mounted it, and he dug his spurs in its flanks and as fast as the horse could gallop he went.

Then the merchant went down to the marketplace and he saw Death standing in the crowd and he came to Death and said, "Why did you make a threatening gesture to my servant when you saw him this morning?"

"That was not a threatening gesture," Death said, "it was only a start of surprise. I was astonished to see him in Bagdad, for I had an appointment with him tonight in Samarra."

It's a highlight of the film, and a great use of Karloff's talent.

POVERTY BREEDS CREATIVITY

Many filmmakers would feel constrained by the limited budget and tight timeframe of a Corman picture, but Bogdanovich saw a real creative virtue in not having much time or money.

"I think," he said, "there's nothing better than being told, 'Look, you've got to do it in three days; you've only got this much money, and do it, kid, or you're not going to get it done.'

"You should have a kind of pressure making movies, that sense of economy. In the old days at Coumbia, for years, they wouldn't let you print more than one take. Now, sometimes that's good."

CAGED HEAT

IIIIIIIIIIIIIIIIIIIIIIIIIIIIIIIIIIIIIIIIIIIIIIIIIIIIIIIIIIIIIIIIIIIIIIIIIIIIIIIIIIIIIIIIIIIIIIIIIIIIIIIII

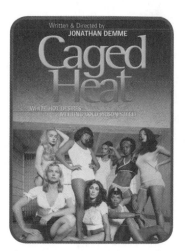

By the time Jonathan Demme got the opportunity to direct his first feature in 1974, the rules of what constituted a "Roger Corman Picture" had been rigidly codified.

Director Jonathan Kaplan, who also worked for Corman around that time, explained the formula this way: "There was a male sexual fantasy to be exploited, comedic subplot, action/violence, and a slightly-to-the-left-of-center subplot. Those were the four elements that were required. And then frontal nudity from the waist up and total nudity from behind and no pubic hair and get the title of the picture somewhere into the film and go to work. And that was essentially it."

Demme's opportunity to work within those guidelines came about in stages, first doing publicity for Corman, and then moving up to more hands-on responsibilities.

"After I did publicity," Demme remembered, "Corman said, 'Why don't you write a bike movie?' Joe Viola and I worked on it and arranged to drop off the script.

"As we were walking away, Roger called us back; he said, 'Joe, you've directed commercials; why don't you direct the movie for me? And Jonathan, you've produced commercials; why don't you produce the movie?' That became *Angels Hard As They Come.*"

Demme went on to handle second unit directing duties on a couple of pictures, which Corman believed was an ideal way to assess a potential director's abilities. "I've always liked the idea of a new director shooting some second unit," Corman explained. "He gets a feel for what's going on, and I get a chance to judge what he can do."

Demme successfully demonstrated his skill behind the camera, and Corman rewarded him with his first feature: the women-in-prison classic, *Caged Heat*.

"We had done *The Big Doll House*, *The Big Bird Cage*, *The Big Bust Out*," Corman reasoned, "and I felt we'd had enough Big, we had to go to something else. Jonathan had been a writer, producer, and second unit director, and it was his turn."

For Demme, a movie about women in prison was an appealing topic. "Ever since my days working with Roger Corman, and perhaps before that," Demme once said, "I've been a sucker for a women's picture. A film with a woman protagonist at the forefront. A woman in jeopardy. A woman on a mission. These are themes that have tremendous appeal to me as a moviegoer and also as a director."

Demme was also attracted to the political statement he could make with the film, which meshed perfectly with Corman's penchant for left-leaning causes. "Roger is a real, sincere bleeding heart," Demme said. "He wants his films to have some sort of liberal slant to them, and he means it."

Before his first day on the set, Demme was treated to a legendary tradition for new directors — a pre-shoot lunch with Corman himself, a ritual that has taken on mythic proportions.

"The Lunch," Demme explained, "is where in the course of about an hour and a half (because time is money, too), you get what is, as far as I'm concerned, the equivalent of four years in film school, just machine gun. The rules and regulations of how to make a very interesting film from a directorial point of view. So it was a spectacular moment in my life as a filmmaker to be able to spend that time. He even picked up the check!"

Demme also relished the relative freedom that Corman bestowed on his directors ... up to a point.

"Having made sure that you accepted the rules of how to make a Corman movie," Demme recounted, "Roger then gave you an enormous amount of freedom to go ahead and do it.

"It wasn't until you started diverging from the formula, or from the approach, or — God forbid — went a moment over schedule, that you heard from him. And, of course, if you did stray from any of the pre-agreed conventions of making Corman movies, then you heard from him in no uncertain terms."

For his part, despite his obvious affection for Demme and pride in the work he's done since *Caged Heat*, Corman takes only a modicum of credit for Demme's subsequent success.

"Jonathan learned from us and then went beyond," Corman said. "I don't want to take any credit whatsoever for the good work he's doing. He's doing it because he himself is a talented and hardworking man. But we may have helped to some extent."

BE DIFFERENT

Although Corman had produced a number of successful women-in-prison films up to that point, he felt that the genre was due for a little shaking-up, and that Demme was just the man to do it. As he would prove again in his later films, Demme has the rare ability to take what might be a traditional, formula film and inject something different into its DNA.

"I'd always felt a little uneasy about these pictures," Corman admitted. "They were incredibly successful, but I'd never really liked the tone of some of them.

"So, knowing that Jonathan was a very good writer, I said, 'Jonathan, isn't there any way we can turn this around a little bit?' And he wrote a very, very good script, which was ironic and funny and satirical, but still delivered the violence and the little bit of R-rated sex that had to be in it."

With *Caged Heat*, Demme successfully turned the women-in-prison film on its ear, with smart characters, strong social commentary, and a distinct point of view, all seamlessly woven into the fabric of the traditional kick-ass genre. Corman, for one, was pleased with the result.

"He made a really good picture that did what I asked him to do," Corman said. "It delivered the elements that the audience who wanted to see that kind of picture would come to see, yet at the same time there was an edge, a coldly humorous look at the film itself."

CONSIDER CAMEOS

Demme took to heart another piece of important advice from Corman, which led to a brilliant casting decision for *Caged Heat* and an important lesson about the value of cameos and how to make them attractive.

"Another thing Corman had said was," Demme remembered, "'Your villain has to be the most fascinating, if not likeable, person in the piece. Notice how *Psycho* worked so effectively. Really pay attention to these things.'"

Demme did pay attention. While that advice would resurface most stunningly with Hannibal Lecter in *Silence of the Lambs*, Demme created a villain for *Caged Heat* — Superintendent McQueen — who was strong enough to attract some name talent to the project.

Corman was delighted with the idea. "He changed the evil warden into a crazy woman," Corman said, "played by Barbara Steele, and she was wonderful.

"She had grown a couple of years too old to be a leading lady," Corman continued, "but she was still a beautiful woman who was a good actress with a striking face and figure, and Jonathan said she would be great as an evil prison warden, and I said you are absolutely right."

Writing a small but attractive part for a known actor is a smart way to get some name value into your movie, assuming of course the performer falls in love with the part and is willing to cut their rate for the project. That is, as long as you don't freak them out too much when you approach them.

"That was just an amazing, bizarre moment in time," Steele recalled. "I was walking down Sunset Boulevard. Nobody walks in L.A. anyway, so it was kind of a feat to be walking anywhere.

"This vast blue car with fins from another era pulled up and out jumped this guy with this really radiant smile and he said, "Barbara Steele! Barbara Steele!!'

"And I said, 'Hello? Yes?' And he said, 'I'm about to make a movie, I've been looking for you everywhere, would you consider doing it? We start shooting in three days! Please say yes, please say yes!' And that was *Caged Heat*."

Barbara Steele as Superintendent McQueen

For Steele, the budget wasn't really an issue. "I'd done so many low-budget movies," she explained, "but of course most of them were in Europe. It was slightly different doing low-budget movies in Italy as opposed to doing them here, because in Italy there is an attendant melodrama to everything.

"In Italy, the crew and everybody actually adore low-budget movies, on one level — not in terms of their salaries but in terms of the drama of it all. The downside is that you're having close-ups after eighteen hours of work, and the lighting suffers because the lighting cameraman is doing a huge amount of set-ups in a very short amount of time."

Despite that downside, Steele had become very attracted to the energy that develops from working on a low-budget project.

"Everybody is in it together, in a *Dog Day Afternoon* kind of way," she explained. "And I like that. You feel like a family in this rush, and you've got to get it done, and it's like you're all pushing at it together.

"You don't have time to worry about your make-up, you're just in there, and I like that. I think it's really great; I must sound demented, but I actually like it."

Regardless of the budget, Steele feels that it's the director's responsibility to create the proper atmosphere on the set. Even at that early point in his career, Demme was establishing the reputation of being an actor's director.

"I think the most important thing is that the actors feel really safe and comfortable," Steele explained. "You can only be as good as you dare to be bad. And if the actor is spooked or apprehensive, they'll just freeze. So the whole thing is for the actor to feel loved, really, and appreciated.

"Jonathan was lovely to work with," Steele continued, "very sweet, very supportive. He had this incredible energy and enthusiasm. He was very passionate.

"I think he's a fantastic director, one of the few directors that really allows a sense of space and creates enormous tension in his silences. I feel most American directors assault and rush you too much, as if the audience has no imagination. You've got to fill it in with your own apprehension. I think Jonathan has a fantastic sense of what's appropriate. He's always making you wait for a little bit more."

LET THEM DO THEIR JOBS

It's not uncommon for low-budget filmmakers to handle every job on their movies — from set dresser to key grip to catering to cinematography — on top of writing, producing, directing and editing.

A key lesson that Demme learned on his first directing assignment was that when you have the money for a crew, hire smart people, give them direction, and then let them do their jobs.

"I tried very hard to get people who are more gifted in their area than I would ever hope to be," Demme explained, "and that extends to both sides of the camera. For me, that's the key to good directing: hire eminently gifted people and let them pursue what they do."

While that approach will result in a happier, more productive crew, it can also yield some wonderful creative results at all stages of production, even in the cutting room. For example, in Demme's world, the first cut of a scene is always in the hands of the editor, not the director.

"I'll never tell the editor how to cut a scene," Demme explained, "because he or she may find a more exciting approach to it than I could ever dream up."

This philosophy has led to a great partnership between Demme and his long-time cinematographer, Tak Fujimoto, which began on the set of *Caged Heat*. It's such a strong relationship that Demme literally leaves

Tak alone to do what he does best — create great images.

"I never discuss the lighting with Tak at all," Demme admitted, "because I know, first of all, his ideas would be far richer than mine; second, I wouldn't understand what he was talking about.

"And there's another thing: when you start shooting a movie, you work so hard every day, you're up at the crack of dawn, you shoot all day, then you have to go to dailies. One of the excitements for me, one of the things that lets me end the day on a high note, is seeing what Tak did on film."

A MOVING PHILOSOPHY

Corman also gave Demme some key advice about camera movement that, like all good advice, was specific to the movie he was about to make, but ultimately universal to all movies.

"I had a long discussion with Jonathan before doing *Caged Heat*," Corman recalled. "We discussed the fact that because the women were confined to the cells within the prison, he was going to be in a very static position, and I simply advised him to go one of two ways: if he used more camera movement than normal and found ways to move actors in conjunction with the camera, he could get more of a fluid look to it.

"Or, if he didn't want to do that, he should 'over-cover' and give himself a lot of angles, so that he could get more movement by cutting. I said just from my standpoint, I like the idea of a moving camera. He chose to go along with the moving camera; other directors have chosen a stable camera but with a great deal of cutting.

"I think, particularly in a low-budget film, unless you go for enough angles so that you have control over the cutting, or a moving camera, you end up with a very static film."

MAKE THE BEST DAMNED [*FILL IN THE BLANK*] MOVIE YOU CAN

The final lesson from *Caged Heat* is one that Demme has applied to every film he's made: Be passionate about your subject and make the best damned picture you can, regardless of what genre you may find yourself in.

According to Corman, that's not only the way to make a successful movie; it's a vital ingredient to a successful career.

"The directors who say, 'Well, it's just a cheap picture, I'm going to knock this off,' are no longer in the business," Corman said. "But the ones who said, 'Whatever the picture, I'm going to do the best job I can,' are the ones who stayed."

Corman agreed that it was that attitude that made him feel Jonathan Demme would have a successful career, even starting with a movie like *Caged Heat.*

"Jonathan told me, 'This is going to be the best women-in-prison movie ever made,'" Corman said, adding, "and it was at least close."

GRAND THEFT AUTO

IIIIIIIIIIIIIIIIIIIIIIIIIIIIIIIIIIIIIIIIIIIIIIIIIIIIIIIIIIIIIIIIIIIIIIIIIIIIIIIIIIIIIIIIIII

Admittedly, Ron Howard's *Grand Theft Auto* doesn't aim high. It's a silly little chase movie that follows the flight of two young lovers as they make their way from Los Angeles to Las Vegas to get married. They're followed on this trek (in the girl's father's Rolls Royce) by an ever-growing horde of crazies, each one itching to nab the couple for a $50,000 reward.

However, as was pointed out in the Introduction of this book, the lessons that Ron Howard learned on *Grand Theft Auto* are lessons that he still uses today on movies that tend to aim a bit higher.

And even the often-stuffy *New York Times* found something nice to say about *Grand Theft Auto*: "Nobody who has ever wanted to see a Rolls-Royce in a demolition derby is going to walk away from this movie disappointed."

Ron Howard's career as a filmmaker started on the set of *The Andy Griffith Show*, when co-star Andy Griffith gave the young actor an 8mm movie camera.

A few years later, while working on the TV show *The Smith Family*, series star Henry Fonda gave him another present: *The Cinematographer's Handbook*, saying of Ron's early efforts at filmmaking, "You should do something with that, boy."

Ron took that advice, and leveraged his growing success as an actor with his love of filmmaking to get his start as a director by joining the Corman school.

MAKE YOUR OWN OPPORTUNITIES

"I was twenty-one years old and itching to direct a film," Ron Howard remembered, "and everywhere I turned I got nothing but sort of patronizing remarks. It was almost as if they were tousling my hair and saying 'Hang in there, kid, when you grow up you might get to direct a movie some day.'"

His dream of becoming a Hollywood film director looked to be dead before it started, until Howard (the actor) got an offer to star in a Corman-produced flick, *Eat My Dust*, and saw in that offer an opportunity for Howard (the director).

"I hated *Eat My Dust*, hated the script," Howard recalled, "but from my film school days at USC I knew that Roger Corman was like a ray of hope for student filmmakers. He was the one guy who would take chances on directors.

"One of the problems in this business, particularly for directors, is that there is no system in place," Howard said. "People go to business school and if they do well they know they're going to be recruited — there's a system in place to lead them on a career path. With film, no such system really exists, and Roger's company has always provided some semblance of that.

"I wouldn't let my agent accompany me to the meeting with Roger," Howard continued, "because I knew I didn't care about the money on *Eat My Dust*, and I wasn't even, frankly, all that crazy about being in *Eat My Dust*, but what I wanted to do was impress Roger with the idea that I would barter this into a directing opportunity of some kind."

Ron's father, actor/writer Rance Howard, remembered how his son pulled it off. "Ron said, 'I will do another movie for you, with one additional job added,'" Rance recalled. "And Roger said, 'What is that?' And Ron said, 'I want to direct. And Roger said, 'Well, Ron, you always looked like a director to me!'"

Corman took the bait, and after *Eat My Dust* proved successful, Ron and his father started pitching ideas to Corman.

"They had to come up with an idea for a script where Ron could be the legitimate lead but not be in that many scenes," Corman said, "so he could spend most of his time directing. We threw out idea after idea until Ron and his father came up with the winner. As soon as they told it to me, I said 'Yes, we'll go with that.'"

"The whole thing was inspired by *It's a Mad, Mad, Mad, Mad World*," Ron Howard recalled, "which is one of my favorite action comedies. And so the idea of spreading out a bunch of crazies and giving them a shared objective and seeing them scramble made for some funny situations and some odd characters."

Corman was impressed with the unique concept the father-son duo had developed: "When Ron said that the climax was going to be a Rolls Royce in a demolition derby, I thought that's the most original idea — or at least one of them — I've ever heard."

"We thought the Rolls Royce would be the perfect automobile for the girl's father to have," said Rance Howard, "and then she would take his car because he had, in essence, taken her car. And then we'd put the car through all the punishment we could, in order to get back at her father, and then finally wreck it at the demolition derby."

"The beauty of the idea was that we could shoot all of Ron's scenes in one or two days," Corman said, "because if you have this chase, Ron and the girl are in the front car and you can shoot all of their scenes in one day. Then he spent the rest of the picture shooting all the people who were chasing after them."

Nancy Morgan, the film's co-star, recounted later: "Ron told me, during the shoot, that Roger had said to him, 'If you do a good job for me on this movie, you'll never have to work for me again.'"

THE FAMILY AND FRIENDS PLAN

Nancy Morgan was surprised by the family atmosphere that Ron Howard created on the set. It was an easy atmosphere to create, because his family was literally on the set. Even his *Happy Days* mother, Marion Ross, contributed a cameo to the film.

"The thing I learned on that movie is that there's nothing like family to pull this together," Morgan remembered. "His mom was in it. His brother was in it. And Rance, of course, co-wrote it with Ron."

Rance Howard concurred. "I think any director likes to use people that he is familiar with and that he can trust and has confidence in," he said. "Both his brother, Clint Howard, and I fit nicely into those categories. And his mother, at that time, had been working quite a lot coordinating extras for other filmmakers. And so she coordinated a lot of the extras for that film."

Another family member also stepped in to help when tensions started to mount on the set ... about the catering!

"We had been feeding the crew Kentucky Fried Chicken for lunch every day," Rance remembered, "and they were getting close to a mutiny, because they didn't appreciate having Kentucky Fried Chicken for lunch every day. And, of course, the reason we were doing it was that it was the most reasonably-priced thing we could give them.

"Ron's wife, Cheryl heard about our problem, and she said, 'Let me cook lunch. Give me the budget that you're spending for the Kentucky Fried Chicken, and I'll prepare a hot lunch for the crew.'

"She enlisted the help of her grandmother," Rance continued, "and they prepared lunches on that budget that — if you run into any of the crew to this day — they will comment on what great food Cheryl provided for that shoot."

Despite the family atmosphere, Morgan was impressed to find that her young director and his co-writer father were taking the movie very seriously.

"There was no partying for them," she said. "You never found them in the bar, sitting around, schmoozing with people. At night they were in their room, looking at dailies. They were looking over every single moment of this film and discussing it like you would discuss an art project. They wanted it to be the best car picture it could be."

GOT THEME?

Despite the broad nature of the story, Ron and Rance did take the film very seriously, and early on established a theme and point of view for the story.

"No matter how silly a movie might be," Ron Howard said, "I've always felt it has to have a point of view, and it has to have a thematic center. Those themes may not be very complex, but they do have to be well thought out.

"My dad and I when we were working on the script, we did see it as a kind of a parable about the power of love."

Establishing that theme early on helps enormously during production, when a director is barraged with thousands of questions and often must make quick decisions.

"So much of directing is managing your compromises," Ron Howard agreed, "and making these quick, knee-jerk decisions that have minor significance on a shot-by-shot basis, but over the course of the entire picture it numbers in the thousands, these kind of choices you have to make.

"And if they are informed or at least fueled by some sort of thematic objective — even if you're having to cut something out or change something on the fly — you're keeping the big ideas in place. And it helps make those decisions more cohesive."

Rance agreed, particularly when it comes to dealing with compromises. "You need to be tenacious," he said. "You need to stick to your guns, but at the same time, you have to be prepared to compromise and negotiate.

"There are a lot of aspects of making a film where you can compromise. In some places, you can't. You need to know what compromises can be made and what compromises can't be made. Coming to that realization is important: understanding that you're not going to get everything you want, you're going to get part of what you want."

CAST WITH CARE

Nancy Morgan had only one other feature to her credit when she auditioned for *Grand Theft Auto*, and she was the first to admit that she didn't have an impressive resume as an actress.

"Back then I used to say to myself," she recalled, "there are a lot of people here who know a lot about acting, but all I really know is that you just have to pretend that it's happening.

"And so, during the audition process, I did as close to what I felt a human being would do under the circumstances, and that was to say the lines like I meant them, and then when Ron was talking to me, react to what he was saying. And that's all I knew — that was about as much acting as I knew."

Her instincts were correct, however, and Howard cast her. "Ron later said to me, 'You know, I interviewed a couple hundred girls. Did you ever wonder why you got it? Because you were the only one who, when you weren't speaking, was still listening.'"

BE PREPARED

In order to get everything shot in the short time they had, Ron Howard divided up sequences in the movie, taking on the dialogue scenes himself and handing much of the action shooting to second unit director Alan Arkush.

Howard storyboarded the entire movie and he and Arkush spent two days before production working out the shots. The two only worked together one day, during the final demolition derby scene.

"I think Alan and I set a record for the most number of set-ups in a day," Howard recalled about the demolition derby scene. "I think we did ninety-eight set-ups between us in one day."

The only way they could achieve that distinction was with thorough preparation.

"I always knew that preparation and rehearsal are extremely important," Rance Howard explained. "But this experience drove that fact home and really solidified that. Preparation is really, really important. Preproduction, really being prepared.

"Ron is a really hard-working, dedicated guy, and always has been," Rance continued. "In order to make the very most out of this opportunity, he spent any spare moments thinking about and working on the production."

For producer Corman, working fast is not necessarily a liability. "You can do it better with more time," he said, "but when you're shooting this fast, there's a certain spontaneity you get. Sometimes when you do it better and bigger, you lose that energy."

Ron Howard agrees. "When you finish directing a movie for Roger, there's two things: If you've enjoyed that, you're going to enjoy everything you ever do, because it is a sort of trial by fire.

"But you're also going to be really well prepared, because that's one of the things that Roger really insists upon, is a game plan, a point of view. An artistic, creative point of view and a practical point of view on how you're actually going to go out and get the shots you need, day in, day out, hour after hour."

PREVIEWS

The final phase before completing the movie was screening it for test audiences, to gauge their reactions. For Ron Howard, this was a key step.

"You can't really know what your film is saying until you put it up in front of an audience," Howard said. "Playwrights have their period of previews, they have that opportunity, so why shouldn't filmmakers?"

Corman concurred: "I'm a firm believer in putting the film, at least one time, before an audience. You always learn something.

"In about half the pictures we've made, they play well in the sneak preview and we send them straight out. In the other half, we will make some edits, some changes, according to the audience reaction in a sneak preview."

This is particularly true of comedies. "Funny is funny," Howard continued. "There is nothing like showing a comedy to audiences to really understand it. Roger was very dogged to making sure we paid attention to what we learned in those preview screenings."

There's one final lesson Ron Howard learned on *Grand Theft Auto*, which was reinforced at the test screenings, but it's a lesson that is key to all filmmaking:

"When in doubt," Howard said, "hit somebody in the groin."

Chapter Two
FIERCELY INDEPENDENT

There are independent filmmakers and then there are independent filmmakers — a special breed you might call the über independents.

These folks are the real deal. Some, like John Sayles, have made a ton of movies. Others, like Eric Mendelsohn, are just getting started.

But they all share a vision that is unique to them, and an unwillingness to let any obstacle prevent them from getting that vision up on the screen.

You may not love their movies (although you probably will), but you have to admire their raw persistence. And you can certainly learn from their experience.

RETURN OF THE SECAUCUS SEVEN

||||||||||||||||||||||||||||||||||||||||||||||||||||||||||||||||||||||||||||||||||||||||||||||||||

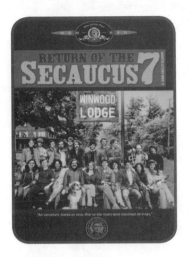

Return of the Secaucus Seven made a pretty big splash when it was released in 1980.

One key reason might have been its paltry $40,000 budget, which put it in stark contrast with Hollywood's biggest movie that year, the $44 million dollar fiasco, *Heaven's Gate*.

The press loves David and Goliath stories, and they loved *Return of the Secaucus Seven*, which made $2 million at the box office, to *Heaven's Gate's* wimpy $1.5 million.

Another reason for the film's success could have been that it tapped neatly into the baby boomers' *Zeitgeist*. Many boomers at that time were beginning to deal with adult issues, while still trying to hold onto their youthful idealism, not unlike the characters in the movie.

Whatever the reason, it launched John Sayles' directing career, or, as he has put it, "I was catapulted from total obscurity to relative obscurity."

Before *Return of the Secaucus Seven*, Sayles had a solid career as a novelist, as well as having achieved success as a scriptwriter for Roger Corman — a level of success, in fact, that few screenwriters find so early in their careers.

"I wrote three movies and three movies got made," Sayles explained, "and that's very rare. Big studios tend to develop twenty or thirty projects for every one that gets made. There are a lot of people who have been in Hollywood for fifteen years and they may have been paid for twenty or thirty scripts, but they have no credits because none of them had been made into films yet.

"Basically, the more you get paid, the more you're working with big studios, the less likely it is to get made," he continued, "because they have the money to develop. If Roger Corman paid you to write a screenplay, he damn well made the movie.

"The nice thing about Roger," he went on, "is that once you've hit the bases you have to hit within the genre, he gives you a lot of leeway to make it

Five of the Secaucus Seven, including Adam LeFevre (center)

funny or good, although he isn't going to give you any more money or time. As long as you have nudity and the helicopter blows up, you can do anything you want."

Anything you want — that is, except direct, until you prove yourself. Which is exactly what Sayles set out to do.

MAKE YOUR OWN OPPORTUNITIES

"John wanted to direct," recalled friend and *Secaucus Seven* cast member Adam LeFevre, "and he kept saying that he wanted to direct, and they would say, 'Well, what have you directed?' and he'd say, 'Nothing, yet.' So the movie was an audition piece for him to show people that he directed and wrote."

"The only way you get to direct in Hollywood," explained Sayles, "is to have a film to show." In order to make that happen, he took matters into his own hands and made his own opportunity by making his own movie. With his own money.

He put together the money he'd earned from writing screenplays, plus money from a short story collection, and with that $40,000, he started writing a movie he could make for ... $40,000.

As it turned out, finding the money and writing the script were the easy parts. "If I'd known how hard it is to make a movie," he said later, "I might not have started."

Although he'd absorbed a lot by watching his Corman scripts get made into movies, Sayles learned on *Return of the Secaucus Seven* just how much he didn't know. "There weren't many film schools or film books at the time," Sayles continued, "so we were inventing the wheel."

Making the movie was a struggle, but at least Sayles was comforted by the fact that it was his movie, made from his script, with his money. And it achieved its primary goal: The film established him as a director.

"The fact that it really took off and did so well," remembered LeFevre, "nobody was thinking of that at that point. We were just thrilled that we were making a damned movie."

WRITE TO YOUR RESOURCES

Sayles realized from the start that with his tiny budget, he'd have to make every dollar count. And that meant writing the script to resources that he knew he could get for little or no money, which even included the actors.

"John had very specifically tailored the script to who he knew he had," LeFevre explained. "He had tailored the movie to people's type and abilities. Because his budget was very limited, it had to be thoroughly plotted out."

"A lot of that movie came out of my experiences of working in a summer theater as an actor and occasionally as a director," Sayles said. "About half of the actors in *Return of the Secaucus Seven* were people who I had worked with in that theater company."

This experience allowed actors to draw on their actual friendships, which Sayles knew would help their performances on-screen.

"Everybody knew everybody and had worked with each other before," LeFevre said, "so there was a level of comfort there and a lot less time necessary to get to know each other.

"I think it was advantageous that we had a shared communal history, and I think, since there was so little time, it was good to have that going in. John knew that and I think exploited that in a very good way."

That experience for LeFevre was unique. "After *Return of the Secaucus Seven*," he explained, "sometimes I'd arrive on a movie set and I'd end up in bed with somebody I haven't met yet. In this case, the working relationship among the core group was already established."

Sayles understood that working with an unknown cast created its own set of issues. Chief among them is the task of introducing the characters to the audience and helping them figure out who's who.

"When you have a lot of characters in a movie, and none of them are stars, none of them are very well-known character actors," Sayles explained, "you're probably going to have to introduce them a couple times, and have those introductions be something about who they are and who they are going to be in the script, so the audience doesn't feel lost."

To that point, Sayles included a key scene in the film where one character names each of the others, while also spelling out their relationship to the rest of the group. Although that may seem heavy-handed, he did it in the guise of having a new character, someone unfamiliar with the group, enter the movie and need to be brought up to speed. In that context, the scene is fast, funny — and very helpful to an audience trying to get their bearings.

Besides fashioning the script to fit his cast, Sayles also tailored it to a location he knew he could get for very little money: a ski lodge that was empty and available for his twenty-five-day shoot. Not only did the lodge provide many of the movie's interiors, he got double duty out of the space by also using it to house the actors and crew.

Another reason the ski lodge worked well as a location was that it didn't take much effort — or money — to make the interiors work for the script, which is always a plus for a low-budget movie. It's a technique that he's used on subsequent films.

"Take advantage of art direction that's been done for you," Sayles recommended. "If there's a great building, if there's a National Guard building with a bunch of tanks parked on the other side of the fence, somebody has horses, whatever, you get a lot of use out of something you didn't have to pay for and your art department didn't have to provide."

Realizing that his budget wouldn't give him much chance to move the camera (you can count the dolly moves in *Return of the Secaucus Seven* on one hand), Sayles designed the script with plenty of parallel action, so that movement would come from cutting between the characters and the various subplots.

He also designed verbal transitions — with a word at the end of one scene dovetailing well with the first word at the beginning of the next scene — to help make up for the visual panache he knew his budget wouldn't be able to provide.

All in all, Sayles took a very exacting approach to getting the movie made for so little money. However, despite his behind-the-scenes precision, the movie itself is very breezy and off-the-cuff — which was also part of Sayles' plan.

"People have said that a lot of it sounded improvised," LeFevre said, "but really very little was improvised, because he didn't have enough money for film to do that. He knew going into it exactly what he had

to get, and he was very diligent about getting shots and moving on, getting shots and moving on."

Looking back on the experience, Sayles feels that there are some advantages to working within an ultra-low-budget. "Sometimes your budget can become an aesthetic," he said, "and you often figure things out that look better than they might have if you'd had all the equipment. And then, other times you don't, and you wish you had the crane or whatever it is."

PATTI ROCKS

||||||||||||||||||||||||||||||||||||||||||||||||||||||||||||||||||||||||||||||||||||||||||||

"12 years later."

Those intriguing words appear on-screen after the opening credits of *Patti Rocks*. To the uninitiated (which is the majority of viewers), the statement refers to an earlier film from the same director and cast, called *Loose Ends,* to which *Patti Rocks* is the sequel.

The idea of making a sequel to a movie that hardly anyone has heard of is just one of the fascinating facets of David Burton Morris' *Patti Rocks*.

The truth is, there never would have been *Patti Rocks* if *Loose Ends* hadn't existed. And *Loose Ends* never would have come about if Morris hadn't been inspired by another low-budget film.

"I saw *Memories of Underdevelopment*, a Cuban film," Morris recalled, "and I rushed home to my wife, Victoria, and I said, 'You know, we can make a movie really cheap. I just saw this great movie, it was black and white. If we can scrape together $20,000, we can make a movie.'

"And so we did. She wrote it. And it shot for two weeks. We went to twenty or twenty-five film festivals, didn't win anything really, but Roger Ebert discovered us and we got these great notices from Vincent Canby and Andrew Sarris."

Using *Loose Ends* as a calling card, and then after shooting another low-budget movie, *Purple Haze*, Morris moved to Los Angeles and graduated to Hollywood studio pictures — where he soon found himself completely miserable.

"I was thinking about getting out of the business because I was really unhappy," Morris explained. "And I realized that the only time I had a really good time making a movie was my first film, *Loose Ends.*

"And I thought, maybe I should think about writing something for those guys and make it back in Minnesota and sort of re-create my enthusiasm for making movies."

The concept he came up with was simple enough: The two main characters from *Loose Ends*, Eddie (John Jenkins) and Billy (Chris Mulkey), meet up twelve years later.

Eddie now has a respectable life. Billy is still at loose ends, but needs Eddie's assistance. He talks Eddie into accompanying him on a late-night car trip, in the dead of winter, to help him talk his girlfriend, Patti Rocks, into getting an abortion.

To Morris, the idea seemed like simplicity itself: "I thought, two guys in a car? How tough can that be?"

"In theory, David was right," agreed producer, cinematographer and editor Greg Cummins. "It was a very simple idea: two guys in a car. But add in the car — a black car, with black upholstery — in the middle of nowhere, in the middle of the night, with minimal equipment, in the cold. It was brutal. Absolutely brutal.

"The camera got so cold most of the time," continued Cummins, "that it was squeaking. When it dropped below -20, the camera ran fine, but there was this high-pitched squeak every few seconds.

"We couldn't figure out what it was for the life of us. It would go away when we'd take the camera into the trailer, and then we'd go back to the car and it would do it again."

As difficult as the film was to shoot, their hard work did pay off: *Patti Rocks* made it into Sundance in 1988, and was nominated for a number of Independent Spirit awards that year (Best Director, Best Screenplay, Best Cinematography and Best Actor).

But, most importantly, it did what Morris originally set out to do: get him excited about making movies again.

"I had a lot of fun making the film," Morris said. "We had our problems, obviously, because of the money and the cold, but it just re-enthused me for making movies again."

IMPROVISE THE EMOTIONS, WRITE THE WORDS

Check out the credits for *Patti Rocks* and you'll see four writers listed, which is usually a bad sign for a movie. However, in this case, the writers were also the director and the film's primary cast (Jenkins, Mulkey, and Mulkey's real-life wife, actress Karen Landry).

The script for *Patti Rocks* grew out of their conversations and improvisations about men, women, and how they communicate.

"It started with some general conversations about what we might do," recalled Jenkins, "and then we started to improv a little bit. David then took that and began to craft a plotline." Then after we had that in place, we got back together again and we spent some more time improvising the script."

"I did a draft," explained Morris, "and I'd give it to them and we'd tinker with it and do some more improvs. Jenkins lived in Chicago, so we flew there a couple times and did some more improvs, and I'd type that up."

"So the script really came out of those improvisations that Chris and Karen and I did," Jenkins added. "Then David would edit and cut and paste and re-arrange. He might add some other dialogue on top of that, but most of it came out of those improvs."

Although he enjoyed the improvisation process, Jenkins experienced a unique situation when it came time to act in the scenes that he had helped improvise.

"It's a funny thing," he noted. "When you're improvising, you're so involved in the problem and the words just flow out. But when you go back to do it again, you've forgotten a lot of that dynamic that allowed those words to flow. So you're left with a script and you know it's yours, but it's hollowed out. You've forgotten the context a little bit."

"It's almost easier to take somebody else's words and to slip on your imagination and work with that, then to go back and do your own stuff. I found that to be a little difficult."

His solution was to treat the improvised text as a new script and approach it like he would any other script.

"I had to do all the actorly stuff and fill it out," Jenkins explained, "sensory work and subtext, to try to get back to that improv state that had been so easy.

"It was just odd. You would think that it would just be a piece of cake, the easiest thing to do, and I found it perplexingly difficult."

IT'S NOT YOUR PROBLEM (IT'S YOUR CHARACTER'S PROBLEM)

After he (and the actors) had written the script, Morris took it to producer Sam Grogg, who was immediately interested in financing the film.

"He had very few notes," Morris recalled. "He just said, 'They have to get out of the car midway through this movie.' I said, 'What do you want them to do? See a flying saucer?' He said, 'I don't know, you'll think of something.'"

What Morris ultimately came up with was a scene in which Billy stops the car to relieve himself, and is sprayed by a passing skunk. Unable to bear the smell of his soiled clothing, he strips down to a pair of boxer shorts (and not even his own boxer shorts; he borrows them from Eddie).

None of this was problematic ... until the shooting schedule changed, and what had been planned as an idyllic summer shoot became a brutally cold winter shoot.

"We got the money in November," Morris recalled, "and I said, 'We're going to make the movie. We've got the money, we're going.'"

Morris wisely didn't alter the script, which made the scenes of Mulkey in his underwear all the better because it was the dead of winter.

"It actually turned into a more interesting film," Morris said of the schedule change, "just because of the look of the snow and Mulkey running around in his underwear in 23 degrees below zero.

"The lesson from *Patti Rocks*," Morris continued, "is when you get the money, make the movie, regardless of what season it is."

CAST WITH CARE

Morris knew who his cast was going to be before they even started the script, so casting the cast for *Patti Rocks* wasn't that big of an issue.

But equally important as the cast is the crew, and Morris feels that as much time and effort should go into finding the right people to help you out behind the camera as in front of it.

"I cast well, including the crew," he explained. "It's such a collaborative art, and they help me get my vision on film.

"If I get the right designer and the right wardrobe person and the right art director, the right director of photography, they can make you look really good, even on those days when you're not so sure about stuff."

FIND THE ANGLE/HAVE A HOOK

When it was released in 1988, *Patti Rocks* stirred up a lot of controversy, primarily due to the way Eddie and Billy talk about women on their long nighttime trip to Patti's apartment.

That controversy about the film's raw language, which helped get the movie publicity, was not accidental.

"We set out to do that," explained Cummins. "The thinking was, these are two guys and this is the way guys talk. If you put two kind of raunchy guys together, this is how they talk. There's nothing unreal about this.

"Sam Grogg felt the language was its strong point," Cummins added, "that's what the film was about."

Although the language helped get the movie noticed back in 1988, Jenkins thinks it wouldn't have the same impact today. "You watch HBO, and you see something like *Deadwood*," he said. "We were tame in comparison. But twenty years ago that was a vastly different time, in terms of what kind of language you could use in a film."

THE FAMILY AND FRIENDS PLAN

Patti Rocks came about because the people who made *Loose Ends* had become friends and wanted to work together again. That level of friendship and trust is a great starting point for any movie.

"Film is a collaborative art, there's no question," Cummins said. "Everybody says that. You can't really do it by yourself, you really need other people, other expertise, other views, other opinions. You need people in the process.

"And the closer you are to those people, the less explaining you have to do, the more intuitive working relationship you can have, the faster you're going to be able to work, the better off you're going to be."

That level of friendship and trust was particularly helpful in one scene toward the end of the film — a love scene between Jenkins and Landry that was rife with possible tension.

"There was a level of trust in the sex scene," Cummins explained. "This is Chris' wife, who's making love with John Jenkins. This is a difficult scene.

"It's difficult to have your wife in a nude scene, it's difficult to be in the same film with your wife in a nude scene, it's difficult to have your wife making love to your friend as a character, but he's a real-life friend. We created a lot of really difficult situations that we were able to get through because of that trust that we had with each other."

"It was difficult to do," Jenkins agreed. "I'm doing a love scene with my best friend's wife — my real best friend's wife. It was potentially explosive. The manners of all that needed to be very, very careful.

"I thought we did handle that part well," Jenkins continued. "We got to the point where both Karen and I felt comfortable to do the scene. We needed to make sure that this had to be business-like, we had to commit to it, but we had to be really, really sensitive to each other about it. I thought we were able to finesse it all right."

Although friendship may be one of the starting points for many films, Cummins cautions that everyone involved understand the real purpose behind many low-budget projects.

"A lot of these small films, they're really calling cards," Cummins said. "You talk to your friends and you say, 'Okay, let's all get together and make this movie and we'll get famous.'

"What it really means is, 'I'm going to move my career forward, and you're going to help me, and if you're lucky, I'll keep working with you in the future and bring work to you.' But you really can't depend on that. You have to do it for the project itself.

"You can't think, 'Okay, I'm going to do this and then this director is going to make my career and give me work down the road.' He won't. He's going to grow into somebody else, he's going to grow past you. Because what he needs from you is your availability and your willingness to work — as a DP or an editor or whatever it is — and if he had money he would hire Haskell Wexler."

Recognizing that fact and finding a way to benefit from the work you've done is up to you, Cummins says.

"You have your own calling card, then, for the field you work in," Cummins explained. "It's an individual opportunity. If you don't take it somewhere and develop it, it's your own fault."

WHAT HAPPENED WAS...

||||||||||||||||||||||||||||||||||||||||||||||||||||||||||||||||||||||||||||||||||||||||

When health problems temporarily sidelined actor Tom Noonan from his Hollywood career (in movies like *Manhunter, F/X*, and *Last Action Hero*), he took an assessment of his life to date and realized what he really wanted to do: make a movie of his own.

"You're not here very long," he said. "It's over before you know it, and it's a good idea to do at least one or two things in your life that you feel are from your heart or that you have a passion for. But I can't take much credit for it; I just had to do it."

Due to his extensive background as a stage actor, Noonan decided that he would first write the movie as a play. "Because I'd never acted in something I'd directed, I thought, 'Well, if I do it on stage for a while, in front of an audience, I'll find out what the thing's about.' And, because I was acting in it, I wanted to make sure that we'd worked out all the acting parts before we shot it."

With the decision in place to write a script, the only question was, what story to tell? He announced an opening day for the play, and then sat down and wrote a script. And another. And another. And wasn't happy with any of them.

Then, as sometimes happens, life handed him a story.

"I went to dinner at a friend's house," he recalled. "During the meal I asked my friend how her brother (whom I'd never met) was and she said, 'Oh, he's such a jerk.'"

She went on to tell a story of a dinner gone wrong, an awkward evening of miscommunication, during which her brother didn't realize that the co-worker who had invited him to her apartment thought they were on a date.

"When the woman told him that she really liked him," Noonan's friend recounted, "he said that he wouldn't have come to dinner if he had considered this a date. The woman blew up and threw him out."

That was all Noonan needed. "I got up from the table and left my friend's house and rushed home and started writing," he said. "Ten days later I had written *What Happened Was....* Three weeks later I went into rehearsal and the play opened, as scheduled, on June 12, 1992."

The play and the movie all take place in real time, in the woman's apartment. For the theatrical version, Noonan created a theater space that actually put the audience right into the apartment.

"When we performed," he said, "the audience walked into what looked like a typical New York apartment — they sat on folding chairs set up throughout the space. I remember one person saying that the experience was like 'seeing a movie in person.'"

One of the goals of the run of the play was to discover how to strike the right balance with the material — to make the audience feel uncomfortable about this awkward situation, but not so uncomfortable that they would bolt from the theater.

"Part of what I would try to do during the play, and in the movie, was to not make people so uncomfortable that they didn't want to watch. I wanted it to be funny and make the characters engaging enough and compelling enough that you'd stay with the story even though it was painfully awkward.

"There were times when I was doing the play when I could tell that the audience couldn't wait for it to be over, because they couldn't stand how awkward it was for the two of us. They just wanted me to leave and let this poor woman go to bed."

IGNORE THE NAYSAYERS

Despite his excitement about the script, Noonan quickly discovered that his enthusiasm was not universally shared.

"Most people who read the script and who are friends of mine, well-known actors who will remain unmentioned, thought the script was stupid," he recalled. "Most of the people I really wanted to do it wouldn't do the movie. I'd written it for my wife who was busy and unavailable, and then I gave it to all these other people who said, 'I like you, but this script is about nothing.'"

However, Noonan had faith in his own writing abilities, which helped him to ignore the naysayers and persevere.

"I'd written scripts for many years before I wrote that script," he said, "and I was a relatively skilled screenwriter, but I never felt I was really writing a reality that was familiar to me, that I felt was fun or interesting to look at. So when I wrote it, I really tried to not worry about what people traditionally worry about when they write a script.

"And when I gave it to people, if they didn't like it, fuck 'em, I don't care. I just liked it so much and thought it was so funny and I had so much fun writing it, that I thought that eventually someone is going to get this. And if they don't, I don't care."

REHEARSE

Having worked extensively on stage and on film, Noonan has a clear idea of the value of rehearsal.

"My general rule is that either you rehearse a lot or you don't rehearse at all," he said. "If you rehearse in the middle, you end up not being authentic."

For the rehearsal process of the film version of *What Happened Was...*, Noonan took a couple of unique steps: He involved the crew, as well as the cast, in the rehearsal process, and he videotaped the movie more than once before he actually shot it.

"The last night of the play, we took out all the chairs, and we shot the script in the theater," he said. "Then, for the next six months after that, before we shot the film, we rehearsed pretty regularly. We rehearsed for eight or nine months before we shot, a couple times a week.

"Most of the people on the crew were all involved in the shooting of the video of the play, and then involved in the rehearsals as we went along, so that by the time we shot, everybody in the crew knew the whole story. They knew what the scenes were about, where the camera moves were. We pre-shot the thing two or three times before we actually shot it on film."

This process made life easier for Noonan the director, and it also made it easier for Noonan the actor.

"When I finally shot the film, they would say, 'It's your close-up, Tom,' and I'd say, 'Okay,' and I'd sit there and just talk. It wasn't like I was acting; I'd done it so often and what was going on seemed so real to me.

"I didn't have to worry about learning the words or learning the blocking or doing any of those things that you have to worry about when you're doing a film. It completely went away. It was just me, just being there. So it felt very real to me."

TIME IS ON YOUR SIDE

There are so many conflicting elements in the moviemaking process, and Noonan wisely removed one of those elements early on — the pressure of time.

"One thing I learned making the film," he said, "is that you have a huge advantage when you have no money, because when you have no money you have all the time in the world. The more money you have, the less time you have to make a film, because you've got to move or you're wasting money.

"So, if you're smart and you're talented and skillful and you manage your time well, you can actually do a whole lot better movie with very little money than you can with tons. Because once tons of money gets involved, you have millions of people trying to put their finger in the pie and tell you what to do and rush you along.

"And I never had that. I wrote this at the pace I wanted to, I shot it when I felt like it, and I edited it for as long as I wanted."

KNOW WHAT YOU'RE SIGNING

Noonan's bliss with the project came to an abrupt halt when it came time to find distribution.

He experienced a myriad of problems — a bad contract that ultimately cost him more than it made him, a distributor who went through bankruptcy, a late video release, and a bad (and misleading) marketing campaign for the video, with a cover photo that had nothing to do with the movie.

"I was not thrilled about the photo," Noonan admitted, "to say the least. Because anybody buying the movie based on that picture is not going to like the movie; and all the people who would like the movie wouldn't get it because of that picture. It's stupid marketing."

More damaging was a small clause in the distribution contract that ended up personally costing Noonan money every time the movie made any money.

"When you sell a film to a distributor," Noonan explained, "there's a certain aspect of the agreement that's called the assumption agreement. It's where the distributor agrees to assume certain costs involved in the distribution of the film, one of which is the residuals for the actors.

"Otherwise, if I sell you the film for $75,000 and I pay the crew and I pay everybody back, and then you go out and sell the film everywhere, the more money you make selling the film, the more money the actors have to get paid as residuals. And, unless the distributor assumes that expense, I end up losing money in the end making the film.

"When we made the agreement, I didn't know that and it was left out of the agreement, or somehow it didn't get signed, so I was left with the bill for the residuals. So besides not making any money, I lost money on the film, paying myself."

Noonan, who is fairly well-versed in the ways of Hollywood, admits that he fell down in this area.

"Distribution is the creepiest part of making a movie, and there are so many ways you can get fucked in distribution. I had someone representing me, it wasn't just me, I had somebody who'd sold a lot of movies and they screwed up a little. I made a bad deal. But it's okay; I loved making the movie."

DO OR DO NOT ... THERE IS NO TRY

Throughout the entire process of making *What Happened Was...*, from the health issues that inspired him to make a movie, to finding the story, to dealing with rejection of that script, and finally to a distribution deal gone bad, Noonan has maintained a Yoda-like attitude about the process that helped get him through it.

Like Yoda, he believes there is no "try," there is only "do."

"To 'try' is to struggle in a powerless situation," Noonan explained. "You can 'try' as an actor to get a part in a movie — the ultimate decision is not yours. But you cannot 'try' to write a script. You either do it or you don't. You cannot 'try' to make a movie. You may not feel ready or you may be afraid to do it but I believe 'trying' is reserved for situations over which you have little control.

"If you're interested in becoming alive through the process of making a movie, then just do it. We so need people to do that. If you have a story you need to tell, then please do what you have to do to tell it. If you have something to say, just say it, whether it's ugly or pretty or wrong or stupid. If you need to do it, please do!

"You make the movie because you want to make the movie, and make it as best you can with what you have. I'm cool making movies for whatever I have. I mean, if I had money, I'd use a crane shot, but if I don't, I don't. That part of moviemaking doesn't interest me a whole lot, the toys and doing fancy stuff.

"I'm a very visual person, but it's all related to the drama and not to showing off. The things that interest me are very simple human interactions."

IN THE COMPANY OF MEN

"Let's hurt somebody."

For writer/director Neil LaBute, that statement was the starting point that ultimately grew into his blindingly funny and bitter comedy, *In the Company of Men*.

"That line of dialogue was the first idea in my mind," LaBute said. "I was attracted to the notion of premeditated agony inflicted on someone. I believe that you can kill characters only once, but you can hurt them every day. It's a simple story: boys meet girl, boys crush girl, boys giggle.

"I was interested in making something that was familiar, but hadn't been seen before," he went on to explain. "I wanted to do a new take on the standard love triangle. I was interested in the idea of a person playing with someone romantically just for the fun of it; I wanted the story to be an ironic examination of office politics."

The film, which won the 1997 Sundance Film Festival Filmmaker's Trophy (which is voted on by the other filmmakers), launched LaBute's career in film while simultaneously launching heated debates among men and women in just about every audience that has seen it.

"The film is not a soap-box lecture on the current state of anything," LaBute believes. "I think it's more of a cinematic inkblot test. Everybody watches the same images and listens to the same words, but what people get from it differs wildly and depends entirely on what they bring to it.

"People seem to love analyzing other people's reactions to the film, but many people would be just as well served by analyzing their own."

The analysis that audiences and the media brought to the sometimes brutal nature of the movie is the first of many lessons found within *In the Company of Men.*

FIND THE ANGLE/HAVE A HOOK

"We've had some really nasty reviews," LaBute admitted. "One critic called it a 'psychological snuff film' and tantamount to watching a rape and doing nothing about it."

The outrage that the movie created, in critics and audiences alike, proved to be, at least in part, a key to its success. As producer Stephen Pevner acknowledged, "A selling point was the controversy."

Even a potential distributor recognized the power of that potential controversy. "*In the Company of Men* — it's so funny that it became successful," remembered Michael Barker, co-president of Sony Pictures Classics, "because it was  so reviled when it was in Sundance.

"I remember someone crossing the street to avoid (lead actor) Aaron Eckhart. And (co-president) Tom Bernard and I were looking at this and saying, 'If so many people hate this film, there must be something to it.'"

Cast members were also surprised by the reaction the movie ultimately received. "When we were filming this," said actress Stacey Edwards, "we thought white men were going to be out picketing this film, not women."

"There's been a lot of women not wanting to see it," LaBute admitted, "And then becoming advocates of it afterwards. I think many women saw it as being a harsh look at men. Whereas men have come out thinking it's funny at the beginning and then kind of holding their heads at the end and thinking 'God, we don't look so good.'"

For executive producer and actor Matt Malloy, the appeal of the movie is simple: "The film pulls you in and makes you an accomplice."

"What's great about the film is that everyone loves to tell you their opinion about it, and it affects everyone differently, because everyone has their own story," said Edwards.

"But I have heard everything," she continued, "including Chad [Aaron Eckhart] being the victim. People come up to me, 'You know who the real victim is? Chad is the victim.' Because they think what an awful life he must have had. It's rare that people think that Howard [Matt Malloy] is the victim, which is interesting."

Even LaBute has taken sides, at least a little. "There are bits of me in all of those characters," he admitted. "It's just whether you choose to use those things. Probably the reason that I dislike Howard more is that he's more like me. Howard's the one I expect a bit more from, he seems to be a bit more normal, he has the ability to make choices and he continually fails. And when he fails I hold him in greater contempt."

Regardless of the controversy, LaBute is pleased to have made a movie that sticks in audiences' minds longer than most of the Teflon-style movies Hollywood produces.

"I'm happy having people think about it for more than five minutes after they've seen it," he said. "I think that so much of what I see, and see people around me making, is so immediately digested, and people move on to the next thing.

"I see myself doing that all the time, watching a film and then going 'Yeah, that was interesting, what do you want to eat?' And that's the last time I ever think about that movie. So it's great to have made something that makes just a slight ripple."

LEAVE NO STONE UNTURNED

To raise the $25,000 budget for the movie, LaBute first began by approaching traditional sources. However, he felt that the size of his tiny budget may have worked against him.

"The first to get hit on were, of course, friends and family members," he said. "I think that people were suspicious that I was not really making a film.

"Understandably, they were wary of the idea that someone could actually make a movie for so little money, so it was difficult to find anybody to put up money at all. I guess people suspected that I might just take that money and go on vacation with a video camera."

Undaunted by lack of success among that group, LaBute cast a wider net. It was this willingness to look under every stone which ultimately paid off and provided him with the budget he needed to get the movie made.

"I had heard that some former students of mine had been injured in a car crash and had received a fairly healthy insurance settlement as a result of this accident," he remembered.

"I called them up and asked them if they wanted to invest any money into a film that I was making, and they said that they would. They put up $10,000 each, and Matt Malloy got one of his brothers to put up $5,000. So we had the $25,000 that we needed and we set off to make the film."

AVOID NAME TALENT

While most producers of low-budget indie movies scramble to add some "name" talent to their cast list, desperately scrounging for any thespian with some small amount of name recognition, LaBute resisted that cliché.

For him, *In the Company of Men* was made all the better because audiences were completely unfamiliar with his three lead actors.

"I couldn't have asked for better actors," he acknowledged, but it really helped that they "were at the beginning of their film work. There's no baggage, that's what's nice. Immediately Aaron becomes Chad. He just is that guy."

LONG TAKES

In the Company of Men contains some stunningly long takes, which was an appealing choice for LaBute.

"The nice thing about shooting in long takes," he said, "is that an actor gets a chance to act. They're not worried about continuity and they get a chance to overlap lines and not have to do things clean. The beauty, I think, is that these actors got a chance to — in big chunks — set the pace for the film, rather than the editor doing it months later."

While allowing the actors to control the pace of the scene via long takes was a positive aspect for LaBute, it did cause production headaches for the producers. Every time a line got blown during a long take, whether it was five seconds or five minutes into the scene, all the film shot for that take was useless.

"That was a problem we ran into all the time," Matt Malloy remembered. "You'd get three minutes into a take and if there was a stumble, we'd eat the film. What we thought was an efficient way, I guess, ultimately moved through more film than they'd anticipated."

The downside of long takes really hit home for the production team when they were informed, three days into their eleven-day shoot, that they had already used up 40% of their allotted film stock. But rather than change their stylistic approach, they simply raised more money and bought more film.

BE PREPARED

There's not much slack in an ultra-short shooting schedule, and LaBute is adamant on one key point: you must do your homework and be prepared.

"Lack of preparation can kill," he warned. "When you have an eleven-day shoot you have no margin for error and you can be ruined by a couple days of rain.

"In that scenario you have to be a little bit lucky, but completely prepared for every contingency that you can think of. I can't stress that enough."

ALL'S WELL THAT ENDS WELL

Some audiences have come away from the movie appalled, more than anything else, by the fact that (spoiler alert!) Chad gets away scot-free and doesn't pay for his horrible behavior.

However, for LaBute, that's the whole point.

"I felt that it was truer to the story that Chad goes unpunished," he explained. "A lot of people are more keen to give what the audience wants, which isn't always the truth, it's perhaps more what they've come to expect.

"We've been conditioned from childhood to expect good to triumph over evil. When someone subverts that a bit, people can get rubbed the wrong way. But all the Chads in this world don't get caught.

"To spend ninety minutes being creative, and then five dashing it all by making the audience feel good about themselves isn't worth it to me."

JUST DO IT

The final lesson from *In the Company of Men* is that you shouldn't wait for just the right moment to take the leap into low-budget filmmaking.

For Neil LaBute, it just didn't matter that he wasn't completely versed in the filmmaking process. In fact, he thinks it helped him get the movie made.

"I think that perhaps my unfamiliarity with the process was what ultimately served me the most. I was pushed toward a 'do it yourself' style of filmmaking — had I known about cameras and lights and cinematographers and grip trucks, maybe I would have been put off from the idea of going out and making my own film.

"But I had heard of all the stories of Robert Townsend or Kevin Smith, who had done projects for small amounts of money that had become very successful, and I just thought, 'What the hell? I'll give it a try.'"

Ultimately, though, it was an unwillingness to give up that made the difference and got *In the Company of Men* completed.

"I think that everyone I came into contact with was crucial in one way or another," LaBute remembered, "but the bottom line is that it was perseverance and hard work that made a difference.

"It was hearing someone say 'no' and not really believing that answer. For me the answer was, 'No, but ...' I had to believe that that person just didn't finish their sentence."

JUDY BERLIN

||||||||||||||||||||||||||||||||||||||||||||||||||||||||||||||||||||||||||||||||||||||||||||||||||||

The writer/director of *Judy Berlin*, Eric Mendelsohn, is a charming and funny man. Asked if he considers himself more of a writer or a director, he replies, "I don't consider myself either one of them. I am just a neurotic with an axe to grind."

That may well be true, but there's precious little axe grinding (however, plenty of neurosis) on view in his debut feature, *Judy Berlin*. The film is a valentine, of sorts, to life on a version of suburban Long Island that isn't often represented in movies.

The film has an outstanding pedigree: a wonderful cast (Edie Falco, Barbara Barrie, Bob Dishy, Madeline Kahn, Julie Kavner, Anne Meara) ... a Best Director award from Sundance ... even the donation of some key technical equipment from Mendelsohn's former boss, Woody Allen.

"I edited the film on his flatbed — the flatbed that he cut every one of the films that Ralph Rosenblum edited," Mendelsohn explained, "which are like, *Bananas* and *Take the Money and Run* and *Annie Hall*. That's what I was using, so there was a lot of history in that machine. It was kind of terrifying."

"The original idea was 'let's do something low budget,'" explained Mendelsohn's friend and producer, Rocco Caruso. "Write something we can do for no money."

"So I wrote a script with seventeen actors, nine million locations, that takes place during an eclipse," Mendelsohn joked, adding, "I had been collecting ideas and characters and moments for a project about an eclipse. That evolved very quickly into *Judy Berlin*.

"I'm a big collector, in real life," Mendelsohn went on to explain. "At one point, I was even collecting versions of the song 'McArthur Park.' And I applied the same ethos to the film: I collected an eclipse on an otherwise beautiful fall day, a tiny suburban town that could almost be something under a snow globe, the harpsichord music, the characters.

"I can't tell you why the second day of school and an eclipse and the music all go together for me. I didn't question it. That was part of the process of writing it for me."

That process produced a sweet, heartfelt little movie, that one critic called "a kind of cinematic haiku," and that another felt was like "David Lynch directing an Arthur Miller script." The finished film, and its filmmaker, offer a number of important lessons on how to get your cinematic vision on-screen intact.

WRITE TO YOUR RESOURCES

When he started writing *Judy Berlin*, Mendelsohn thought he was writing a small script to fit their small budget. However, as soon as they got into preproduction, he found he had been mistaken. Or, as he put it more succinctly, "I'm an idiot."

"Multiple-character, ensemble pieces are not simple to shoot in a limited time frame with actors who have established careers," he explained. "It's really hard to do upper-middle class people, with jobs and cars and school rooms and offices. It is very difficult to accomplish and have it look seamless."

While he recognized the issue in retrospect, it wasn't apparent until very late in the process.

"The problem was," he said, "I thought, 'Well this seems like a little film, it's in a contained area of one town, it takes place over the course of one day.'

"But in reality it's an ensemble cast, in an upper-middle class suburb, and everybody needs a house and everybody needed a car. And we were using established actors, people who had careers and lives and television shows. Trying to coordinate all of that — the schedules of the actors — and the quantity of story lines was overwhelming."

Although he learned this lesson too late to help him on the production of *Judy Berlin*, it did teach him a greater lesson about filmmaking in general.

"I realize why independent films always revolve around a bunch of idiot kids sitting on a curb somewhere doing drugs," he said. "Because you have one story line, you can shoot all hours with them, and the actors never have to go home."

NO MONEY = MORE CONTROL

The film's small, $200,000 budget provided Mendelsohn with something that he couldn't buy with a bigger budget – more control over every aspect of his film.

"People were offering us a lot of money to make this at a higher budget," he recalled. "However, the low budget was a way for me to maintain control."

Mendelsohn learned during the financing stage of preproduction that whenever outside producers offered to finance the film for more money, they also wanted to change elements that he was unwilling to alter.

"They wanted to make the film at a higher budget," he explained, "but could we get rid of Madeline Kahn? They wanted to make it at a higher budget, but could Judy Berlin be played by such and such a Hollywood star?

"But when you have nothing, nobody cares about you and that's great. So I had control with my little budget, I had absolute control."

The benefits of that low budget were not wasted on the film's leading lady, Edie Falco, who has found the atmosphere on low-budget productions to be often more conducive to creative results.

"There are so many advantages to working on a low-budget project," she said. "I feel totally comfortable with the idea of trying something and having it not work.

"I feel a sense of freedom to just go for it, because money is not at the forefront of everything that goes on with these things. You don't have a producer standing over you saying, 'We gotta make the day!'

"Everybody's just flying by the seat of their pants and I feel a sense of freedom that I don't when money is being talked about. It's been my experience that nothing but good stuff will come out of that."

TIME IS ON YOUR SIDE

While Mendelsohn clearly didn't have much money to work with, he did have something of equal or greater value — time. He could take all the time he wanted to plan out the shoot in meticulous detail.

"I worked on films my whole life and I have been a crew member my whole life. So I knew every trick," Mendelsohn explained. "I knew what we needed was preproduction. It was put together like a little army. It wasn't just knowing where we were headed every day; we also had at least two fallback positions for everything. This was months and months and months of preproduction."

Mendelsohn recommends taking a long, long time in preproduction, particularly if you have a tiny budget and an ambitious shoot.

"It's sort of unheard of, but I knew that if you don't have money and you don't have any more manpower than anyone else has, you need time," he reasoned. "So I just kept adding in preproduction time, because that was something I could afford."

FIX PROBLEMS QUICKLY

While he recommends taking the time you need on preproduction, there is one area where Mendelsohn advocates moving with all due speed — when you see a problem arising.

"The problem that you have two weeks before the shoot is better solved right then," he believes, "rather than on the set.

"If you have a sucky technician or a terrible, mean-spirited, lousy actor, two weeks or a week or a day before you shoot — it's a nightmare to replace. But that problem becomes a nightmare a hundred-fold the day you start shooting."

There's a tendency to rationalize your way out of it, rather than take immediate action, and according to Mendelsohn, you have to fight that impulse.

"You think, 'Well, it's two weeks before the shoot, it's too close.' Or, 'It's a day before the shoot, it's too close.' Nope, that's not the right thinking. Cut your losses even though you're about to shoot. It's better than watching the problem play out during the actual shoot."

FEWER TAKES, MORE SHOTS

It's not uncommon, particularly with directors who are just starting out, to shoot take after take, as if some unseen hand will sprinkle magic dust on a scene if you just shoot it enough times. Mendelsohn warns against this practice.

"Do fewer takes and shoot more shots," he suggests, because the reality is "you probably got it on the first or second take anyway. And when you get to the edit, shots — angles, set-ups — are elements that progress the story. Takes are just repetitive."

"You get a lot of directors who are nervous and they don't trust themselves or they don't trust the process," Falco added. "So, they might end up doing a lot more takes than they need, as if the actor is an infinite source of these things.

"But at a certain point I know I'm not doing work that I'm proud of anymore, I'm just exhausted. And they are just too afraid to say, 'Okay, let's move on.' And so you'll do another four, five takes, and I start thinking, 'Oh, this is not what I meant to do, this is not the take I want.' So that's a little rough."

THE FAMILY AND FRIENDS PLAN

Mendelsohn learned an important lesson on an earlier project that he successfully applied to the making of *Judy Berlin*.

"I had this crazy idea at the beginning of my short, *Through an Open Window*," he recounted. "I thought I'm going to try to make this *everyone's* film. Meaning the grips are going to feel involved and the craft services person is going to feel involved and passionate and want to work on it because I'm going to include everyone.

"It was a terrible decision," he said of that experience, "because films aren't democracies. They're monarchies. And the grip on your film isn't going to go to a festival with you; they're going to go on to a new job and be a grip again. They do not, and cannot, be expected to have the same passionate involvement as you do. They shouldn't. They should have professionalism."

That passion you need to help you get through production can often be found close to home. That's why key roles in *Judy Berlin* — the producer, the DP, the lead actress, among others — were all filled by close friends.

"If you use your friends," Mendelsohn said, "they can be expected to have a level of passion above and beyond a paycheck. They have an active interest in your success and the success of the project. And you can't buy that. You can't put an ad in the paper and get that. Those people who are there with you who are your friends have a vested interest that is just priceless."

Falco, Mendelsohn's long-time friend, agrees: "A lot of the films I've done I've done with friends and family. The advantage is you go in there feeling no obligation to prove yourself. There's a camaraderie and a trust that is inherent in just all of you being there together. It makes all the difference in the world. I know they trust me and I trust them. It gets that all out of the way so we can get down to work."

USE REALITY TO YOUR ADVANTAGE

Although filmmaking is usually about creating fake realities for the audience, there are times when a dose of actual reality can help make a scene more ... well, real.

A key moment in *Judy Berlin* takes place when Judy (played by Falco) stops by the grade school where her mother (Barbara Barrie) works, to say goodbye before Judy leaves for Los Angeles. The two women have a distant relationship, and Mendelsohn wanted to make sure the awkwardness of the mother/daughter dynamic made it to the screen.

His solution was unique: He kept the two actresses, who had never met, apart until just before the scene was shot.

"I didn't want them to become comfortable with each other," he explained, "and spend the

An awkward moment between mother (Barbara Barrie, right) and daughter (Edie Falco)

entire day chatting and getting to know each other. I thought the best way to do it — because it was a scene where two people are awkwardly meeting — was to let all the natural feelings that good actors have access to in moments of real awkwardness come out. And they did."

Falco was not aware of Mendelsohn's plan during the shoot. "I thought it was just a matter of scheduling," she said. "I thought, 'All right, I won't meet her until the day we shoot.' That's the way these things are."

When she learned of his plan after the fact, she thought it was a smart way to help both actresses in the scene.

"I think in retrospect it did help," Falco admitted. "She was a woman around whom I was unfamiliar. You hold your body differently; eye contact is different than with someone that you're comfortable around.

"I think physically the relationship that Judy and her mother had sort of mirrored that of strangers. In that regard, the subconscious stuff that was already taking place probably only fed what was happening in the script. And I imagine that was his intent."

Mendelsohn was happy with the finished scene. "It was nice to find that it worked," he said, adding, "I'm not a big fan of tricks unless they play out on-screen, otherwise it just makes a great back-story. This was just a shorthand way for me to get more out of the scene."

FAKE IT 'TIL YOU MAKE IT

The final lesson from Mendelsohn concerning his *Judy Berlin* experience is a basic lesson in how to be a director, and it's simply this: if you act like a director, people will believe you are a director.

"If you do not naturally have the kind of personality that is comforting, parental, and self-confident," he advises, "then act as if you do. That's it. Let no one know that it does not come naturally to you.

"People want so badly to believe that you're in charge," he continued, "that if you simply act as if you are in charge, even the worst imitation of being in charge actually goes over, and people believe it.

"You smile and act as if you're a confident person. It's how children learn and it works — you just pretend. I'm not kidding. You just smile and say, 'Hi, how are you? Good to see you. Now listen ...' And you think no one's going to buy this, this is the worst imitation since Lucille Ball pretending that she knows how to play the bongos at the Club. This is so pathetic.

"But the funny thing is, you'll find that everyone is listening to you, everyone's doing what you say, everyone's at your beck and call and people are comforted by the fact that you're in command.

"Then you go in the bathroom and have diarrhea."

Chapter Three

OUT OF THIS WORLD

Movies are a wonderful vehicle for taking us out of the real world and depositing us safely onto amazing worlds and lands heretofore unseen.

The movies highlighted in this chapter prove conclusively that a big budget is not required to create these otherly worlds.

In fact, it's the very lack of budget that made these filmmakers dig deep, creatively speaking, to come up with the visions that they fashioned — visions that, in some cases, still haunt audiences years after the films were first unveiled.

CARNIVAL OF SOULS

|||||||||||||||||||||||||||||||||||||||||||||||||||||||||||||||||||||||||||||||||||||||||||||||||

If there's one lesson to be learned from *Carnival of Souls*, it's that you can't keep a good movie down.

It's the ultimate irony that a film that explores how the dead walk among us rose from the dead itself, years after its presumed demise. What's more, in a world of successful low-budget movies, *Carnival of Souls* is a classic movie that's probably best-known for being unsuccessful — at least in its first incarnation.

Director Herk Harvey put it succinctly. "It's a heck of a note," he has said, "when a film that has failed financially is your total breadth of success in the feature film market."

That wasn't their goal when they started out. "We didn't set out to make a classic," explained cinematographer Maurice Prather. "We just wanted to make a movie that would make a little money."

Actor Sidney Berger agreed. "It never occurred to me that *Carnival of Souls* would last beyond its initial showings," he confessed. "None of the people involved thought that it had any kind of future.

"The life the film has taken on since then is absolutely mind-boggling to me. It's this obscure, small, black-and-white movie, and people just adore it. I have no idea why it has had the effect it's had."

At the time it was shot, in 1962, Lawrence, Kansas was a hotbed of film production, at least on the corporate industrial side. And local filmmakers were itching to try something a little more challenging.

"Robert Altman, also an industrial filmmaker at that time, had just completed a feature film, *The Delinquents*, in Kansas City," Harvey remembered. "And we figured, if he can do it, we can do it."

Unlike many first-time filmmakers, Harvey didn't have much trouble raising funding for the movie. It probably helped that he wasn't asking for all that much money.

"I talked to a couple of local investors, who then talked to other people," Harvey recalled. "And the sum of $17,000 was raised over a weekend, which I thought was really pretty amazing, because in those days that was a fairly good sum. Although the idea of doing a 35mm feature film for $17,000 was a little staggering, even then."

With deferred salaries, their total cost for production was only about $30,000. And there was no mistaking this for anything but a low-budget production.

"There were no dressing room facilities, catered food, makeup people, stand-ins, special effects or stunt crews," Harvey explained. "We made do with what we had and we had to accept what we got. No retakes. We filmed, basically, on a 3:1 shooting ratio."

The end result is a unique, one-of-a-kind movie that still works today, in its own dream-like way. Employing interesting locations and camera angles, along with some innovative editing (check out the cut from turning the car key to turning the organ knob early in the movie, or the simple pan to black at the gas station that becomes the inside of the rooming house door), Harvey and his team created a low-buck classic that still haunts people today.

"People have asked why *Carnival of Souls* is still around, playing in theaters thirty years after it was made," said screenwriter John Clifford, "when hundreds or even thousands of other low-budget, black-and-white films have been long forgotten. I think it has something to do with the fact that we didn't try to copy anyone else's past successes.

"From the writer's angle," Clifford continued, "I was freed by the fact that I had no need to worry about Hollywood formats. I didn't have to conform in any way. It is, for instance, one of the few films from that period, or even today, that has no love story or romance, even as a subplot."

Carnival of Souls broke many rules, some that helped the film and some that hurt it, and many of which provide lessons for filmmakers today and well into the future.

EXPLOIT THE UNIQUE

One of the many advantages to working outside the Hollywood system in general, and outside the Los Angeles geography in particular, is the interesting look you can give your movie by using locations that haven't been done to death in other films.

For Herk Harvey, a unique location he stumbled across became the spark that started the whole process.

"It was sunset and I was driving back to Kansas from California when I first saw Saltair," he recalled. "It's an amusement park, located at the end of a half-mile causeway out into the Great Salt Lake.

"I felt I had been transported into a different time and dimension. I couldn't believe what I was seeing. I stopped the car and walked out to the pavilion. The hair stood up on the back of my neck. It was the spookiest location I had ever seen.

"When I got back to Kansas," he continued, "I discussed Saltair with my friend, co-worker and writer John Clifford. We agreed that with the Saltair location, and others that we had locally, we just might be able to develop a script for a feature film."

John Clifford picks up the story there: "Herk described to me a strange outdoor ballroom he had seen rotting on the shores of the Great Salt Lake, and said he'd like to make a film about creatures rising from the lake and doing a dance of death in this pavilion. That was the image he had and he asked if I would create a script encompassing that."

Clifford stewed on the idea for a while. "While thinking about a character and a story," he said, "I was also trying to think of locations that would put atmosphere on the screen at little expense. And one of the places I thought about was the Reuter Organ Company here in Lawrence, Kansas. Reuter builds church pipe organs — and I had seen the room where they assemble and test these exposed pipes.

"I liked the weirdness of the atmosphere," he continued. "I decided to make the girl an organist. That was the key for me, the catalyst. Everything flowed from that on my mental screen. It was one of those things where you write by instinct rather than anything else. The script took only two weeks."

Once the script was written and the money raised, the next step was finding the right cast.

FIRST IMPRESSIONS / SECOND CHANCES

Local actor Sidney Berger was cast first, in the role of the nerdy rooming house neighbor, Mr. Linden (a performance that Roger Ebert called "the definitive study of a nerd in lust").

When casting the female lead locally proved impossible, Berger, who was headed to New York for a few days, offered to find an actress there. Harvey agreed, explaining to Berger what he was looking for: "I wanted a girl who had an ethereal quality and yet was pretty," he recalled.

However, when he finally met the actress, Candace Hilligoss, his first impression was so negative that he immediately regretted handing the casting chores off to someone else and was convinced that he would have to recast.

"When Candace got off the plane in Kansas City," Harvey recalled, "I thought Sidney Berger had done us in. She looked and dressed like a flower child of the sixties; she was very quiet and projected zilch. All that night I agonized over how to tell her that she wasn't right for the part."

Harvey had succumbed to a common casting misconception: He expected to see the character of Mary Henry step off the plane. What Harvey hadn't taken into account was that Hilligoss was an actress, hired to play a part.

"The next morning she was to read for us," Harvey said, "and when she came in, her hair and features sparkled. She projected coolness and confusion. She was an actress. And she was Mary Henry."

And that's when he learned the value of giving your first impressions a second chance.

GO LOW-TECH

Many supernatural movies try to wow the audiences with state-of-the-art effects, but *Carnival of Souls* took the opposite approach, relying on mood and minimal special effects to create a creepy and other-worldly atmosphere.

This decision was made early on. "We decided the film would feature someone being chased," Clifford explained, "and since there wouldn't be much budget, we couldn't indulge in a lot of expensive effects."

Director of Photography Prather agreed: "We had basically no special effects whatsoever. The only 'special effect' per se is the time Mary Henry rolls up her car window and the ghost (played by director Harvey) appears on it."

Although the effect is impressive, not a lot went into its creation. "We created that in the studio ourselves," Prather recalled. "We did it with a mirror."

KNOW WHAT YOU'RE SIGNING

While it's often difficult to pinpoint exactly how a "lost" film is re-discovered, in the case of *Carnival of Souls*, it's quite clear why and how it got lost in the first place.

The filmmakers' lack of knowledge of the movie industry, which actually helped them create the movie, was their downfall when it came time to distribute the film.

"In the early days of independent productions, it was very hard to find anybody who would distribute a film. Herk found this small distribution company," Prather recalled.

"We finally ended up with a distributor in California," Harvey explained. "We had high hopes for a return on our investment, which would enable us to produce more films."

Harvey signed the distribution papers and then took off to South America, to shoot a number of geography films for the company he worked for in Kansas.

"When I returned, I contacted the distributor," Harvey said. "They said, yes, they owed us money and that they would send us a check. When their check arrived, it bounced and I knew we were in trouble. They were out of business."

With the distributor out of business, the lab that had made all the prints seized the film.

"The deal with the laboratories is if you don't pay for the product, it becomes their property," explained Prather, "and they can sell it to anybody they damn well please. That's what happened to Herk's film. The worst part was that the film was never copyrighted. We didn't know much about copyright laws."

Harvey realized his limitations too late. "It was a big mistake," he admitted. "At the time, we had all the experience necessary to produce films, but not the knowledge of the business end of distribution."

Harvey had mixed feeling about the experience. "Making the film had been very exciting," he recalled. "Distributing the film had been agonizing. We bowed our heads and went back to our regular filmmaking activities."

The lab later sold the film to another lab, which then sold it for television broadcast, which was where this lost gem was eventually discovered by a new generation of film fans.

Unique as *Carnival of Souls* is, its director considers the film's very existence to be something of a fluke.

"Looking back," Harvey recalled, "I was surprised that we even had the guts to shoot it. If I have one message, it's that you can do anything when you make your mind up to make a film. The stress and strange luck will always come together on your side."

NIGHT OF
THE LIVING DEAD

‖‖‖

"Romero's groundbreaking film was like a box of rattlesnakes delivered to a tea party."

Stephen King

Mr. King is dead right. George Romero's *Night of the Living Dead* shook up unsuspecting audiences like no film had ever done before. There was no template for this experience, no past cinematic memory for audiences to cling to.

In short, they'd never seen anything like it.

King described the unfamiliar elements that this film presented to movie-goers: "The hero of *Night of the Living Dead* was a young black drifter; the heroine was insane after the first ten minutes, all the main characters die — all but one of them eaten alive — and the reinforcements come too late."

Like many classic works of art, *Night of the Living Dead* is deceptively simple: A group of strangers gathers in a deserted farm house to fend off the lethal attacks of the newly dead who have risen from their graves with a hankering for human flesh. Like the living dead in the title, the film is formidable and relentless.

As with many independent films, it started with a group of friends who shared the desire, and the filmmaking skills, to make their own low-budget feature. And, like many filmmakers before and since, the decision was reached in a bar. At least, that's the way co-screenwriter John Russo remembers it, recalling George Romero's enthusiasm for the idea.

"'We're going to make a movie!' George yelled, and banged his fist on the tabletop so hard that the bottles, glasses and ashtrays rattled," recalled Russo. "All the customers in the bar heard him and turned to gawk at us. But we were laughing and ordering more beer, doping out the initial details of our big venture."

"Ten of us formed a corporation called Image Ten," director Romero explained, "and advanced the seed money to begin production." All they needed was an idea and a script. Romero felt he had what they needed.

"I had written a short story," Romero said, "an allegory inspired by Richard Matheson's *I Am Legend*, which dealt with the mass return from the grave of the recently dead and their need to feed off the flesh and blood of the living.

"I was in the process of converting the idea to a shooting script, but was only half finished when the company was ready to begin shooting. John Russo took over the task of script writing."

While Russo wrote, Romero and his crew tracked down their primary location: a deserted farmhouse. "We found this old farmhouse that they were going to tear down," Romero said, "so we said, 'Let us do that for you. Give us a try.'"

They decorated the house with $50 worth of furniture from Goodwill and started shooting. Once shooting was completed, the final step for the group was choosing a title.

"Our first finished 35mm print bore the title *Night of the Flesheaters*," Russo recalled, "but we had to change it when we got threatened by a lawyer whose clients had already made a picture by that name.

"The next title was *Night of Anubis* — George's brainchild — Anubis being the Egyptian god of death," Russo explained. "It wasn't until the picture was ready for release that it was given its final title, *Night of the Living Dead*."

The movie went on to become a classic in the genre, and is now part of the permanent film collection of New York's Museum of Modern Art.

For Romero, there really was just one downside to the experience of making *Night of the Living Dead*: "The only problem," he said, "was that this movie made it seem like the movie business was pretty easy."

CAST WITH CARE

The cast of *Night of the Living Dead* is uniformly excellent, but one cast member — Duane Jones, who played the male lead, Ben — received extra attention from critics, primarily because it was one of the first times that a black male was the lead in a picture that wasn't concerned with race issues. His casting is a great lesson in the value that colorblind casting can bring to a project.

For their part, the Image Ten folks weren't trying to set any precedents. They simply wanted as strong a cast as possible.

"The truth of the matter is that Duane was the best actor who auditioned for that part," explained producer Russ Streiner. "Originally, a friend of ours, Rudy Ricci, was supposed to play that character, and even Rudy voted to give the role to Duane after he saw his audition."

"We cast a black man not because he was black," explained Romero, "but because we liked Duane's audition better than others we had seen. The socio-political implications of Ben's being black have been studied and pondered and written about in various journals, and it caused one critic in his exuberance to write that he heard the strains of 'Ole Man River' in the music score when Ben meets his fate.

"Perhaps *Night of the Living Dead* is the first film to have a black man playing the lead role regardless of, rather than because of, his color, and in that sense the observation of the fact is valid, but we did not calculate that this would be an attention-grabber. We backed into it."

"He just turned out to be the best person for the part," Streiner added. "He would have gotten the part if he were an Asian or an American Indian or an Eskimo."

IT'S NOT YOUR PROBLEM (IT'S YOUR CHARACTER'S PROBLEM)

Accidents happen. And when they do, it's the smart filmmaker who can turn that accident into an advantage.

In the case of *Night of the Living Dead*, the accident in question was a car crash that happened to the car they were using. The car belonged to producer Russ Steiner's mother.

"Between the first day of shooting in the cemetery and the second day of shooting in the cemetery, which was some time later," Streiner explained, "a car ran into my mother's car and dented the front fender pretty badly. We decided we could either pay to repair it, or work it into the story."

They opted for the latter, making the car crash the character's problem, while getting some free production value in the process.

"We made it look as though this had happened when Barbara, chased by the cemetery ghoul, crashes the car into a tree," Russo said. "That way we could have a 'car wreck' in our movie without paying for it."

HOLD ONTO YOUR VISION

Holding onto your vision of your movie is one of the trickiest parts of the process, because there are so many points where you can be pulled off track.

For the team who made *Night of the Living Dead*, part of that vision was the film's ending, which came into question when they started showing the movie to distributors.

"We showed the film to distributors in New York and Los Angeles," Romero recalled. "American-International liked it, but they said it was too unmitigating. They said, 'How'd you like to change the ending?' They wanted an up ending. They wanted the black guy to survive."

The filmmakers didn't want their main character to survive, which lost them a potential distributor. However, they ensured that their vision — and this particular plot point — would remain intact even during postproduction, by only shooting one possible ending for the film.

"We had talked for some time about the possibility or the necessity to shoot a second ending," Streiner explained, "and then we decided — collectively — to not do that; to just shoot the ending that we thought the movie had to have, and that way we wouldn't be tempted by some distributor to change it."

MAKE THE BEST DAMNED [*FILL IN THE BLANK*] MOVIE YOU CAN

One of the primary reasons that *Night of the Living Dead* remains a classic to this day is that the filmmakers didn't look down on their subject matter.

There is no tongue-in-cheek joking, no nudge-nudge to the camera, no sense that what we're seeing isn't an absolutely realistic depiction of how people would behave in that situation.

Or, as horror expert Stephen King put it, "At its best, *Night of the Living Dead* feels more like a Frederick Wiseman documentary than a horror flick."

That feeling was created by design, with the filmmakers consciously deciding to make the best movie they could, regardless of the subject matter.

"We were dealing with a fantasy premise," explained Streiner, "but deep down inside we were all serious filmmakers and somewhat disappointed because we had to resort to horror for our first film.

"We then tried to make the best, most realistic horror film that we could make on the money we had available. In all aspects of the production we treated it as a serious film, although sometimes it's hard to treat that kind of premise seriously. I think that overriding viewpoint is displayed in the final product. Once you buy the fact that the dead come back to life, it's treated in all other regards as a serious film."

"The philosophy of our movie-making group," said Russo, "was that not only did the terror have to be believable, but so did the people confronting it. They had to think and act the way ordinary people really would behave in a crisis."

"And I think that's one of the reasons the film has been so successful and attained classic status," Streiner added. "I think the audience senses that energy.

"For all of the flaws and everything else that we know are in the movie, and the low-budgetness of it, there is still a human energy that is involved in this production that budget can't replace."

DARK STAR

||||||||||||||||||||||||||||||||||||||||||||||||||||||||||||||||||||||||||||||||||||||||||||||||||||

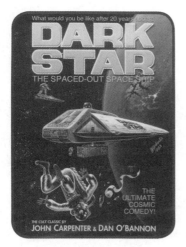

The quirky space comedy *Dark Star* launched a number of careers and trends in the movie business.

The film put director/co-writer/producer/composer John Carpenter and co-writer/production designer/actor/editor Dan O'Bannon on the map; it introduced the concept of a "used future" to moviegoers; and it also gave some early experience to a handful of special-effects artists who would shape the way movies looked for many years after.

A quick glance through the credits of *Dark Star* reveal such familiar names (familiar, at least, to special-effects geeks) as Greg Jein, Bill Taylor, Ron Cobb and Jim Danforth — artists who would later have an impact on movies as varied as *Star Wars, Alien, Aliens, Back to the Future, Escape from New York, Blade Runner, Spaceballs, 2010, The Thing, Cape Fear,* and *From Hell.*

However, *Dark Star* might not have been more than just a blip on the interspace radar screen if not for the perseverance of Carpenter and O'Bannon.

The idea for a film about a spaceship in the deeper reaches of space blowing up potentially unstable planets came from an unlikely literary source. "At the start, Dan O'Bannon and I conceived of the film as a *Waiting For Godot* in outer space," Carpenter has admitted.

Upon completing their fifty-minute film at the University of Southern California (USC), the pair found that — like the fictional Godot — their finished movie was in danger of never appearing in front of an actual audience.

"When we took it to the USC Cinema department and started talking to them about taking it to festivals," O'Bannon said, "We were told it was too long — that it should have been twenty minutes long, and then they would have taken it around to festivals. But because it was fifty minutes long, they couldn't do anything with it.

"John and I were pretty upset about that," O'Bannon continued, "because it meant nobody would see it. We only had one option — go ahead and shoot some extra scenes. Expanding it meant we were going to have to shoot a lot of scenes that were filler, and that would lessen the tightness of the story and make it into an episodic film. It was kind of disappointing, because that meant we had to go from the most-impressive student film ever made to one of the cheapest features in history."

The film is still well-regarded for its humor, visual design, performances (particularly O'Bannon as the plucky yet prickly Sergeant Pinback), and the many lessons it affords filmmakers throughout the galaxy.

TIME IS ON YOUR SIDE

Although the length of their finished movie was initially an issue, the amount of time it took them to complete the film was always a positive aspect of the project.

Time can be your friend or your enemy in low-budget filmmaking, and in the case of *Dark Star* the filmmakers found a way to use time to their advantage. In fact, in O'Bannon's view, they couldn't have done it any other way.

Unlike traditional movies, with a cast and crew on salary and the clock ticking on equipment and location fees, Carpenter and O'Bannon, using USC resources, made the film at a relatively leisurely pace.

"The only thing that made it possible with the small amount of money that we had is that we would shoot for a few days, then we would stop for a couple weeks while we scraped together enough resources and money to shoot another scene or two," O'Bannon said.

"If we hadn't had those long time gaps, I don't think we could have done that picture on that budget."

GO LOW-TECH

Upon realizing that their budget wouldn't allow them to imitate space classics like *2001: A Space Odyssey*, O'Bannon and Carpenter decided to make their lack of funds part of the joke and create a spaceship that looked as lived in as a college dorm.

Although it's a common image today in science fiction movies, making a futuristic world look old was a new idea in the early seventies.

"I believe that I am the inventor of the used future," O'Bannon said. "We were very much under the trance of *2001*, John and myself.

"*Dark Star*, in a lot of ways, is a joke on *2001*. And since *2001* was big and spectacular and shiny and clean, we decided to go the opposite way and make *Dark Star* small and grubby and funny. This was the seventies, and everyone was grubby with long hair anyway. We figured we'd put a bunch of hippies out in space and make everything look rundown."

Besides the humorous aspects of this production design decision, there was also a strong creative motive behind it. To O'Bannon's eye, the world they were creating simply looked more real the more he beat things up and added junk to the set.

"I was getting more dissatisfied with high-tech stuff in science fiction movies, where the models just didn't look real for some reason," he recalled. "I finally hit on the fact that everything was too clean when they depicted the future.

"So I got the idea that if you wanted to fool the audience with scale, if you dirty it up a lot, there might be the shock of recognition and it might look bigger."

While this approach seemed to work while they were shooting, O'Bannon wasn't thrilled with the results on screen. "When we looked at footage, the actors (including me) looked grubby enough, but the sets — which I had grubbed up pretty good — didn't look all that grubby. The ship didn't look anywhere near in as bad shape as I thought I made it. After we got through lighting it and shooting it and editing it, it just wasn't that prominent."

It wasn't until he got to the set of *Alien*, which he scripted (sharing story credit with Ronald Shusett), that he saw how it needed to be done.

"When *Alien* came along and Ridley Scott took over the reins of directing," O'Bannon explained, "he picked up on the used future idea and he knew some things I didn't know.

"He knew that if you wanted the audience to actually see that the details of the set were kind of grubby, you had to build it five times exaggerated, or the camera wouldn't even pick it up.

"When they started dressing the control room set, I walked around and saw all the broken things hanging around and I started getting concerned. It looked like a bad joke. But then when I saw some dailies, I thought, oh, it looks just right. Ridley knew how to get that on the screen."

Due to the passage of time, some set dressings that might have produced laughs in *Dark Star's* first release aren't recognizably funny to today's audiences. For example, Sergeant Pinback's video diary is actually an 8-track tape, and the machine he uses to record it is really a microfiche machine, jokes that are lost on a modern audience.

However one prop is still as funny today as when the film came out: the alien that is the ship's mascot, which is played with great menace and humor by ... a beach ball.

As it turns out, beach balls were not an uncommon item on the *Dark Star* set, because they were used as the starting point for planet models.

"What we would do with this giant beach ball is use bathroom plungers to hold it up, paint it, and photograph the top of its surface," Carpenter explained.

"Someone who was helping on the film was carrying this inflated beach ball," he continued, "and O'Bannon and I immediately looked at each

other and said, 'What if the alien who is supposed to be on board looked like a beach ball with legs?' Then we imagined that one of the characters had to take care of it. That was the genesis of it.

"We spray-painted the beach ball, put monster claws beneath it, and got Nick Castle behind it to be the claws and give them some sort of life."

Although the beach ball alien is a highlight of the film, some people found the image disturbing. And one of those people was George Lucas.

"When I did a few little special effects on the first *Star Wars*," O'Bannon recalled, "Lucas had seen *Dark Star*, with the beach ball alien. He was very disturbed; it was the most disturbed I have ever seen Lucas. He said, 'It was just a beach ball!' I said, 'That's right, George, it was just a beach ball. Best we could do.' He wanted it better than that. Well, I wanted it better too."

(Discerning viewers will find a nod to Lucas in *Dark Star*, when some space debris flies by the camera, bearing the lettering "Toilet Tank THX 1138.")

Carpenter and O'Bannon used another low-tech trick for one of the added sequences in the longer version of the film: Sergeant Pinback's frightening ride clutching the bottom of the ship's elevator, while dangling near the top of the long elevator shaft. After they wrote the scene, they had to figure out how to shoot it safely and for very little money.

"The first thing we thought was that we'd go find an elevator shaft somewhere," O'Bannon explained, "but that didn't get very far before we realized — never mind whether it was practical or impractical — it was dangerous.

"So we finally came up with the idea of let's just do it on its side. What the hell. At least we can do it that way, and maybe if it's funny and exciting people won't care."

Carpenter explained how the illusion worked: "The elevator shaft was built on a sound stage, about eighty feet long. It was horizontal. We turned the camera on its side and shot both sideways and upside down.

"When you see him dangling from the elevator, he's merely lying on a platform sticking his feet up to appear like he's in danger of falling. The elevator itself was a crab dolly with a piece of masonite in front of it, painted silver. You only see the bottom of it."

O'Bannon agreed that this was the safest way of pulling off the shots, but the endeavor was not without its consequences.

"I ended up having an appendectomy right after I shot that scene," he recalled. "I just had that board down to my butt, and I had to keep my legs up, waving around in the air. Sometimes I think that I forced some food or something into my appendix from all that stress."

O'Bannon admits that, despite how safe they made it, it's a stunt he wouldn't attempt today. "I was twenty-six years old, and you really don't think what that sort of thing is going to do to you," he said. "You just have a good idea and you start to do it. And then you find out how hard it is.

"Today I wouldn't be able to do it all, even if I were willing to try, which I wouldn't be."

MAKE YOUR OWN OPPORTUNITIES

Although *Dark Star* helped launch his career, Carpenter is the first to admit that it wasn't necessarily talent that opened the door for him.

"The most talented directors that I knew in my class at school never got a chance," he recalled. "They were better than me, and they never got a shot at it. Why is that? I can't say for sure. Maybe they didn't push hard enough.

"You gotta go out and make it happen for yourself," Carpenter continued. "That's really the answer that every director who ever came to film school and lectured to my class gave. You have to make your breaks. You have to go out and do it.

"You have to show them one way or the other that you have what it takes. It may take you years to prove it, and you may indeed fail, but if you want it to happen you've got to try, you have to make your own breaks."

NO MONEY = MORE CONTROL

Despite the difficulties they encountered in bringing *Dark Star* to life, O'Bannon still feels that working at that low-budget level has many advantages over the higher-budget films he subsequently was involved in.

"One of the advantages to having no money is that you could do anything you want," he said. "You don't have some asshole standing there, saying 'We want a re-write.' Or, 'That's in bad taste,' or 'We've been talking it over, and we think you should —' No. Fuck you.

"John and I wrote a scene, and if we both liked it we went out and shot it," he said. "In that regard it beat all subsequent filmmaking hands down.

"You could just do what you wanted to do. It may have been hard, and you may not have had resources and it was a challenge, but you didn't have some butt hole sitting on your back like Sinbad's Old Man of the Sea, with his arms and legs wrapped around your head, telling you how to ruin your film."

π

||||||||||||||||||||||||||||||||||||||||||||||||||||||||||||||||||||||||||||||||||||||||||||||||||||||

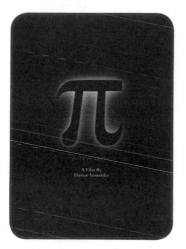

Creating strange, alien worlds isn't just about traveling through outer space. Inner space can be just as mysterious, cheaper to produce, and often a lot more interesting than the standard, cliché-filled science fiction movie we've all seen a million times before.

Director Darren Aronofsky's feature, π, grew from an arresting image that he found intriguing.

"I have a single image," Aronofsky wrote in his journal, "of Sean Gullette, my actor friend from college, standing in front of the mirror, his head shaved bald, digging into his skull with an X-acto blade for an implant he thinks is there."

That image grew into a tight thriller about paranoia, mathematics, computers, and the formula that explains the universe. Made for a mere $60,000, it was sold to Artisan Entertainment for $1 million, snagging the Best Director prize for Aronofsky at the Sundance Film Festival along the way.

"The core of the film is a thriller," Aronofksy explained, "but I wanted to merge genres. I grew up on Hollywood movies and was looking for something new. I was getting bored with a lot of the indie films, too, some of which were art house but repetitive.

"π melds elements of a psychological thriller with tinges of science fiction — not as in effects-driven, futuristic films like *Star Wars*. We don't need to see things blow up anymore, we have seen everything blow up from plants to planets."

Aronofsky looked to the past as well as the future while designing his story, referencing several ancient myths, including that of ill-fated Icarus, who fashioned wings to fly. One theme of his script is "If you fly too close to the sun, you get burnt."

Aronofsky pointed out another myth that influenced his script. "It's Prometheus: If you steal fire from the gods, they send giant birds to come out and eat your liver. It's that typical Faustian journey, a retelling of this old mythology for the digital, cyberworld age."

Mixing the old and the new, the mundane with the mythic, is a core part of Aronofsky's filmmaking philosophy.

"Personally, I don't believe there are that many original ideas," he explained. "The originality is when you absorb them into your own interpretation.

"To me, filmmakers are like blenders. We take different ideas, which are like different fruits — bananas, cherries, strawberries — and stick them in a blender to make a big smoothie that's our own creation. The ingredients in the smoothie are all out there in the world; it's simply the filmmaker's choice as to which ones to use."

FIND THE ANGLE/HAVE A HOOK

Rather than waiting until the film was in the can, Aronofsky came up with a marketing hook for his movie even before he started writing the script.

"I want to call the movie π," he wrote in his journal. "When the idea came to me, it made so much sense.

"Plus it's a great marketing angle. I can see it now: πs everywhere — stenciled on buildings and street corners, billboards, napkins, matchbooks, beer coasters.

"I'm super excited because a symbol hasn't been used for a movie title. It will make people think. People will see the symbol and say, 'What's that?' Then the hook is in and we just need to give them the info of how to get to the theater."

IT'S THE SCRIPT, STUPID

Max, the main char- acter in π, is a brilliant mathematician who approaches the system of mathematics — and the world in general — with an extremely structured, rigorous, thought process bordering on madness.

Aronofsky adopted a similarly rigorous plan for writing the script for π, steering clear of the madness but laying out a very strict approach to getting the work done without whining or excuses.

The rules he drafted were for his own purposes, but they also provide a reasonable set of guidelines for getting your script written quickly and efficiently:

1. Always move forward. If you have a problem, type through it.
2. Only take a break after something good happens on the page or you accomplish a goal. No breaks for confusion: type through it.
3. Ten pages a day minimum.
4. Only go back to add something. Do not remove contradictions, just make a note.
5. Do it. Suffer, live, cry, struggle.
6. Have fun.

GOT THEME?

Even though the finished movie is highly stylized, the stylization for π was developed to support the movie's story and its theme, and not simply for the sake of stylization. For Aronofsky, that's a key filmmaking principal.

"Basically," he explained, "what we try to do is discipline ourselves to never use stylistic techniques unless it pushes the narrative forward."

Knowing your film's theme, and recognizing how that theme can mold and shape every aspect of the movie, including style, will have a big impact on the finished product.

"You start with your theme and your story," Aronofsky explained. "Whenever you know what your theme is and what your theme is about, there's only one place to put the camera. There is only one place that you tell the story from. The film is very clear once you understand that.

"That is my whole schooling. Akira Kurasawa is my god, an extremely disciplined filmmaker. Wherever he places the camera, it's the right place to place the camera, there's no other place to put the camera, it's in the right place.

"That's what I search for when I go onto a set: what angle is going to really tell this. Then I have every department approach it that way."

Although he followed that approach on π, Aronofsky was surprised to learn something about his theme while in the midst of making his movie.

"While working on this movie on paranoia," he recalled, "I started to realize that the filmmaking process is a paranoid experience. Because they always tell you in filmmaking that every single scene should relate to your main character, relate to your theme.

"And that's exactly what paranoid schizophrenics think their world is. That the entire world relates to them. So filmmaking is a paranoid experience."

THE FAMILY AND FRIENDS PLAN

Aronofsky used the production of π to test and confirm a number of his philosophies about filmmaking: the importance of theme, the blending of genres, the approach he took to the scriptwriting process. The movie also allowed him to put another philosophy into action: Work with your friends — people who are as passionate as you are — to achieve your goals.

"I know all this may sound soft," he admitted, "but the fact is that nothing can make up for creative partners. I spent many years struggling by myself to push the bus over the hill, but with partners I'll be damned if that crest ain't coming soon. And then — besides some potholes and bumps — it's all downhill."

He felt that with the support of two key friends — co-writer and producer Eric Watson and actor and co-writer Sean Gullette — they were virtually invincible.

"I believe the three of us will make a firm base for this monster collaboration,"he noted. "A triangle holding up a giant circle. Our personalities blend and contrast enough so that the most obvious weaknesses are covered. If any of us stumble, we'll have two friends to pick us up."

SHARE THE WEALTH

Aronofsky also felt that *anyone* who worked on the film deserved to benefit from any success it might achieve. As he noted in his journal: "Eric and I have decided to put our commie leanings to the test. Fifty percent of the film's profits will go to our investors. The other fifty percent will be divided amongst all the filmmakers."

"That's the only way to get it done," Aronofsky explained later. "On a film made for $60,000, the only way you get it done is with a tremendous amount of favors.

"Every single person on the film, from the P.A. to me to Sean to the producer to the first A.C., are all equal profit sharers in the film. There's a pool of 50% of the film which all of us share equally. That's the way to do it. That's how we got their passion."

With that philosophy in place, they dove into their first day of shooting. But not before starting the day (and the film) with a short ritual.

"The entire crew and cast joined hands and we all formed an economic and artistic partnership, a socialist collection," Aronofsky wrote in his journal.

"I made a speech from my heart. I thanked all and offered everyone a chance to take risks, a chance to make π their own, a chance at meaningful collaboration. I almost cried. My mom did. (She's doing craft services.) Now we shoot — no more excuses."

TAKE A BREAK

The movie production process — long hours of writing, scouting, money-raising and preproduction, followed by two to four weeks of grueling eighteen-hour days of shooting, followed by weeks or months of painstaking editing — can take a physical, emotional and creative toll on a filmmaker.

During that process, you have to find ways to recharge your batteries. For Aronofsky, nothing does that better than taking a few hours off to see a movie.

His production diary has one chapter entitled, *Sometimes You Gotta Just Go See a Movie*. In it, he notes: "I gave the editing crew the weekend off. After a fantastic push, the crew has earned it. We're all a bit exhausted, and a break is exactly what I needed. Today I will go see Woo's *Face-Off* and hopefully have a good time. I am broke."

GO LOW-TECH

A primary character in π is Euclid, the super-computer that Max has built for his numerical studies. Euclid is a big character, not just in the sense of the impact the computer has on the story, but in size as well. It is nearly as large as Max's small apartment.

When it came time to design Euclid, Aronofsky knew immediately what he didn't want.

"When you watch any of the old sci-fi films," Aronofsky said, "my big problem with them is that they date because they try to project what the

future will look like. It's really hard to do that, because you're always wrong.

"So what we tried to do was take technology that we all know, but say it has special abilities because of its size and its wiring."

Using old technology to evoke the future is not a new idea, and Aronofsky admits exactly where the spark for the idea came from: Terry Gilliam and a little flick called *Brazil*.

"We tried to learn from a master," Aronofsky said. "The whole idea was we took Terry Gilliam's brilliance and tried to copycat it a little in the sense of taking old technology and putting it into a hyper-future reality.

"If there's a throwback to old technology, then people accept it more that this is an alternative world. We did that with everything from the dot-matrix printer to the old disk drive and the old keyboards. Yet, Euclid was more powerful than any computer in the world."

DUMPSTERS ARE YOUR FRIENDS

Aronofsky found the parts to build Euclid in a serendipitous manner, just this side of dumpster diving. He had done some video work for a local corporation and made a discovery when he went to their offices to get paid.

"When I was picking up my last check from the Evil Petroleum Empire," he wrote in his journal, "I noticed a room filled with old computers and parts.

"I told them they could keep the $500 they still owed me if they let me empty their room. They were more than thrilled. I sent for Franklin and the van, and we packed the shit out of it."

POVERTY BREEDS CREATIVITY

From the moment he started π, Aronofsky knew he had a big challenge ahead of him. People don't usually set out to make highly-stylized, science-fiction thrillers for $60,000.

"People normally perceive science fiction as effects-laden and high production value," he said. "We wanted that high production value, but we didn't have the money to spend, so we basically tried to take our physical limitations and turn them to our advantage.

"By recognizing what we couldn't do, we accepted that and just made what we could do as good as we could.

"Everyone was sort of laughing at me for the concept of 'we're trying to do a science fiction film with no money.' But if you stop exploring outer space and explosions, which science fiction has sort of been captivated with for the last twenty years, and you start exploring inner space — in the tradition of Philip K. Dick and Rod Serling — you can do things with less money."

Chapter Four

IN A LEAGUE OF THEIR OWN

The filmmakers in this chapter are from what some might call the "don't try this at home" school of filmmaking — artists who have transcended the medium and are working at a level way above the rest of us.

What they've created is often so original that you'd be inclined to think there is nothing that we mere mortals could glean from their work. Well, you'd be wrong.

For all their originality, they faced the same obstacles and the same problems that filmmakers have always faced.

The difference is, they found ways to overcome those problems while simultaneously creating something amazing and original. They have much to teach us.

95

SHADOWS

||||||||||||||||||||||||||||||||||||||||||||||||||||||||||||||||||||||||||||||||||||||||||||||||

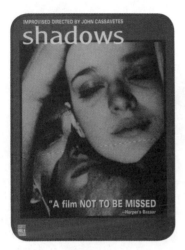

John Cassavetes was, undeniably, a unique actor, but he shared one emotion with his fellow thespians: the frustration actors feel about how little control they have about the parts they're offered and how little say they have in the direction of the projects they work on.

This dissatisfaction with the acting process pushed him into directing and creating his first film, *Shadows*.

"As an actor you don't get the freedom to function the way you'd like to," he once remarked. "I couldn't stand the idea of sitting around for a couple of years waiting for the phone to ring. It drove me crazy. So I found other people that it drove crazy too and we started working together. It saved me from going off the deep end."

He found relief in a loosely organized acting workshop that he began in New York. Doing scene work and improvisations was just the beginning; soon a project began to grow out of the work they were doing.

"*Shadows* began as a dream in a New York loft on January 13, 1957," Cassavetes remembered. "One particular improvisation exploded with life. It was about a black girl who passes for white. It was a basic melodramatic situation in which she was seduced by a young man, who then realized that she was colored. The wild dream grew that this improvisation could be captured on film."

Although he had acted on television and appeared in a handful of movies, Cassavetes didn't want to follow traditional paths on this project. Instead, he wanted to work in a non-traditional, non-Hollywood manner. That applied to all aspects — the writing, the casting, the shooting ... and, to begin with, the money-raising.

"I went on a radio show," he recalled, "and I said, 'Wouldn't it be terrific if just people could make movies instead of all these Hollywood bigwigs who are only interested in business and how much the picture was going to gross and everything?' The next day, two thousand dollars in dollar bills came in."

Using that start-up cash, his own money, and equipment borrowed from other New York filmmakers, Cassavetes began the long process of bringing *Shadows* to the screen.

"Over a period of three years we worked on this film," he said. "And none of us knew what to do; I mean we didn't know anything about filmmaking at all. I had made movies as an actor, but I was only interested in myself. I didn't care where the camera was. All I heard was, 'Roll 'em, action, print that,' so I would say, 'Print that.' But there was no one to write that down."

Despite his protestations, Cassavetes clearly had a pretty good idea of what he was doing. The film won the Critics Award at the 1960 Venice Film Festival, and even the *New York Times* found something nice to say about *Shadows*, calling it "fitfully dynamic, endowed with a raw but vibrant strength."

Cassavetes was hooked and an amazing career was on its way. "I don't even think of myself as a director," Cassavetes has argued. "In fact, I'm probably one of the worst directors around. But I do have an interest in my fellow man."

IMPROVISE THE EMOTIONS, WRITE THE WORDS

Although he initially allowed people to believe that the entire movie was improvised because it helped get audiences interested in seeing the film, as the years went on Cassavetes eventually became more open about how the film came into being, saying, "The emotion was improvisation. The lines were written."

Cassavetes was a strong proponent of improvisation as a key step in the creative process. However, in his mind, it was not a tool that stood well on its own.

"I believe in improvising on the basis of the written work and not on undisciplined creativity," he said. "When you have an important scene, you want it written; but there are still times when you want things just to happen."

It could be argued that creating a film set where things could just happen was the secret of Cassavetes' success. Peter Bogdanovich put it this way: "The only way a director can create an environment in which actors will take the kind of emotional risks that they did in John's movies is if you are an extraordinarily open, loving, giving and receptive audience."

Actress Lelia Goldoni, the female lead in *Shadows*, found that to be true. "I felt totally safe," she said. "And for an actor to feel safe is astonishing. But it also allows you such freedom. Freedom to do — and freedom not to do."

No one loved to be surprised by something an actor did more than Cassavetes, and once they realized that, actors gave their all in order to surprise him. "He never got his nose out of joint because it wasn't what he expected," his wife, actress Gena Rowlands, recalled. "He loved things he didn't expect."

Actor Ben Gazarra agreed, adding, "John was more interested in the surprised moment than he was in the planned moment."

However, the surprise was balanced with a strong script, and Cassavetes used improvisation to make his scripts that much stronger.

"For each scene I give the basic idea of the scene," he explained. "First we improvise to get the feel of the characters; then as the actors become easy in the roles we go back to the text. If it doesn't work out, then we go back and improvise some more; and again return to the text.

"We keep working like this until we feel complete identification between actor and role. Once they relaxed and gained confidence, many of the things they did shocked even me, they were so completely, unpredictably true."

THERE'S NO SHAME IN RESHOOTING

After finishing the movie and screening it for audiences, Cassavetes did one of the hardest things for a filmmaker to do: he took a cold, hard look at the film and realized that he had missed the mark.

"I could see the flaws in *Shadows* myself: it was a totally intellectual film, and therefore less than human," he recalled.

"I had fallen in love with the camera, with technique, with beautiful shots, with experimentation for its own sake. All I did was exploit film technique, shooting rhythms, using large lenses, shooting through trees and windows. It was filled with what you might call 'cinematic virtuosity' for its own sake, with angles and fancy cutting and a lot of jazz going on in the background."

However, the film was not a total loss; he felt there were salvageable elements. "The one thing that came to me after I had laid it aside a few weeks was that now and again the actors had survived all my tricks," Cassavetes said.

"My producer, Maurice McEndree, and Seymour Cassel got together and said, 'Now look, John, we're going to have to do some reshooting. We have all the faith in the world in you, but you're an amateur.' So I decided to reshoot it."

That was a bold move, and a move that proved to be successful. "We started again, and I tried to shoot it from an actor's standpoint," Cassavetes recalled. "And I think we succeeded because the actors are wonderful, whereas before you couldn't see them for all the trees and cars."

Cassavetes ended up reshooting about three quarters of the movie in two weeks, and he was glad he did, feeling that the new version was much closer to his original vision.

"The second version is completely different from the first version," he said. "In my opinion, it is a film far superior to the first. The cinematic style which was so prominent in the first gives way to the emotional experiences that the characters encounter.

"The emotional expressiveness of the first version dissipated in its generality — the emotions were not precise and particularized. The second version was more exact."

POVERTY BREEDS CREATIVITY

Although his budgets grew after *Shadows*, Cassavetes always worked with available resources and felt that on a film set, money wasn't the answer to the problems he was trying to solve. Money might help feed the crew, but it didn't feed the creative process.

"Money has nothing to do with film," he said. "I think that it, in the end, kills you from being creative and from inventing. Finding a way to do it makes you think. It makes the crew think. It makes everyone think."

"John wanted to be in a struggle to make his films," Peter Bogdanovich said, "because if it's too easy, it won't be any good.

"He believed in limitation being inspiration to quality and art. He worked under constant limitation: money, time, resources, everything. Yet look at what he did. He didn't need a penny more."

SYMBIOPSYCHOTAXIPLASM: TAKE ONE

||||||||||||||||||||||||||||||||||||||||||||||||||||||||||||||||||||||||||||||||||||||||||||

In the standard, stereotypical vision of filmmaking, the director is the all-knowing one. The man with the vision. The man with all the answers.

But what if a movie were being made by a director who had no clue? And what if the crew eventually realized that they were essentially being led nowhere by their clueless commander? What would a professional film crew do in such a situation?

In the case of William Greaves' classic movie, *Symbiopsychotaxiplasm: Take One*, the crew literally took over and started making their own movie.

Shot in 1968 but not widely released until 2005, Greaves' amazing movie follows a real film crew around and through Central Park as they attempt to shoot a series of screen tests with various actors over a period of several days. Their fearless leader (Greaves himself) keeps the crew moving with endless re-takes and digressions, while unbeknownst to them doing everything in his power to make them crack.

The film was legendary, if hard to find, before its current release. Even a renowned film buff like director Steven Soderbergh had trouble tracking it down.

"I first heard about it through my colleague, Larry Blake," Soderbergh explained. "He went to Sundance in 1992, and when he came back he said he saw this really crazy movie. In the middle of the movie screening in Park City the projector broke and the director walked up the front of the theater and said, 'This may or may not be part of the film.'"

"Larry said, 'You have to see this movie, it's really amazing.'"

"I didn't see it until four years later, when finally I managed to track down the tape. I just thought it was one of the most amazing things I'd ever seen. I couldn't believe how great it was and that it wasn't famous, I mean *really* famous.

"It's the ultimate reality show," Soderbergh continued. "The difference being, in this case, that nobody was in on the joke. And that's what makes it so brilliant. When you do a reality show on TV today, you know you're part of a show and that they're going to start creating obstacles for you or try to complicate the situation purposefully and consciously.

"Here, you're just watching a situation where people are absolutely convinced that Bill is out of control, doesn't know what he's doing, and you're a fly on the wall. And then the ultimate mutiny takes place. It's really incredible."

Soderbergh was so impressed with the film that he and actor Steve Buscemi went on to executive produce Greaves' sequel, *Symbiopsychotaxiplasm: Take 2 1/2*, which also co-starred Buscemi. Both were taken by Greaves' exploration into ideas that one doesn't usually find in a feature film.

"The title comes from symbiotaxiplasm," Buscemi explained, "which was coined by social scientist Arthur Bentley.

"Symbiotaxiplasm has to do with interchange of dialogue, how environment shapes human behavior and how human animals affect their environment, how we alter our environment and how those alterations then affect us. Bill inserted the 'psycho' part of it to sort of explore creative thinking and what role that plays in the interchange of dialogue.

"If it sounds like I don't know what I'm talking about," Buscemi concluded, "I don't."

BE DIFFERENT

For this film project, Greaves was given something most directors can only dream about: carte blanche. He could make any movie he wanted to make.

But rather than follow the traditional path (horror film, coming-of-age story, film noir, you name it), he bravely decided to create something entirely new and different.

"I taught acting for quite a while in Canada," Greaves explained. "One of my actors became very wealthy in the real estate business in Miami. He said, 'Listen, you're a very talented fellow and you have a lot of ideas. You're just as good a director as anyone coming out of Hollywood. Why don't you do a feature?'

"I said, 'These things cost money.' And he said, 'What does it cost?' I told him and he said, 'Do it. I'll back it.'

"So I asked him what sort of subject he wanted me to concentrate on — a whodunit or a romance, or what? And he said, 'Anything you like. Whatever you want to do, Bill, you do.'

"So, with that blank check I reflected on a lot of things that that I had been thinking about over the years."

His reflection covered a wide range of areas.

"The Heisenberg Principle of Uncertainty fascinated me," Greaves began. "Heisenberg asserted that we'll never really know the true basis of the cosmos, because the means of perception — the electron microscope — alters the reality it observes. It sends out a beam of electrons that knocks the electrons of the atoms being observed out of their orbits.

"I began to think of the movie camera as an analog to the electron microscope. The reality to be observed is the human soul, the mind, the psyche. Of course, as the camera investigates that part of the cosmos, the individual soul or psyche being observed recoils from the intrusion. On-camera behavior becomes structured in a way other than it would have been had it been unperceived — a psychological version of the Heisenberg Principle.

"Another scientific theory that interested me," he continued, "was the Second Law of Thermodynamics, which describes the flow and distribution of energy in any given system.

"I said to myself, 'What would happen if I got talented and extremely intelligent people together and set up these basic unconventional circumstances that would lead to a certain amount of conflict? What would come out of their expressing themselves in the context of what was going on during this ostensible, obnoxious screen test that we were shooting?'

"This film was an attempt to look at the impulses, the inspirations of a group of creative people who, during the making of the film, were being pushed to the wall by the process I, as director, had instigated. The questions were, 'When will they revolt? When would they question the validity, the wisdom, the conventional logic of doing the scene in the first place?' In this sense, it was a metaphor of the politics of the time.

"*Symbiopsychotaxiplasm: Take One* is about revolution against political power and convention. It expresses the mood of the 1960s in America with respect to the Vietnam War, the civil rights struggle, the need to escape from suffocating conventional lifestyles. The film is a metaphor for this revolt."

CREATE CONFLICT

One of the principle building blocks of drama is conflict. A character needs an obstacle to overcome, a villain to defeat.

The biggest challenge Greaves faced in shooting the movie was how to become that villain and give his crew an obstacle to overcome, without tipping his hand that a scheme was afoot.

"One of the elements of my characterization was my inscrutability," Greaves explained. "Try and try as much as they could, they couldn't decode my motives. That was calculated to elicit a degree of tension and anger and anxiety in the crew.

"I set up a series of situations that they couldn't possibly live with," he continued. "We were violating a lot of conventions of traditional Hollywood film procedures, with its very specific rules and regulations of how you should shoot a film and where the camera should be and all of that sort of thing."

"He was looking for some form of rebellion," agreed soundman Jonathan Gordon. "'Oh. Let's go over here.' 'Oh, this isn't working, let's go over here.' 'Oh, this isn't working, let's do this,' 'Oh, well that isn't working. Let's do that ...' Just infuriating the crew, who like clarity.

"Creative people, they don't necessarily want to be told exactly what to do," Gordon continued, "but they do want clarity. And Bill was the opposite of clarity. He presented a kind of muddled approach, which drives professional people crazy."

"I was hoping to have any conflict to what I was doing played out in front of the camera by the crew challenging me or criticizing me or whatever," Greaves explained. "But that didn't happen."

Well, it didn't happen in front of Greaves, but it *did* happen in front of the camera.

Unbeknownst to him, the crew began to gather at night after the shoot, to complain about the production and about their clueless leader. And, because they were a film crew in the sixties with seemingly limitless raw film stock, they filmed their encounter sessions.

Production manager Bob Rosen's on-camera rant against Greaves is typical of the mood of the crew: "If you ask him what is the film about," Rosen told the group, "he gives you an answer that's vaguer than the question. It's just so vague that it would be better if you hadn't asked the question in the first place."

Then, when the production finally came to an end, Rosen handed Greaves the footage they had shot, saying, "Bill, we have a little present for you."

"When I saw this material," Greaves recalled, "I was just elated. They had this closet revolt and it was terribly exciting to me, because I was afraid that the film was not going to work out, because it didn't have enough conflict."

The crew provided him with the conflict his story needed, and they did it in a way no one had ever done before — by taking over the film and putting their own spin on it.

"Luckily for Bill," Soderbergh observed, "they took it to 11, by filming the sessions at night on their own.

"I think when he was presented with that material, he must have felt like the cinema gods were smiling on him."

WHAT'S YOUR CLEARANCE, CLARENCE?

For Jonathan Gordon, and many of the crew, working on the movie was a perplexing assignment and one that made it difficult to maintain a consistent professional perspective.

"I think that one of the things that happened, because of our innocence, and because of the newness of the medium," Gordon said, "is that we could not define our roles with complete clarity.

"Yes, of course, we're professionals and we do this for a living, so in that sense we know who we are, we know what we're doing.

"But I think that because of the strangeness of it and because of the way in which we were not brought completely into Bill's plan, I do think that there was a confusion, a mixture of the role of the normal observer in a situation and the role of the filmmaker."

The role of professional crew member was challenged late in the film by the arrival of Victor, a drunken homeless man who wanders into the midst of the film shoot like a character right out of Shakespeare. When told that he's in the middle of a movie, he barks, "It's a movie? So who's moving who?"

The crew is clearly stunned by this arrival. "Here once again is that division," Gordon explained, "where one part of you is operating as a human being and the other part is operating as a filmmaker.

"And you aren't quite sure of who you are. Are you a normal person, or are you a filmmaker? The normal person just stands there, witnessing this incredible performance. The filmmaker runs after Victor to get a release."

As luck would have it, the professional side of the crew came to the fore and they quickly got Victor to sign a release form while on camera, ensuring that his remarkable performance could become a part of the finished film.

Despite the mayhem of the production, the frazzled crew had the wherewithal to get a signed release from someone who had simply wandered onto the set ... and who ended up being one of the most memorable moments in the film.

"I was very happy with the fact that there was confusion," Greaves admitted. "If you notice me with Victor, the homeless guy at the end, I have a kind of private smile. That feeling comes out of the fact that the thing was going my way: There was confusion, or conflict, or some new unpremeditated development that was important for the life and success of the film.

"That's the way life is," he continued. "Life is full of a lot of lucky moments, as well as tragic moments. And our mission was to capture as many lucky moments as possible."

MONTY PYTHON AND THE HOLY GRAIL

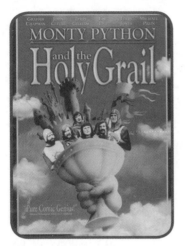

When *Monty Python and the Holy Grail* first premiered in the U.S. (with promotional taglines such as "Makes *Ben Hur* Look Like an Epic!" and "At Last: A Film for the Squeamish"), many Americans had no idea who (or what) a Monty Python was. While some people had seen the television show in those cities where it ran on PBS, the majority of us were in the dark.

In Minneapolis, where I saw the movie, the theater was giving away free coconuts to the first one hundred customers. I saw it well into its second day of release, and they still had about 75 coconuts to unload.

From that perhaps less than auspicious beginning, the film has gone on to become one of the best-loved comedies of all time, filled with nearly countless quotable lines ("Are you suggesting coconuts *migrate*?") and even spawning a Tony Award–winning Broadway musical.

The movie was funded primarily with investment money from members of successful rock groups, chief among them Pink Floyd, Genesis and Led Zeppelin.

The script was written by all six members of the troupe. Directing chores went to two Python members, Terry Jones and Terry Gilliam, almost by default, because none of the other members wanted to do it. Neither had directed before, and they weren't entirely prepared for what they were getting into.

"We were learning as it went along," Gilliam explained. "It was a film school, and we just went in there every day and learned something new, learned something not to do, and got better.

"I think that's the only way to learn how to direct a film: get the job of director and then go out and do it. Either you survive or you don't."

They not only survived but thrived, and in the process provided a few very important lessons about comedy: how to make it and, more importantly, how to make it funny.

IT'S NOT YOUR PROBLEM (IT'S YOUR CHARACTER'S PROBLEM)

After Holy Grail's opening credits (complete with Swedish subtitles that tell a story all their own), we're treated to a classic beginning to a medieval adventure story: a mist-covered forest and the sound of a knight, approaching on horseback.

It's only after he crests a hill that we realize what's wrong with this picture: He's only pretending to ride, and his trusted servant, Patsy, is making the *clomp, clomp* sound of a horse by banging two coconut halves together.

From this we move into the first dialogue scene, in which Arthur must justify the availability of coconuts in this climate, all the while trying (and failing) to get a word in edgewise about his quest.

This hilarious opening sequence not only sets the tone for the entire film, but also solved a key problem for the directors — how do you shoot King Arthur and his knights when you can't afford horses on your meager budget? The answer was to make it Arthur's problem.

"The coconut gag was the original gag that sparked the whole thing off," Terry Jones recalled. "We did talk about having horses at one point and then we quickly dismissed it, because we thought it would be funnier not to and because we couldn't afford horses anyway."

Michael Palin, like the other Python members, agreed with the logic behind the idea. "This device was funny," he said, "but it turned out that it was also cheap, and it got us out of the problem of how do we teach all the Pythons to ride horses. Horses cost an awful lot of money."

Terry Gilliam felt that not having money for the horses was ultimately a good thing for the movie. "If we'd had the money," he said, "we would have had real horses.

"What was wonderful was the limitations put on us by the budget. We couldn't do all those things so we had to get clever and thank God, because the coconuts saved our ass. We would never have gotten through that movie with real horses."

Terry Jones was surprised that the audience laughed at the joke, then got on with the movie. "It's funny how you get used to them not having horses," he said. "It doesn't seem to be a joke; you just accept it as a convention after a while. It's only occasionally when they dismount that you suddenly remember, 'Oh, of course, they're not riding horses.'"

All in all, Gilliam is still pleased with the choice they made. "It makes a wonderful leap because with that opening shot you accept the kind of lunatic logic that's there," he said.

"Arthur is incredibly serious, never a blink, and then in the background you've got all this stuff going on. It's one of those things that's, in retrospect, brilliant."

MORE TAKES / LESS STOPPING

When they made the move from producing a weekly television series to producing feature films, the Python members discovered that the traditional process of shooting a film can often kill the energy needed to make humor happen on camera.

Or, as John Cleese succinctly put it: "In movies everybody concentrates on the fucking technical aspects! And they don't matter when you're making comedy; what matters is whether it's funny!

"In filmmaking you can find yourself being made completely subsidiary to all the technical requirements," Cleese continued, "and then when they've got a take that everyone is happy with because it's in focus and the sound was all right, they want to move on. It's absolutely putting the cart before the horse.

"I remember doing one of the best takes in my life, with Eric," Cleese said. "Terry shouted, 'Cut.' I shouted, 'How about that!' because I was really exhilarated, and I heard this comment, 'Not enough smoke.'

"Now this is for me the perfect example of the tail wagging the dog," Cleese explained, "of getting your priorities all wrong. I remember getting quite sarcastic then and any time anybody said, 'Cut, that was a good take,' I said, 'Well, was the smoke funny enough?'"

The solution to this problem, according to Cleese, is to forget the technical stuff for a while and just let the actors do what they do best.

"When I'm working," Cleese explained, "I will sometimes say, 'All right, we've got the technical stuff settled, now it's the actors' turn. Let's do four or five takes back-to-back.' Because what happens is you get warmed up.

"What normally happens is you do the first take and then it all stops while somebody adjusts this bulb, this light, somebody adjusts the position of the lamp, somebody else comes and takes some fluff off your jacket, somebody else is worried about the fact that there's a bit of a glow on your nose. By the time you're ready to shoot again, you're cold again."

Taking the time to let the actors do their thing, and not continually stopping for technical issues, can really make a difference in the end result.

"A take can vary tremendously," Cleese explained, "from being dreadfully, embarrassingly unfunny to being hilarious. And it all depends on whether you go into that particular take with the right energy and the right degree of focus."

PREVIEWS

It's hard to believe that one of the arguably funniest movies of all time wasn't considered to be even mildly amusing by the first few audiences who saw it. But such was the case with *Monty Python and the Holy Grail*, and without the benefit of previews (lots and lots of previews) it might have never become the classic we now know and love.

"The first showing of *Holy Grail* was a total disaster," remembered Terry Jones. "It was a disaster, an absolute disaster. People laughed for the first few minutes, then just silence all the way through the rest."

"It was one of those evenings when Python flopped," Michael Palin explained. "There was some laughter and there was some enjoyment and there was polite applause at the end which felt like a spear in the guts, because it was clear that the audience had been, by and large, disappointed."

The problem, they determined, was that in their quest for medieval realism, they may have gone too far.

Executive Producer John Goldstone explained it this way: "What had happened was, Terry Gilliam and Terry Jones decided to make it as real as possible, to have a soundtrack that was very real, bone-crunching and everything.

"It was all as authentic as they could possibly get. Neil Innes did the music, it was a sort of semi-religious chant that in fact was kind of too real. And so it wasn't getting the response from the audience that we'd expected."

The troupe re-grouped quickly after the early screenings, to discuss what worked, what didn't, and what was needed to make the movie as funny as they knew it could be.

"That's the good thing about Python," said Eric Idle, "you'd say, 'Here's what's wrong: a, b, c, d and e. We have to fix these points.' And I think that film had some good close attention from the comedy makers to make it right.

"I always felt this thing of 'three previews and you're done' is just not long enough. Comedy has to be dragged to the audience. Listen to them, where are they laughing? Where did they stop laughing? Why have they stopped laughing?"

John Cleese agreed, adding, "I don't think I realized in those days how late it is in the course of making a movie that you actually know whether it's going to work or not," he said. "In those days I thought if all the individual bits worked you had a movie and the answer is you don't.

"There's some strange process by which in the end it either integrates or it doesn't and it's almost impossible to tell whether it's going to do that until quite late on."

"There were thirteen screenings of *The Holy Grail*," recalled Eric Idle. "We dragged it towards being funny."

For co-director Terry Jones, the solution was simply a matter of "less is more." "I was sitting there thinking, it can't be that unfunny," he said, "and I thought maybe the soundtrack is somehow flattening the comedy."

His solution was to reduce all the realistic sound effects, take out Neil Innes' traditional score and replace it with stock heroic music.

"There was the realization that you can just pull the soundtrack off," explained Eric Idle, "and put on a sort of classic bad Hollywood soundtrack. It's all pre-recorded music on *Grail* and that really helped it, because it lifted it into the area of swashbuckling parody. It's a parody soundtrack that gives the parody film a base, so we can recognize what's going on, and that really helped."

Thirteen previews turned out to be the film's lucky number, because from that point on the film worked and became the classic film we know today. However, at least one of its makers thinks it's a feat that he couldn't — or wouldn't — repeat.

"When I look back at *Grail*," Gilliam said, "I can't actually believe we made it in the time and for the money we did. I don't think I could do it now. It was just the act of very naïve, ambitious, obsessed people.

"I think you do those things once in your life and then you realize how painful and awful it is and try to spend the rest of your career avoiding that again. But there's a kind of mad energy that's produced in those moments."

ERASERHEAD

||||||||||||||||||||||||||||||||||||||||||||||||||||||||||||||||||||||||||||||||||||||||||||||||||

"My original image was of a man's head bouncing on the ground, being picked up by a boy and taken to a pencil factory. I don't know where it came from."

David Lynch

From that decidedly bizarre vision grew one of the great cult classic films of all time — David Lynch's *Eraserhead*.

The beauty of the film — and, despite its grotesqueness, or perhaps because of it, it is a truly beautiful film — every viewer brings their own explanations to the story. "It is a personal film," Lynch said, "and no reviewer or critic or viewer has ever given an interpretation that is my interpretation in twenty-five years."

The idea for *Eraserhead* was born from the feelings Lynch had when he lived in Philadelphia.

"*Eraserhead* is the real *Philadelphia Story*," Lynch has said. "Philadelphia was really a frightening city. It has an atmosphere of fear, just all-pervading fear.

"One time I was walking around at night with a stick with nails driven through it, and a squad car pulls up alongside of me, and a cop says, 'What've you got there?' And I showed him this stick with nails driven through it. He said, 'Good for you, bud,' and took off."

Lynch created the film while enrolled at the American Film Institute (AFI) in Los Angeles. The school discouraged students from attempting to make feature films, but since Lynch's original script for *Eraserhead* was only twenty-one pages long, the faculty assumed (incorrectly, as it turned out) that he was working on a short that would run about twenty-one minutes.

Honest to a fault, Lynch told them, "I think it's going to be a bit longer than that."

The movie was filmed in the unused stables on the AFI grounds. "We had about five or six rooms," Lynch recalled, "and this giant loft where all the other sets were built — a miniature soundstage and studio."

It started out as a set, but before long it became ... home. "I started living in the stables in 1972," Lynch confessed. "To live and work in the same place is the best, so it was a perfect scenario. I lived in Henry's room. I lived there off and on for two or three years. It was illegal what I was doing."

The illegality aside, it was a perfect, if bizarre, set-up. He had a tiny but loyal crew. They only shot at night. And David had to duck out every evening to go to work. But only for an hour.

"I got this paper route and I delivered the *Wall Street Journal*," Lynch remembered. "That's how I supported myself.

"We only shot at night, and my route was at night. So at a certain point, I'd have to stop the shoot and go do the route. But I had the route down so fast that I was only gone about an hour and eight minutes. Sometimes it would be fifty-nine minutes, but I was going flat out to make the hour."

"David was always in charge," remembered crewmember Catherine Coulson. "He always knew exactly what he wanted, but he had each of us feeling like we were really part of it.

"It was a real artist's film," she continued. "He had a clear, strong vision tempered with enough consideration to let people help him to realize it, but always with enough ego to make it very clear that it was his film."

"I once said it was a perfect film," Lynch recalled. "Well, it was just that one day. I might have been very relaxed, and it was a long time ago, and it just struck me as, you know, perfect. But nothing is perfect. You can shoot for it — you've got to shoot for it — but there's just no such thing as a perfect film."

DUMPSTERS ARE YOUR FRIENDS

Lynch earned $48.50 a week from his paper route, and although he had access to AFI's cameras and lights, he still had to pay for film, processing and other production costs. So he looked for bargains wherever he could — even in the dumpsters of nearby Hollywood studios.

"We didn't have any money for sound stock," Lynch explained. "Somehow we heard that there were bins of sound stock that the sound editors from Warner Brothers would throw away. Big trash bins filled with it.

"We got on the lot and found these bins. In preparation I'd removed the backseat of the Volkswagen, and we filled every square inch of that Volkswagen full of almost totally clean reels. So all the sound stock for *Eraserhead* came from the throw-away bins at Warner Brothers."

He had similar luck with the sets and many of the props for the film, again relying on the excesses of the Hollywood studios, spending a mere $100 for all those elements.

"One day Jack Fisk and I found out that a studio was being shut down. We rented a 35-foot flatbed and drove over to this place. This was an ancient, real deal studio, and they were selling stuff for nothing.

"When we drove out of there, we had thirty-five feet long, twelve feet high of flats. Bales of wire, kegs of nails, thirty-foot by forty-foot black backdrop, I can't remember all the things we had. Radiators, and things I needed for the film.

"All the sets were built with those flats. And since I had a paper route, if there were holes in them, I would just do papier-mâché patches with the newspapers — *Wall Street Journal* and flour and water. All this stuff — one hundred dollars."

IGNORE THE NAYSAYERS

While making a low-budget movie, there often comes a time when you need to show a rough cut or some assembled scenes to a potential investor, in order to raise the necessary funds to finish the movie.

This was the situation Lynch found himself in while in production on *Eraserhead*, and it demonstrates the perils of showing an unfinished piece to someone outside of your production circle.

"We showed it to one guy who was a friend of Terrence Malick, his financial backer, I think," Lynch recalled. "So we organized several scenes, and this man came in and sat down and I was, you know, trembling.

"And in the middle of this thing, the man stood up and screamed: 'PEOPLE DON'T ACT LIKE THAT! PEOPLE DON'T TALK LIKE THAT! THIS IS BULLSHIT!' And out he went. But, like, really upset.

"So I thought, 'Man!', you know, 'This is gonna be really difficult.'"

TIME IS ON YOUR SIDE

The original shooting schedule for *Eraserhead* was pretty typical. "It was supposed to take a few weeks to shoot," Coulson recalled. "I think the original shooting schedule was six weeks."

That six weeks stretched on ... and on ... and on. Ultimately, the film took nearly four years to shoot.

"After a film's going for a couple of years," Lynch said, "you sort of find your rhythm. We normally did about one shot a night. A 'master shot' would definitely be lighting all night."

There were certainly benefits to such a leisurely schedule. "What we lacked in monetary resources, we had in time," recalled Director of Photography Fred Elmes. "We could take the time to build something right. We could shoot a test, and if it didn't look right, we'd go back to the drawing board and build it again."

The downside to such a long schedule were issues like maintaining vision and energy, and dealing with minor problems, like continuity issues.

"There's one particular shot," Lynch recalled, "when Henry (actor Jack Nance) walks down the hall. He puts his hand on the doorknob and turns it, and there's a cut. A year and a half later he comes through the door!

"Those things can be extremely frightening, to think about holding a mood and a correctness, something that will stick together after five years. It's pretty hard.

"There were some dark moments," Lynch continued. "At one time I was thinking about building a small eight-inch Henry and stop-motioning him through some small cardboard sets to fill in the blanks. Just to get it finished."

"It just turned into this monster we couldn't finish," Nance said. "It was a killer, but Lynch wouldn't give it up. We couldn't give it up. So we kept shooting."

Although he was happy with the final result, in retrospect Lynch felt that four years was just too long to devote to one movie.

"I feel now that I shouldn't have spent so much time on *Eraserhead*," he admitted. "I should like to have made more films in that time, but it wasn't happening. I couldn't do anything new because *Eraserhead* wasn't finished. I didn't have anything to show anybody. So I just saw the world going by and tried to raise money and, little by little, I did it.

"The thing is, the film isn't done until it's done."

Using the Los Angeles film festival, Filmex, as a forced deadline, Lynch finally finished the movie, to the relief of his cast and crew.

"My parents came to the first screening of *Eraserhead*," Lynch said. "Afterwards, someone sitting next to my mother told me, when the lights came up, she said, 'Oh, I wouldn't want to have a dream like that.'"

"At the end of the screening," Nance recalled, "there was a complete dead silence. And I knew that it worked. I said to Lynch, 'You see, I told you it would turn them into zombies.' People were stunned, and there was this long, shocked silence. Then a huge burst of applause. It was beautiful. I'd been waiting five years for that applause."

KILL YOUR DARLINGS

Seeing the movie with an actual audience also inspired Lynch to do something very difficult — cut some favorite scenes, totaling about twenty minutes of running time.

"The pacing is slow in *Eraserhead*, and that's great," Lynch said. "I love the feel of it, but I think some scenes were dragging it down to where the pacing was painful. It was pushing you out of the film. It was just too long. So that night, I made a decision.

"In my heart, I knew that some of these scenes had to go. I'd never been able to quite do it, but when you feel an audience not reacting, then you can do it. So out they came.

"After that screening, I drove over to Fred Elmes' house. I sat in the car with Fred, and I told him every scene I was going to cut, and exactly where it was gonna be cut, so I wouldn't forget it. And the next day, I cut this composite print, which you're not supposed to do. But I just cut it and rearranged it, because I'd been wanting — needing — to do it. It was so long this other way, it was not working. It's still long for a lot of people."

KEEP SOME SECRETS

Nowadays, there are no secrets left in movies. Nearly every bit of information of how a movie is made is revealed, often before the movie is even released. With film magazines, behind-the-scenes specials, DVD commentary tracks, and books like this one, there is little that appears on film that is still a mystery.

Except the baby that appears in *Eraserhead*.

Lynch has steadfastly refused to divulge the secrets behind the baby, and he feels that people are better off without that knowledge.

"Magicians keep their secrets to themselves," Lynch said. "And they know that as soon as they tell, someone will say, 'Are you kidding me? That's so simple.' It's horrifying that they do that.

"People don't realize it, but as soon as they hear that, something dies inside them. They're deader than they were. They're not, like, happy to know about this stuff. They're happy not to know about it. And they shouldn't know about it. It's nothing to do with the film! And it will only ruin the film! Why would they talk about it? It's horrifying!"

SHARE THE WEALTH

The final lesson from *Eraserhead* is a testament to Lynch's kind heart and devotion to his hard-working crew. To reward their (literally) years of work, he gave each crewmember a percentage of the film's profits, sharing the wealth with the people who helped bring his unique vision to life.

"Because he couldn't pay us," Elmes said, "David offered us a percentage of the profit of the film — if and when it should ever make money.

"I certainly wasn't in it for the money, and we were all certain that it was not possible for the film to make any substantial amount of money. So, it's a welcome surprise that there's some money coming back."

"There was a sense of collaboration," Coulson added, "which is why David gave us all such a nice percentage of the film — something we did not even write down until after the film started making money.

"The reward artistically and emotionally was great, but to be able to get some money back from it — a healthy check each quarter — is a real rarity in this particular business."

SOMEONE TO LOVE

"You have a different way of making movies than almost anybody else. Certainly very different than mine."

Orson Welles

The great Orson Welles makes that observation, on-camera, to his dear friend Henry Jaglom, in Jaglom's quasi-documentary, pseudo-narrative feature, *Someone to Love.*

Someone to Love, like many of Jaglom's films, mixes documentary interviews with improvised dramatic scenes, to explore a theme about what it means to be human. In the case of this film, Jaglom looked at the idea of loneliness, primarily because he had recently found himself single again.

"I was alone, and I didn't understand why I was alone," Jaglom explained. "And I looked around at my friends and I realized that I was part of a whole generation of people that were alone.

"It was a function of something that was happening at that period in the '80s and the '90s, where people who always assumed that they would be married and have families found themselves somehow in the middle of their lives on their own.

"So I thought I would try to make a movie about it, but what I would do is go through my phone book and actually pick out people I knew who were alone and put them together in some central location."

That central location was a soon-to-be demolished theater, and over the course of a long day, Jaglom's cast chats about loneliness while they eat, flirt and interact with each other.

There is no action. Only talk. Lots and lots of talk. Which is just the way Jaglom likes it.

"There will never be an action sequence in my movies," Jaglom declared. "I've been lucky enough not to have had too many action sequences in my life. The life I lead and the lives of people around me have to do with talking, feelings, words, emotions. I want my films to be as much as possible about life.

"Most people spend their time not dealing with car chases," he continued, "not dealing with creatures who arrive from outer space.

"Most of us deal most of the time with two people sitting in a room having a conversation, exploring issues that they deal with: love, loss, desire, romance, happiness. I want my films to reflect the real life that I feel around me."

Admittedly, some critics and audiences don't like movies that deal with real life and real issues, but for Jaglom there's no point trying to capture anything else.

And in his films, nothing — nothing — is off limits. "There's no such thing as too personal," he declared. "If there's one thing I'm trying to prove with my movies, it's that there's no such thing as too personal."

To his credit, Jaglom has found — created, developed and perfected — his own unique niche in the movie business, and he's discovered a method of making movies which satisfies his artistic aspirations without costing an arm and a leg.

"I figured out once that I made one of my movies for what Spielberg spent on lunches for one of his movies that same year," he boasted.

One additional benefit of making *Someone to Love* was the opportunity it provided Jaglom to introduce the world to the real Orson Welles.

"He allowed me, finally and for the first time — and, sadly as it turned out, for the last time — to show the world what Orson Welles was really like behind the mask," Jaglom said.

"In *Someone to Love* you really meet Orson the way you would have met him if you had had lunch with him. It is the charming, sweet, lovely, supportive, brilliant but totally vulnerable, interested, curious, young Orson Welles."

Welles not only kicks off the movie, but he also brings the movie to its conclusion, stopping the action (or, rather, lack of action) once and for all.

"I thought it was fitting, somehow," Jaglom explained, "that the last word Orson Welles should say in the movie, after fifty years, starting with 'Rosebud' as his first word, the last word should be 'Cut.'"

REHEARSE? NEVER!

"I hate rehearsal," Jaglom has said, loudly and frequently.

"In the case of *Someone to Love*, because the entire thing was about somebody making a film, there could be no preparation," Jaglom explained. "It would be absolutely wrong for me, from my point of view, to have anybody know anything in advance of what anybody was going to say, including Orson.

"The most truthful moments, it seems to me," he continued, "are the moments that just happen and even surprise the person themselves as they're saying something, because they don't know they're going to be saying it. If you rehearse, no matter how good you are, you know you're going to be saying it.

"If you surprise yourself and you surprise the other actor and you therefore surprise me, the director, while it's happening, you're going to surprise the audience. It's going to be fresh and exciting.

"The best stuff in the world can happen the first time. Why give it away and then say, 'Shit, I wish I had a camera here.' Get it the first time."

GOT THEME?

Although he opted not to prepare, write a script or rehearse, Jaglom didn't go into this movie blindly. Story took a backseat and instead the entire process was driven by the theme of loneliness.

"I had a plan, a super structure," he explained. "I knew what I wanted to talk about in terms of loneliness and relationships, but I was actually seeking the movie as I was in the movie.

"I decided I would just do it that way and then when I got back to my editing room, I would look at what everybody gave me and find a way to put it together into a narrative.

"I didn't set out to work this way," he added. "It's the way I like finding stories."

This approach — letting the theme drive the train and finding the story only once you get into the edit — is for Jaglom a risky but ultimately rewarding way to work.

"Orson always said that the difference between me and other filmmakers," Jaglom recounted, "was other filmmakers write their film and while they're writing it they try to find their theme. I decide on my theme and hammer away at the theme until I get the story. The story is always very secondary to me."

THE FAMILY AND FRIENDS PLAN

As we discovered frequently in this book, there are many reasons for working with your family and your friends on your movie projects: Trust is already established, working habits are understood, and communication can be reduced to simple shorthand.

However, none of these were the reasons Jaglom used his friends, a potential new girlfriend, his ex-girlfriends and even his brother in *Someone to Love.*

"I knew all the people in *Someone to Love*," Jaglom explained, "and the advantage is that I'm playing someone in that film who knows all those people, so I know when they're being evasive or certain intimate things, buttons that I can push to get responses — that's the biggest advantage. I love doing that."

That type of — let's call a spade a spade here — *manipulation* might not be well received by most people. But, by all accounts, Jaglom is such an attentive, supportive, motivational and inspirational person that his friends are more than willing to allow their private selves to be exposed in this manner. It's all part of the process of being friends with Henry.

Or, as actress and friend Candice Bergen put it, "If I had had Henry as a father or a husband, I probably could have taken Poland."

POVERTY BREEDS CREATIVITY

Due to his early years working in and around the Hollywood studio system, Jaglom understood a key value of working with a small budget. "I keep the economics down," he said, "so that I can have complete freedom, so nobody is looking over my shoulder."

However, on *Someone to Love*, he learned a greater lesson about the value of poverty in a creative situation.

"I was complaining about not having more time, not having more money to do something I wanted to do," he recalled, "and Orson said this line that I now have over my editing machine. He said, 'The enemy of art is the absence of limitations.'

"That was just about the most important thing that has ever been said to me, because if you don't have limitations you start throwing technology or money at a problem. But if you have a limitation, you have to find a creative solution, and therefore you create art.

"If you don't have any limitations you become Spielberg, you become Lucas, you make great special effects movies and big things because you can throw money at every problem. If you have no money to throw and no time to throw, you're have to find a creative solution.

"For me the most valuable lesson from Orson, and it happened during that movie, was make whatever happens work. It's good to have limitations, because you have to find an artistic or creative way to surmount them. And it's more fun."

NEVER NEED HOLLYWOOD

One final lesson that Jaglom applied to *Someone to Love*, and to all the films that he made after he began his friendship with Orson Welles, was simply this: Never need Hollywood.

"Never depend on it for your financing, for support, for your ability to make films," Jaglom said. "Get your backing as far away as possible from what they proudly call their 'Industry' if you have any intention of being an artist.

"Co-existence cannot occur, as Orson's last two decades sadly showed. He needed them till the end, and they rejected him till the end. And a half-dozen or more brilliant motion pictures never got made as a result. And a magnificent artist could never get back to the canvas that they had pulled out from under him."

Unlike filmmakers of past eras, Jaglom believes today's film-maker is in a perfect position to avoid all the traps and trappings of Hollywood.

"This is a great time to be an independent filmmaker," he said. "There are more venues than ever before, there's a bigger, ever-growing audience, there's an ever-growing economic system to support it now that videos exist, there are endless distribution opportunities. It is the best time to be a truly independent filmmaker.

"But the other thing is to be true to yourself, not to sell out the first second you have a chance. Because when you become part of the system, your movies suffer.

"I really am the only person I know in this town that's happy," he continued. "All my friends that I grew up with in this business are constantly complaining, 'They screwed me, they're messing me up in the accounting, they're not giving me this money, they won't let me shoot the movie I want to make, they're forcing me to use this actor.' I don't have any of those problems.

"From watching Orson deal with Hollywood, I learned never to depend on them. I learned that if you want to be an artist in this town, you've got to get your financing away from this town, you've got to be independent of this town.

"You can be friendly with this town, but you can't be of it, because if you're of it, you're buried by it and they don't want you anymore. Every frame of every Henry Jaglom movie is the way I want it.

"You may love my films, you may hate my films, but they're my films. I'm the only free person in this town."

Chapter Five

FAKE OUT!

There once was a time when you could count on reality.

And then in 1967, a little "documentary" called *David Holzman's Diary* came along, and all bets were suddenly off.

The birth of the "mockumentary" changed the way people looked at movies. They suddenly realized that if something that looked so real was actually fake, then didn't that mean that something that looked fake might actually be real?

This blend of fake reality and real fakery has given us a new category of films — and filmmakers — from which to learn.

DAVID HOLZMAN'S DIARY

||||||||||||||||||||||||||||||||||||||||||||||||||||||||||||||||||||||||||||||||||||||||||||||

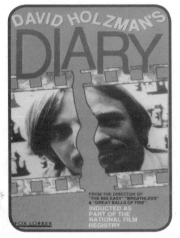

It's at least a little ironic that one of the first, and arguably one of the best, fake documentaries of all time — *David Holzman's Diary* — came about as a result of overexposure to some of the top documentary filmmakers of the 1960s.

"I was very interested in cinéma vérité," remembered director Jim McBride. "Kit Carson and I were going to write something for the Museum of Modern Art about cinéma vérité, and we interviewed all these filmmakers — like the Maysles brothers, Ricky Leacock, Pennebaker, even Andy Warhol — who were making films that purportedly were for the first time entering into real life and finding out the truth.

"People were really passionate about this idea," continued McBride, "that you could find the truth with this new, lightweight equipment and faster film stocks and synch sound — all the stuff that was very new in the sixties.

"So at that time I was very interested in all of that, and at the same time I felt there was something wrong here."

L.M. Kit Carson, McBride's friend and the star of the movie, recognized that McBride was having trouble accepting this new reality.

"We set about doing this book for the Museum of Modern Art, called *The Truth on Film*, and halfway through the book, Jim said to me, 'There is no truth on film. Once you put the camera there, everything changes.'"

This conclusion led McBride to want to do a movie about someone who was — for better or for worse — seeking truth on film.

"There was always in my mind an image of a guy with a camera on his shoulder, filming himself in a mirror," McBride said. "And that image seemed terribly profound to me. I'm not sure I could explain why.

"At the same time, I was also very interested in banality — the banal facts of a person's daily life. I was living in circumstances similar to David Holzman's, and I suppose the film was partly about me.

"If you take the image of a guy filming himself in a mirror and you put that together with the other elements that I mentioned," McBride reasoned, "you come up with a diary as a logical form."

"Jim had conceived this idea to do a film called *David Holzman's Diary*," Carson recalled, "which was this guy who starts the movie by saying 'My life is all fucked up, and I'm about to be drafted, and I figure it's time for me to try to figure what's going on. And if I shoot every day and look at the rushes of every day, I can find the plot again because I've lost the plot.'

"The interesting thing is that, at the time, I was also studying the roots of the English novel," Carson continued, "which are these fake diaries, like *Robinson Crusoe* and *Pamela*. It was the first way they figured out to do long-form fiction, by making diaries out of it.

"So that also informed what we were attempting to do, because a diary is something that feels like it's real time, but you know, if you think about it for two seconds, 'Oh, yeah, he's edited this together.' So it's not really happening in front of you. It's been examined and purposed, structurally, to be this way."

Using the money they'd received to write the book on cinéma vérité for the Museum of Modern Art, they instead turned their focus on getting David Holzman on film.

"On my Easter break from college in Texas," Carson remembered, "I came to New York. And since I didn't know how to do it any other way, I just became the character. I lived in the editing room, I slept in the closet, and I lost my girlfriend who at the time thought I was nuts — just like Penny in the movie thinks I'm nuts. So it worked."

"Over a period of three months," McBride said, "including one big four-day weekend when we shot all the footage in the apartment, we filmed *David Holzman's Diary*.

"Then, over another couple of months, I put it together in the evenings. When it was finished, I didn't know what to make of it. It was a pretty good approximation of what I wanted. But I had no idea of whether that was worth anything to anybody else at all."

"I came back from Texas," Carson said, "and Jim had put the film together, sort of, and he had [Martin Scorsese's long-time editor] Thelma Schoonmaker come in and take a look, because Thelma was everybody's pal at that time.

"What Jim had done was take the worst takes of the two or three that we had made, because he felt that was more truthful to the character. And Thelma said, 'Fine, that may be more true, but it's horrible, so you have to use the best takes. Otherwise it's really painful.'"

McBride re-edited the film — using the best takes — and the end result was an instant classic. The Museum of Modern Art, still a bit ticked that they never got their book on cinéma vérité, almost immediately added *David Holzman's Diary* to their permanent collection.

Despite this early acclaim, McBride to this day isn't entirely sure what all the fuss is about.

"I know that this film is an important film to a lot of people," McBride admits, "and I am always constantly surprised when people come up to me and say, 'I saw your film when I was in college.'

"My own experience with the film is that it's never had any kind of commercial release; it's never shown in theaters. It really only has a life at film festivals and colleges. So I'm always surprised that more than seven people have seen it."

The attraction of the film may best be expressed by Pepe, a character in the film who looks at Holzman's early footage of himself and provides this on-camera critique:

"You don't understand the basic principle: as soon as you start film-ing something, whatever happens in front of the camera is not reality anymore. It becomes part of something else. It becomes a movie. And you stop living somehow. And your decisions stop being moral deci-sions, and they become aesthetical decisions. And your whole life stops being your life and becomes a work of art — and a very bad work of art this time."

THERE'S NO SHAME IN RESHOOTING

As unique a project as *David Holzman's Diary* was, it was not McBride's first attempt at the concept. His experience proves, yet again, that not only is there no shame in reshooting — there's often a better movie to be found in the process.

"In 1966 I was working at a company that sold land in Florida, and they did it through films," recalled McBride. "I was serving an appren-ticeship there, learning to shoot, learning to edit, stuff like that. I got this idea for what was later to become *David Holzman's Diary*, and they let me borrow their equipment on weekends.

"We shot a bunch of stuff, almost all of it improvised — and not very well, I should add — and then as we were shooting, I got fired. So I packed it all up into a box and put it in the trunk of my car, and I went around looking for a cutting room that someone would lend me so I could put these pieces together.

"And when I finally did locate a cutting room a couple of weeks later, I went to the car and opened it up and discovered that someone had stolen the film.

"In those days," McBride continued, "16mm was associated with porn, so my guess is that's why somebody took it. They must have been ter-ribly disappointed. And I was terribly disappointed myself, but as time went by, I was kind of relieved because it really sucked.

"But somehow the experience of doing it made me realize how I should have done it differently."

"So all of a sudden, two events happen," Carson added, continuing the story. "Jim says there's no cinéma vérité, and then Jim says, 'Come have dinner, I want you to audition for me to play David Holzman because I've shot the film, and now I've lost it.'"

Eight months later, the camera rolled again on the second version of *David Holzman's Diary*.

IMPROVISE THE EMOTIONS, WRITE THE WORDS

There never was a written script for *David Holzman's Diary*. All the monologues were improvised.

However, these key scenes weren't improvised in front of the camera; instead, they were created in controlled improvisational sessions, so that McBride and Carson always knew what was going to happen in any given scene.

"For those parts of the film that took place in his apartment," McBride explained, "we spent several days beforehand with just a tape recorder in a room.

"I would give him a sense of what I wanted to have happen in a given scene, and then he would put it into his own words, and then we'd listen to the tape, and I'd say 'I like this, I don't like that, change this.'

"He would do it again, and together we refined each scene. We didn't transcribe it. We just listened to it, again and again, until we both had a fairly clear idea of what was going to happen when we were actually pointing the camera at him. It never got down to a word-by-word situation.

"And when we started shooting, it was always better than it had been in the taping sessions. He always threw in a little zinger for me that he hadn't told me about."

"We were satisfied that we had the shape of the scene," Carson said. "We knew the beginning, middle and end. But I said to Jim, 'I want to surprise you.' I had no idea what I was saying when I said that, but the idea was to keep that instant alive, the instant when anything can happen.

"I like the idea of not filtering the moment, not knowing what I'm going to do."

This technique worked well for this movie, but McBride admits that it might not be the best approach for more traditional films.

"It's a lot simpler when it's just one person talking into a microphone than two or three actors trying to do something dramatic together," McBride said.

"It was very much controlled improvisation, and by the time we actually went to shoot the scene — although it wasn't written down — we all knew exactly what was going to happen.

"Because we didn't have a lot of film to fuck around with, we had to get it on the first or second take. So it was pretty carefully rehearsed."

THE LAST BROADCAST

||||||||||||||||||||||||||||||||||||||||||||||||||||||||||||||||||||||||||||||||||||||||||||

A small group of people venture into the woods searching for evidence of a supernatural entity, bringing along video cameras to document their experience. Something bad happens. Most of them end up dead. And all that remains is their video footage, which may or may not reveal what happened to them.

Produced a year before *The Blair Witch Project* rocked the indie world, *The Last Broadcast* set some records of its own, including being the first digital feature to skip the traditional transfer to film and hit theaters digitally, pioneering a digital satellite broadcast to theaters in five cities across the USA.

For filmmakers Stefan Avalos and Lance Weiler, it all started with the news that desktop editing was finally a reality.

Weiler recalled, "Stefan and I got excited about the prospect of being able to edit on your desktop, so we built some systems and then started making this movie almost as a lark, to see how little we could make it for."

When it was all finished, they were truly surprised. "I remember the shock when we totaled up the receipts," Weiler said. "We rounded up, but it was very close, maybe within 28 cents, of $900."

"We had wanted to make a movie for no money," Avalos added, "but we missed the mark by 900 bucks!"

Both filmmakers agreed that they felt real advantages to working with virtually no money.

"Not having any money made us be more creative," Weiler said. "I think sometimes there's a tendency to fall back on money as an answer to a problem, where we found ourselves brainstorming and trying to find ways to make things work without the money."

Avalos concurred. "Having no money gave us a carefree attitude that I've never had before or since when making movies. We didn't have a producer breathing down our necks concerned about a budget that was spiraling out of control. It's ironic that having no money gave us that freedom."

That freedom produced a handful of important lessons.

IGNORE THE NAYSAYERS

"We had no shortage of people telling us that we were going to fail, at whatever point we were at," Avalos said. "Right along the line, from the moment we said we were going to make a movie until the moment the movie was on HBO. From beginning to end, people were always saying, 'That won't work.'"

"Throughout the process, we were always told 'No, you can't do that,'" Weiler added. "We were told, 'No, you can't make a film on a desktop computer,' 'You're crazy if you think you can make it for $900,' 'You're crazy if you're not going to take it to film,' 'There's no way you can show it at festivals that way.'

"And we just kept not listening to those people and kept pushing through as though we were on a mission."

In addition to the satisfaction of successfully finishing and distributing their movie, they both also had the satisfaction of proving all those naysayers wrong.

GOD IS IN THE DETAILS

One of the elements that makes *The Last Broadcast* so much fun is that it looks and feels genuine. You really believe that you're watching an actual documentary.

Avalos and Weiler knew they didn't have enough funds to get every detail right, so they achieved this authenticity for very little money by simply focusing on a few key details in each scene.

"We called it Theater of the Minimal," Avalos said. "It's amazing how little it takes to convince people. You only need small clues to make something seem convincing. Which is what we were commenting on in the movie: What's reality, what do you believe?

"And I found it amazing how readily people believed the movie, based on just a couple little pseudo-realities within the movie. I think a lot of documentary filmmakers were perturbed by that."

Many of those convincing details were found in the numerous newspaper articles and legal documents that appear in the movie — none of which ever existed as hardcopies, but were instead created electronically, using Photoshop and other off-the-shelf programs.

Photoshop also came in handy for touching up still images of the victims. Rather than go to the time and trouble of applying make-up to the actors for autopsy photos, they simply took shots of the actors and added the make-up and gore electronically.

Bloodstains were added to other images electronically, saving the trouble of ruining perfectly good clothes for one quick shot in a movie. This made strong, economic sense, because in many cases those clothes were their own; you see, in addition to writing and directing, Weiler and Avalos cast themselves in key roles in the movie.

"We knew that if we cast ourselves in it," Weiler explained, "that we were guaranteed to show up. And we knew that we would work cheap.

"We also structured the movie so that we would be shooting and doing a lot of the sound work ourselves; a lot of the movie consists of us actually on-camera and holding mics in the scenes. So I think it was a very conscious effort to try to work within the limitations that we had."

Avalos agreed and added, "We joked that the first thing we tried to get rid of when we made this movie was film, which is why we shot digitally. The second thing were the actors, because you have to feed them and hope they show up."

WHAT'S YOUR CLEARANCE, CLARENCE?

Despite their nearly non-existent budget, Weiler and Avalos were quick to make sure that all the business aspects of making their movie were handled professionally.

"I would hope that a filmmaker has figured out the clearance issues," Avalos explained, "Because it's such a basic, easy problem to avoid."

Weiler was quick to agree. "Having good legal representation is always very important," he said. "Having somebody who can read over contracts and agreements for you. And really taking the time to clear everything in the movie — the basics — the stuff people really don't think about when they get going making a film.

"The only way you're going to continue to make films is if you take control over what you do and treat it responsibly, in terms of clearing rights, music, legal representation.

"A lot of times when people are making films for no money," Weiler continued, "they think that later on somebody else will deal with it. 'Somebody else will take care of it for me.' And, in very rare cases, that happens.

"The reality of making films, especially on a low-budget level, is that you're going to have to wear a lot of hats. You're going to have to juggle a lot of balls. So you might as well try to protect your interests as much as you can.

"Sometimes people get caught up in their vision and think 'I'm creative, and because I'm creative, somebody else will take care of the business aspects of it.'" Weiler simply doesn't agree, adding, "That's the downfall of a lot of projects."

PREVIEWS

Editing the movie took around nine months. But before they declared the movie done, the team held some preview screenings, not to see if people liked or disliked the movie, but to make sure that audiences were seeing the same story the filmmakers were making.

"I think when you know a story really well in your own head," Weiler remembered, "there are certain little connecting things that maybe other people don't pick up.

"The test screenings we did made us a little more aware of certain things that we took for granted, because we already knew them. It was pretty much where we wanted to go, it just needed some tweaking after that.

"But it's always good to get some feedback, because you're kind of in a vacuum."

ALL'S WELL THAT ENDS WELL

Endings are key.

It's the last thing that the audience takes with them when they leave the theater or turn off the TV, and if your ending hasn't brought your audience to the conclusion of an emotionally-fulfilling journey, their

opinion of everything that has come before it — as wonderful as it might have been — can be seriously jeopardized.

For the ending of *The Last Broadcast*, Avalos and Weiler opted to take a big creative risk, which may or may not have paid off, depending on who you ask.

Audiences are split on the ending; the people who love it really love it, and the people who hate it loathe it. (One website review of the movie opened with this heading: "*The Last Broadcast*. Worst ending ever? Maybe.")

Without giving away any twists, I can say that the ending turns what appears to be an objective documentary into a subjective narrative, with a twist that is surprising and original (although not strictly logical).

For their part, the filmmakers couldn't be more delighted with the controversy.

"The ending was one of the first things we thought of for the movie, to do this genre switch." Avalos said. "Instead of breaking down the fourth wall, we were putting the fourth wall up. We were really excited by that idea."

Avalos compared their ending to the reaction he first had when he saw another famous fake documentary. "I was hoping people would be as pissed off with the ending of our movie as we were with the end of *David Holzman's Diary*.

"When I realized that that movie was a fake, when the end credits rolled, I was so angry. I hated it. I hated it. But very quickly it became one of my favorite movies. So that reaction was something we were trying to get with our genre switch."

For Weiler, the ending is the perfect encapsulation of the theme of the movie. "The movie really takes you on this ride," he said. "The point we were trying to make with the film was that you can't necessarily believe everything that you see.

"And when we twisted it at the end, we really wanted it to feel like a punch, to leave you breathless. That was a very bold choice on our part, to all of a sudden break that wall and go into what was, effectively, a narrative.

"I think people have trouble with endings sometimes when they don't get what they feel is a final resolution or a final answer," he continued. "I think people like things wrapped up, in nice, cohesive packages.

"I'm still very proud of that ending; I think it was very effective. And I think anytime that you have something that moves people to either love it or hate it, that's pretty cool."

BE DIFFERENT

Although they were approached with offers for theatrical distribution, Avalos and Weiler didn't think that was necessarily the right direction for their movie.

"Because the movie didn't cost anything to make, and we didn't owe anybody any money," Avalos said, "that was one of the things that let us arrogantly disregard theatrical distribution.

"There were people who did want to pick the movie up and blow-up the film. At that point it was our movie and we really didn't want to give it up. And because we didn't have costs to recoup, we could go down that road of trying something new."

The "something new" they wanted to try was digital distribution — beaming the movie directly to theaters by satellite, thus sidestepping many of the costly elements of traditional distribution.

Weiler explained: "We started thinking, 'we've been digital this long, why not just keep it that way?'

"So we started thinking about ways we could show it in more than one theater at the same time, and that led to the idea of satellite. And so we took it a step further and started looking at people who were familiar with that technology.

"We put together this crazy sponsorship and convinced these companies to get involved in this groundbreaking event, and it didn't cost us anything. In fact, we made money, and in the long run, made cinematic history.

"We were right on the edge of that technology wave," Weiler concluded, "which was horrifying and exhilarating all at the same time. We did actually make history, and it's ironic that *The Last Broadcast* actually became the first."

THE BLAIR WITCH PROJECT

||||||||||||||||||||||||||||||||||||||||||||||||||||||||||||||||||||||||||||||||||||||||||||

If you made a movie about the making of *The Blair Witch Project* and its subsequent success, no one would believe it. The story is simply too far-fetched.

This unassuming little fake documentary, made for around $35,000, hit it big at Sundance, made the cover of *Time* magazine, fueled Internet controversy for months, then went on to take in about $240 million at the box office.

And, to this day, there are still people who insist that the movie is real.

Co-director Eduardo Sanchez agrees that the film's trajectory was, at best, improbable.

"When we did the film," Sanchez said soon after the film's release, "we hoped for a video or cable deal. When Artisan told us the film would be released in theaters, we were thinking, 'Man, if we make $10 million, it'd be a dream come true.'

"But to do $29 million in one weekend was so beyond our comprehension. If anyone had said that a year ago, we would have had him committed."

"Ed and I were both fans of the *In Search of...* series and movies like *The Legend of Boggy Creek*," explained co-director Daniel Myrick, talking about the genesis of the film. "There were all kinds of these UFO, Bigfoot faux-documentary television shows and features that walked the line between fact and fiction. And we always found them very scary and haunting and they resonated with us.

"I think *The Blair Witch Project* was born out of wanting to re-visit that and recreate that, with a more contemporary video language.

"We just wanted to make a scary movie," Myrick continued. "Naïve group goes into woods. They get in over their heads and eventually realize the error of their ways. We just felt that it was a solid, fundamental structure for a frightening film. It's pretty basic when you really think about it."

These two filmmakers only set out to make a movie, not a cultural phenomenon. So Myrick and Sanchez were just as amazed as anyone when *The Blair Witch Project* entered the national psyche with the force of an atomic blast.

"For most of that ride, we were on the outside looking in like everybody else and were as fascinated by the evolution of the whole *Blair* phenomenon as anybody else," Myrick recalled.

"We had an inside look at what was going on, but to this day I look back at the confluence of events and the timing and the Internet and the reality approach we took to this — how everything intersected and what happens when it does. I find that fascinating to this day.

"I definitely think it was a convergence of old and new media," Myrick continued. "Whether there was something new to learn or not is arguable. I don't think we re-invented the wheel or taught anybody any new lessons."

Determining if the lessons found in *The Blair Witch Project* are new or not is fine fodder for an argument; however, it's clear that the lessons found in the movie, like the filmmaker's footage found in the woods, are both intriguing and valuable.

WRITE TO YOUR RESOURCES

Writing to your resources is not just about saving money at every step of production (although that's a big part of it). It's also about *scale*, about understanding what your money can and can't buy you, about creating a movie that fits your budget and doesn't make a mockery of it.

Roger Corman, a man who knows a thing or two about making a movie for a buck, saw in *The Blair Witch Project* a movie made by filmmakers who understood the value of scale.

"I think *The Blair Witch Project* is an exceptionally well-conceived and well-made film," he said. "It's well-conceived for this reason: they understood what their budget was and they wrote the script and made their picture to do the best possible job they could on that budget.

"One of the worst things you can do is have a limited budget and try to do some big-looking film. That's when you end up with very bad work. They accepted their limitations and tailored their film to those limitations."

CAST WITH CARE

The Blair Witch Project put a lot of pressure on its cast. The three actors were required to create conflict, provide exposition, add humor and be scared out of their minds — all without benefit of a script or a director within sight.

Sanchez and Myrick understood those requirements before they started the film, and as a result spent months, and months, and months looking for just the right three people to send out into the woods on their own.

"I think Hitchcock once said that 90% of direction is casting," Myrick observed, "so if you find really good, talented people, and take great pains to do that, and then let them do their thing on set, you'll come away with some really great material that you couldn't possibly script. And that's what we applied to *The Blair Witch Project*."

Sanchez agreed: "Start off with a good idea, start off with a good script, and work from there. If you don't have the actors then you stop and you continue to cast because there is somebody right out there; you just gotta find them."

HONESTY IS THE BEST POLICY

And once you do find that cast, you have to be honest about what you have planned for them. In the case of Myrick and Sanchez, honesty wasn't just the best policy — it was the only policy. They made it very clear to potential cast members that they weren't signing up for a week on *The Love Boat*.

"I read an ad in *Backstage* in New York, which is where I was living at the time," recounted actress Heather Donahue. "You know what it said? 'An improvised feature film, shot in wooded location. It is going to be hell and most of you reading this probably shouldn't come.' They used every possible deterrent."

"When we signed on to do the project," actor Joshua Leonard recalled, "one of the first things they told us was, 'Your safety is our concern. Your comfort is not.' And they made that blatantly clear from the very beginning."

USE REALITY TO YOUR ADVANTAGE

"We hated a lot of traditional fake documentaries," Myrick explained, "because there was always some sign or red flag in them that would be a little telltale sign that it was scripted or faked in some way.

"The camera would happen to be in the right place at the right time too many times. A line of dialogue from a testimonial just sounded too scripted, too convenient."

Myrick and Sanchez were convinced that the only way to make a fake documentary seem real was to turn it into — insofar as possible — a real documentary. "We took the Method approach to the acting and the filming over eight straight days, 24-7," Myrick said.

"Our theory was, let's shoot this like a documentary as much as is humanly possible," Myrick continued, "and set the stage for our actors to play in character within this documentary, so hopefully when we come out the other end we have, effectively, a documentary."

"Pretty much everything you see being done to the actors was done," explained Production Designer Ben Rock. "We really did have the baby sounds on tape players outside their tent, and they never knew what we were going to do to them until it happened."

And while the actors slept in their tent, "We'd go out on our raids and score them — wake them up, leave things behind. We basically played the Blair Witch," said Sanchez.

The result was footage — hours and hours of footage — from which the team found the best, most real moments.

"I think we came away with what looked very natural and what looked like very unpredictable footage," Myrick said. "Then we cut, from that footage, the story that ultimately became *The Blair Witch Project*."

KILL YOUR DARLINGS

Myrick, Sanchez and the rest of the team who created *The Blair Witch Project* made some excellent decisions during their preproduction and production process.

However, one of the best decisions they made — and the one that probably made the film the success it was — came in postproduction, when they took a clear-eyed look at what they had shot and decided to, essentially, throw away two-thirds of their movie.

"We initially shot two phases of *Blair Witch*," Myrick explained. "One was kind of a framing device, which was more like a traditional documentary, where you had interviews." The other phase was all the "lost" footage of the filmmakers in the woods.

"Initially when we went out to shoot, we were only hoping to get fifteen or twenty minutes of the students' footage in the woods," Myrick said, "never anticipating that we'd have enough to cut an entire feature.

"It was always our goal to get just a handful of really good moments within the construct of the storyline, and then much like *The Legend of Boggy Creek* or an *In Search of...*, have it sprinkled throughout what would be more of a traditional documentary.

"And when we came back with so much great footage, and because w had scripted our time out in the woods with a complete narrative arc, came back to the edit and said to ourselves, 'You know, we have a movie in just this footage. It's a very risky movie, but we do have a movie.'"

"We knew it was different, and a risk," agreed Sanchez. "But as rough and as raw as it was, we knew we should leave it alone."

Changing direction like that, at such a late date, is not a small step and should not be taken lightly. However, the editing process is all about listening to what the footage is trying to tell you, and creating the best story from the footage you have. And sometimes you have to kill your darlings (i.e., get rid of the original framework for your movie and all the footage

that went with it) in order to make the strongest movie possible.

"It was a very tough decision for us to jettison that original concept for the film," Myrick admitted. "I was more resistant to jettisoning that stuff. But once we did, I was really glad that we decided to do that, because ultimately, that became the movie."

PREVIEWS

After they made the decision to radically alter their original plan for the movie, the filmmakers tested their new idea on a very reliable source: an audience.

"Once you get so close to the editing process, it's hard to remain objective," Myrick explained. "So we had to screen it for a non-biased audience for feedback.

"We screened a very long cut of the student's footage," Myrick continued, "and it was set up like a very traditional test screening, where we called in all of our friends and their friends and whoever would give up a couple hours of their afternoon and come check out this film.

"We handed out questionnaires, about what they liked and didn't like.

And from those questionnaires you can draw a consensus about what people are turned on and turned off by.

"And we had more than a few comments telling us, 'You know, this really is your movie. We don't really want to break away from the narrative story of what's going on here.'

"That test screening was really helpful in that respect."

KNOW WHAT YOU'RE SIGNING

The final lesson from *The Blair Witch Project* is directed to all filmmakers, whether your finished movie is destined to break box-office records around the world ... or merely show up at 3:00 a.m. on your local cable access channel.

Flush with excitement about a distributor's bid for your movie, you may be inclined to think that they have your best interests at heart. Nothing could be further from the truth.

The deal you make with a distributor is one that can affect your career for years to come, and not always in a positive way. So learned Myrick and Sanchez.

"We had this three-picture deal, post-*Blair Witch*, with Artisan that we thought was our guarantee to making movies into the decades to come," Myrick recounted.

"And we found out that a lot of those so-called 'three picture deals' are ways to just leverage you later down the road, whereas you effectively sign off the rights to your next two movies, which are two of your pet projects, to the distributor and then they can, in turn, hold that as leverage to get you to do, or try to get you to do, *Blair 2* for example.

"That's a specific example of us learning a hard lesson where we signed off a couple of our best ideas because in the heat of the moment we thought our distributor was going to line them up and starting making these movies with us, and then we come to find out that their primary interest was just making more *Blair* movies.

"And that wasn't where we wanted to go creatively at the time."

LISA PICARD IS FAMOUS

||||||||||||||||||||||||||||||||||||||||||||||||||||||||||||||||||||||||||||||||||||||||||||||

"Truth is really, really small. That's why it's so hard to find."

David Holzman

Our friend, the fictional David Holzman who kicked off the fake documentary revolution with *David Holzman's Diary*, makes a brief but important return appearance in Griffin Dunne's faux doc, *Lisa Picard Is Famous*.

His sage advice (delivered, oddly enough, while shooting Polaroids of his lunch), about the size of truth and the difficulty of tracking it down, is just one of the many pleasures to be found in this movie about fame, the people who seek it, and what it does to them when they finally get it.

The film tracks actress Lisa Picard and her fellow thespian, Tate, as they struggle to make careers for themselves in New York City, followed by a documentary crew headed up by the film's actual director, Griffin Dunne. The script was written by actress Laura Kirk, and her fellow thespian, Nat DeWolf.

"It started with just some monologues," Kirk explained, "talking about these acting jobs that — I am serious — were great jobs. And then, all of a sudden, the character of Tate just started to grow. We just started meeting and writing this stuff down.

"We had about twenty-five pages, and I'd always have it in my back-pack; you know, in New York, you're always walking around with a backpack. And I ran into Mira Sorvino, who was in our acting class. She said, 'What are you up to?' And I said, 'You know what? I think I'm writing something with Nat.'"

Sorvino (who eventually went on to produce the movie) looked at the script-in-progress, liked what she saw, and encouraged Kirk to keep writing. Eventually, Sorvino went so far as to set up readings of the script.

"About fifty pages later," Kirk recalled, "we started having readings of it in her living room, with other people from our acting class. And we'd just furiously take notes.

"At one point we did a reading with Quentin Tarantino; he read the part that Griffin ended up playing. Then, when everyone was giving all their comments, he said, 'Everybody, this is not a finger-painting. You don't all get to mess it all up.' He was really encouraging us to keep our own voice as we took criticism and suggestions."

"When I first read what Nat and Laura wrote," Dunne said, "it was just about 'I hope I get the job.' I really wanted to put much more of a social spin on it, about how fucked up people get about fame."

To give it more of that social spin, Dunne sprinkled interviews throughout the film with people talking about fame and the effects it's had on their lives.

The interviews Dunne added include conversations with Carrie Fisher, Fisher Stevens, and Buck Henry (who kicks off the movie by asking, "Did you know that 'fame' has the same root as 'famished?' It's all hunger, isn't it?").

"I just thought it needed a bigger perspective beyond their small world," Dunne explained. "And it would be great to have interviews with people who had dealt with fame in a very direct way, who really had fame and had lost it or were at the various ous points that these two kind of desperate characters were trying to be."

Kirk agreed that the interviews were a smart addition. "A lot of the criticism that we faced was that the film would be too 'inside,'" she explained, "but Nat and I felt this was about anybody who has a dream and is just absolutely blindly having to pursue it, and it could be applied to anything. Griffin, through the interviews, really explained what we were doing."

Although L.M. Kit Carson, as David Holzman, appears only fleetingly in the film, he did have an influence on the movie as a whole.

"They did the first cut, or maybe the second cut," Carson recalled, "and Griffin invited me to take a look at it. And they had a problem."

The problem Carson saw was that Griffin's character in the movie had not included himself in the self-examination style of the film — he was just an uninvolved observer.

"Afterwards I said, 'Griffin, you have to implicate yourself. You can't get away with this,'" Carson said. "So he went back and re-shot stuff and put himself more in the film.

"That's what I learned from *David Holzman's Diary*: If you're the film-maker, you can't get away with not exposing yourself."

GO DIGITAL

Early on, it became apparent that *Lisa Picard Is Famous* was an ideal project to employ digital technology, for a number of reasons.

"The digital video thing had just begun and we knew that we were perfect for it," Kirk explained, "because it would be the right look for it."

Besides being the right look, the technology also became an important part of the filmmaking process.

"The exciting thing for me about making a digital documentary, or whatever you want to call this genre," Dunne said, "is the line between satire and reality the director can straddle.

"I was fascinated by how long people would sit still for my questions just because I had a DV camera pointed at them. I never called cut or ~tion — I just kept shooting until the tape rolled out or the battery ~t down, and that was the end of the scene.

~s a new and wonderfully uncomfortable process."

DON'T BE PREPARED

In order to truly capture a documentary feel for the film, Dunne set aside one key directorial requirement: preparation.

"A director's job is to be the most prepared," Dunne explained, "and this was an exercise in leaving a real part of your creative process to being unprepared and open to accidents. And I was able to keep those 'let's see what happens' balls in the air for most of the picture."

The nature of the movie, and the technology he was using to create it, made this the perfect movie to leave to chance and luck.

"It struck me that working digitally with a small crew," Dunne continued, "I could lay out a general plan and hope for mistakes which would create something more than satire and something less than truthful reality."

Taking this leap of faith was no small step; it involved being willing to set aside much of what he'd learned on larger-budget projects.

"With movies I'd done before," he said, "everything was about preparation, so that there would be absolutely no mistakes, because mistakes would cost so much time and so much money.

"So you plan everything, if you're really doing your job right, so you're not going to be felled by weather or any of the billions of things that can go wrong. You try to plug every hole before anything sets in.

"With this movie, I approached it, before I started shooting, that it was about the lack of preparation, about being open to accidents and disasters.

"So, if she's running to catch the train and she accidentally catches the train and I don't want her to catch the train, then we shoot her catching the train. If she doesn't catch the train, then we shoot that."

WHAT'S YOUR CLEARANCE, CLARENCE?

Product placement works both ways. A company can ask your permission to feature their product in your movie. Or, you can ask their permission to feature the product.

The key word in those two scenarios is "permission." You have to get it before you proceed.

A key element of *Lisa Picard Is Famous* — and the incident that convinces the (fictional) director that this (fictional) actress is going to be famous and therefore worthy of a documentary — is a simple Wheat Chex commercial that gets a little out of hand.

Lisa's appearance in what turns out to be a very *sexy* commercial was a major plot point in the script. But before they could shoot, they needed to find a company willing to put their product in the movie. Finding that product was not a simple task.

"I remember that we changed it to yogurt at one point," Kirk recalled, "and I remember Nat and I having an emergency meeting with Griffin, trying to talk about yogurt. I think we tried plastic wrap and aluminum foil.

"But then we went to Wheat Chex and they just thought it was really funny and a good thing. They sent lots of Wheat Chex."

Once they received permission from the company to feature Wheat Chex in the movie, Dunne proceeded to shoot the scene. And as glad as he was that they were granted permission, he still isn't entirely sure why the company went along with it.

"How did we get clearance?" Dunne said. "I have no idea. It just blows my mind. I will always eat Wheat Chex. I couldn't believe it.

"I kept saying to our producer, 'Are you sure they know about this?' They thought it was funny. Who would have thought the people at Wheat Chex would be so dry?"

BEWARE THE CUTTING EDGE

"Like most real documentaries, this film was definitely found in the cutting room," Dunne explained. "But, since we were going where no filmmakers had gone before, with respect to the software, it was much more problematic."

Lisa Picard Is Famous was one of the first features edited on an early version of Final Cut Pro, and Dunne and company definitely paid the price for being first in line at that rodeo, learning first-hand the dangers and pitfalls of working on the cutting edge.

"Everything that could go wrong, did go wrong," he said. "It was complicated for a number of reasons.

"I was under the delusion that since it's digital, you can shoot as much as you want. And I shot a lot; I never even said "action" or "cut," because I didn't want actors to feel like they had to key up. I didn't want them to be aware of the camera. And William Rexer, my DP, was just incorrigible. Sometimes he would shoot long after I thought we were done shooting.

"So, because of all the footage I shot, it really was baptism by extreme fire. Consequently, the system crashed a lot. And it always seemed to crash right at a fix you were trying to make. It was very difficult, and we lost a few days."

Despite the postproduction difficulties, Dunne recognized that the problems they had — and solved — helped to made life easier for subsequent films and their makers.

"We were the soldiers who other soldiers stepped over."

Chapter Six

THE
NEW
ESTABLISHMENT

Not all filmmakers want to work outside the system. Many, in fact, seem to want to get inside as quickly as possible.

The films in this chapter are the ones which opened that door for their respective filmmakers.

What sets these filmmakers apart from other similarly-talented peers is that as soon as that door was opened, they wasted no time moving in — and then started re-arranging the place to suit their needs.

The lessons they learned on the way in are lessons they're still using today — albeit on exponentially higher budgets.

157

SEX, LIES AND VIDEOTAPE

There's very little doubt that *sex, lies and videotape* created a lot of change in the independent film community, while earning more than a bit of spare change for its funders.

For one, the film launched Steven Soderbergh's career, not only putting him on the map, but basically naming the map after him, at least for a while. There are few directing/writing debuts as self-assured as this one.

For another, the movie re-charged the independent film scene, making it (seemingly) financially viable. The incredible success of *sex, lies and videotape* was used for years as the primary example of just how profitable an independent film could be.

Or, as über producer's representative John Pierson described it, "If I had a nickel for every prospectus that I've received that highlighted *sex, lies and videotape's* $100 million dollars in worldwide gross on a $1.2 million budget, I'd be a rich man."

(I believe that I owe Mr. Pierson at least a nickel, as I'm sure I quoted those figures in a business plan for a feature project years ago. He may claim the coin from me at his earliest convenience.)

And, for better or for worse, *sex, lies and videotape* is credited by some as irrevocably changing the Sundance Film Festival. If you don't like what Sundance has become, feel free to pin the blame on *sex, lies and videotape*. Lots of other people do.

As film guru Robert Hawk put it, "After *sex, lies and videotape*, the festival was never the same. It was just a phenomenon. Up until then, it had this low-key Redford aura and was more manageable. Afterward, it really became more of a zoo."

Soderbergh received an Oscar nomination for his screenplay, and the film also won the Palme d'Or at the Cannes Film Festival, putting it in very good company: other past winners of the Palme d'Or include *The Third Man, Wages of Fear, The Conversation,* and *Taxi Driver.*

There are many important lessons to be mined from *sex, lies and videotape*; however at the time it was released, Soderbergh cautioned anyone from taking him, or the film, too seriously.

"Having made only one feature film," he wrote, "I don't feel comfortable or justified in putting forth any real filmmaking 'theories.'"

That being said, he then went on to offer some solid advice:

"It's my *feeling*," he wrote, "that nobody has the market cornered on good ideas, and that you should be open to suggestion and keep your eyes and ears open at all times.

"It's my *belief* that there should be a chain of command on a film set, but not a chain of respect (I have worked as the lowest member of a film crew and been treated like a no-class citizen by the 'above-the-line' people. The experience was unpleasant but illuminating.).

"But it's my *guess* that no two filmmakers work alike, which is as it should be. Personally, I like to have a good time. I mean, it's just a movie; we're not solving world hunger, right?"

FIRST IMPRESSIONS / SECOND CHANCES

While the cast for *sex, lies and videotape* seems perfect in retrospect, during preproduction Soderbergh had to learn an important lesson about casting: Look at what an actor is capable of doing, not just at what they've already done.

"I think you have an idea," he explained, "and you stick with that idea until you're confronted with the fact that there's something better than your idea. I think the smart play is to go with the better idea."

To begin with, he had trouble imagining Andie MacDowell in the role of Ann.

"In the case of Andie," he said, "I was laboring under the illusion that she was not much more than a model and couldn't deliver what was required. Fortunately for me, she came in and proved me wrong. And I was happy to be proven wrong."

But then when James Spader expressed interest in the part of Graham (after hearing about the script from his agent), Soderbergh experienced the same tunnel vision.

"I was ambivalent when his name was first brought up," Soderbergh said. "He'd been very good in everything I'd seen him in. I just hadn't seen him in anything like this, and being the neophyte dilettante that I was, I assumed that if he hadn't done it, he couldn't do it. I assumed the same thing about Andie, and look what happened."

The casting choice paid off handsomely. James Spader was brilliant in the film and was awarded the Best Actor prize at the Cannes Film Festival. And, perhaps the greatest compliment of all, Spader himself was pleased with his performance, a rare admission from any actor. "Jimmy gave me the best compliment an actor could give me," Soderbergh recalled. "He said he felt like I cut his best performance together. That's a great thing to hear.

"From now on," he continued, "I'll assume an actor can do anything I require until he/she proves otherwise."

This is a lesson that Soderbergh continually revisits, even years later.

"It happened to me the other day on a movie we're starting next month," he recounted. "It's a supporting role, and one of the people who came in was someone I know and who, on first blush, I would have said, 'No, I don't think he's really right for this.'

"Sure enough, when I sat down and looked at what he did, I immediately said, 'Oh, that's the guy.'

"He did something that was different from what I'd seen him do, and different from what other people were choosing to do, and suddenly he seemed like the only guy who should be doing it.

"So you have to keep your prejudices in check."

REHEARSE

Once he had his cast in place, and before shooting started on *sex, lies and videotape*, Soderbergh arranged for a full week of rehearsals.

While some look upon rehearsal as a time to block scenes and run lines, for Soderbergh it serves a much more primal function.

"Rehearsals for me are not about exploring the piece," he said. "They're about finding out how I can communicate with the cast. Because I need that shorthand."

That shorthand can come in very handy when you're working with four very talented but very different actors, each with their own way of working. That week of rehearsal helped Soderbergh learn how to effectively communicate with each of his cast members, which now included Peter Gallagher and Laura San Giacomo.

"This quartet was a classic example of how each actor requires a different director," Soderbergh explained. "Jimmy is very, very thorough, very rigorous, likes to talk a lot, has a lot of questions, likes to have a dialogue.

"Peter: ready to do it, running on instinct. Andie wants to talk about everything *but* the movie. And then Laura was sort of in-between. It was her first movie, and she wasn't really sure how much we should talk."

Taking the time to learn how to communicate with the cast helped Soderbergh maintain focus during production, so that he was able to keep all the elements of the film on track, which is a tricky art in itself.

"If you drift off compass a couple of degrees, thirty days later you're *way* off compass, but you don't even know it," he explained. "And then you put the movie together and it doesn't work, and you don't know where it went wrong."

NO MONEY = MORE CONTROL

Despite the nearly universal acclaim that the film ultimately received, Soderbergh had less than high hopes when he started the project.

He was sure it wouldn't go anywhere. Although they were guaranteed a video release, he had doubts it would ever be picked up for theatrical distribution. He tended to look upon *sex, lies and videotape* as "a feature-length resume piece that would get me a job making a real movie," he said.

While that perspective may seem negative, it actually had the opposite effect. With so few expectations, everyone was able to experiment and take some creative chances.

"The great thing about that was that all of us felt pretty free to do whatever occurred to us," Soderbergh concluded. "There was no pressure and you felt like no one was watching you."

So, in spite of the low budget and the relatively quick thirty-day shooting schedule, he felt he had more control than he would later experience with larger productions.

"On that movie," Soderbergh said, "I felt I had more time to do the work than I have had since on any movie. That was the only movie where I never once felt rushed and felt like I had all the time I needed to do the work on a given day. And every film since then, I've felt like I didn't have enough time.

"*Out of Sight* cost $49 million," he continued, "And every day you felt like you had a gun to your head."

TAKE A BREAK

In the midst of shooting a low-budget movie — sometimes working six or seven days a week, with what few hours you have in the evenings spent looking at dailies – there seems to be little time to kick back, relax, and get charged up about movies.

Soderbergh, however, sees the value in putting aside your movie for a few hours and getting lost in someone else's cinematic vision.

On his only day off one week, in the midst of shooting *sex, lies and videotape*, he took a break and went to see a movie.

Here's how he recorded it in his production journal: "Day off felt good. Saw *Tucker: The Man and His Dream*, which (I'd) been dying to see. Unfortunately, I was engaged aesthetically but not emotionally … It literally was one of the best designed and photographed films I've ever seen."

Getting outside of yourself and your movie — at least for a couple hours — is a good way to recharge your creative energies and get you ready to dive back into the grind of preproduction, production, or postproduction. And it's a method Soderbergh still uses to this day, although now he creates that space by working on several projects simultaneously.

"I'm more and more finding ways to create pockets of time to step away, so that I can come back and be less precious. I think the biggest lesson I learned over the years, especially with the first four films, is that preciousness — thinking too highly of your own material — is to be actively attacked.

"The benefit of having several projects going at once is that I move from projects on a day-by-day or night-by-night basis. It keeps everything fresh. You never get bored with what you're doing and it doesn't feel like an obligation. You come back to something and say, 'Oh my God, why is *that* in the film?'"

ANTICIPATE SUCCESS

You've got to hand it to Steven Soderbergh: despite his feeling that *sex, lies and videotape* would end up being nothing more than a resume piece, when opportunity did come knocking, he was ready with an armful of ideas.

Before the movie had even hit Cannes, he was approached to do another feature and had three projects set up quickly, all based on material he had loved for years: *The Last Ship* with Sydney Pollack at Universal; *King of the Hill*, another book, set up with Robert Redford; and *Kafka*, a script he had read previously and really loved.

"It's all very personal and a function of your character," he explained. "I certainly had spent a lot of time thinking about what would happen if somebody came to me and said, 'What do you want to do next?' So I had some answers.

"As my career has gone on, I've gotten more and more aggressive about keeping my plate full. I've got so many things that I want to do, so many ideas that I'd like to pursue, that's it hard to find time to do all of them. I'm mystified by directors who say, 'I can't find anything I want to do.' I look around and I want to do everything. There are stories everywhere.

"For those aspiring to a career in the film business, I offer this equation: Talent + Perseverance = Luck. Be ready when it happens."

KEEP IT ALL IN PERSPECTIVE

Finally, Soderbergh's greatest gift during the success of *sex, lies and videotape* — and, I suspect, throughout his career — has been the ability to keep it all in perspective.

"I think the reason a lot of suddenly successful people get screwed up," he has noted, "is because they think they should feel better and be happier, and when they aren't, they think there must be something wrong with themselves, so they indulge in self-destructive behavior.

"My definition of success is being continually engaged by whatever film is in front of me."

SLACKER

|||||||||||||||||||||||||||||||||||||||||||||||||||||||||||||||||||||||||||||||||||||||||||

If *sex, lies and videotape* reinvigorated the independent film movement, then it's safe to say that *Slacker* announced to that same community that their own backyards could easily be transformed into locations for a new generation of independent movies.

Slacker, writer/director Richard Linklater's lazy-Susan of a movie, follows a few minutes each in the lives of a couple dozen Austin, Texas residents on a prototypical summer day. The film signaled to the world that a real movie could be made on less than a shoestring, using items that you could probably find lying around your house.

For filmmaker Kevin Smith, it was the movie that would inspire him to make *Clerks* just a couple of years later. "I was awed by *Slacker*, that it existed," Smith recalled.

"And Richard's story was kind of compelling too," he continued. "This guy from Austin, Texas — not from Hollywood, not from New York — had made a film that's playing here in New York and look at all these people here to see it! And he'd made it for such a low amount of money.

"But by the end of the film I was thinking, 'I could definitely do this!'"

As with many great ideas, the genesis for *Slacker* struck Linklater out of nowhere, like a bolt out of the blue.

"I remember I was driving to Houston at about two in the morning," he recalled, "and it just hit me, why couldn't I make a film that just went from character to character, kind of an early radical idea about narrative?

165

"I sat down and went through my notebooks," Linklater continued, "and in about a twenty-four-hour period started writing scenes and finding the connective tissue and came up with the basic outline for what would be *Slacker*.

"So the structural idea always stayed with me and to me that's what the movie is really about, storytelling and different ideas of narrative. It was sort of an experiment in storytelling."

And the beauty of the structure was that if you didn't like what you were watching, that was fine, because you wouldn't be seeing it for long. "That's one thing about the movie," agreed Director of Photography Lee Daniel. "If you're bored with it, five minutes later you'll find something maybe more interesting."

Slacker has become so identified with Austin, and Austin with *Slacker*, that it's hard to separate the two. Or, as Linklater put it, "What *Bullit* is to San Francisco and *Night of the Living Dead* is to Pittsburgh, *Slacker* is to Austin."

However, that's not to suggest that the behaviors of the characters in the movie are strictly limited to that Texas town. "People are crazy everywhere," Linklater admitted. "I just think in some places they're slower to put them in jail or lock them away."

Although many outrageous theories and opinions are spouted in the movie, what makes it all so appealing is the absolute ordinariness of the people and their environment.

"I always felt regular life was worthy of a movie," Linklater said. "I think people feel alienated from most movies because it's far from what we experience. You come away thinking, 'My life's no good, let other people entertain me, and tell me what's important.'

"*Slacker* is a celebration of day-to-day life. Especially the last scene, with the all-night partiers driving around and filming each other. It's a microcosm of the whole film, ordinary people saying, 'Hey, my life's worthy of cinema.'"

BE DIFFERENT

Every time you start a new movie, you stand at a crossroad. You can either do what's been done before ... or you can throw off the shackles of tradition and venture into the land of the unknown.

Due to economic consider-ations, you don't see Hollywood ambling down the latter path too often. But independent, low-budget movies aren't required to take the road more traveled. And they shouldn't be. If you don't have much to spend, the theory goes, you really don't have much to lose.

"If you are going to do a low-budget film, you can't compete with Hollywood," Linklater agreed. "It's better to do something that is unique, that no one else is doing, that no one else could do.

"No one could make a film like *Slacker* in the system. It was a total experiment that could very well have not worked. It's the kind of risk you could only take on an underground, no-budget level.

"*Slacker* was made exactly opposite of the way you are supposed to do things," Linklater continued. "There was no real official-looking script, we used mostly nonprofessional actors, we never got permits to shoot on city property, no one got paid. If you want to make movies that are different, I think it's okay to make them differently."

Of course, bear in mind that the movie-going public as a whole (and often mainstream critics, as well) don't have a great history of embrac-ing works of art that go against the grain of tradition. So, as you launch your new vision into the world, be prepared for reactions of confusion and outright disdain. That was certainly the case with *Slacker*.

"My favorite review was in *Playboy*," Linklater remembered. "The reviewer said, 'There's nothing else like it, but the question is, should there be?'"

Cast member Whammo (The Anti-Artist) also recognized that the main-stream is often slow in appreciating something wildly new or different.

"I remember watching Siskel and Ebert doing the actual critique of *Slacker*," Whammo said. "One guy was thumbs up, one guy was thumbs down — I think Ebert was thumbs down and Siskel was thumbs up.

"And Ebert was like, 'Nobody has conversations like this. Everybody in this town isn't that clever.'

"Well, yeah, but nobody can fly, either, and nobody bitches about Superman."

POVERTY BREEDS CREATIVITY

Okay, so you have no money and you don't see any likelihood of money coming in. You have two choices: You can sit around and complain about it ... or you can stop whining and make your movie.

Not having any money was not a deterrent for Linklater. In fact, it seems to have spurred him on. "We pulled off stuff with this movie that you couldn't even do with a budget," he said with pride. "Or you wouldn't think to try."

The key is to take a level-headed view of what's possible and what isn't. "Your limitations dictate everything," Linklater said.

Clark Walker, the film's assistant camera and dolly grip, agreed: "Make your liabilities into your assets," he said. "We talked a lot about that

before starting. When no one's looking over your shoulder, you can make the kind of film you want to make."

"Filmmaking is an unfold-ing process," Linklater said, "where you have to be able to turn on a dime and go with Plan B or C. If the meaning and the spirit of the film is right, then it is okay to change things.

Creative solution meetings can be really fun. Money solutions are never an option to us, only outwitting the problem."

Although his approach is grounded and pragmatic, there's a strong philosophical underpinning to the way Linklater works.

"The biggest obstacle is yourself," he said. "There's a sort of psychic process involved.

"If someone were to give you money, say three hundred thousand dollars, that doesn't mean anything. They might be cursing you for life by letting you demonstrate for all to see just how much you have to learn. The films by rich kids who get out of film school and make features with their parents' money are usually terrible. You can hire a cinematographer, a production designer, a professional cast and crew, throw millions at it, and you'll have a movie. It just might not have anything to do with cinema.

"So I think the best way to get a film made is to have a film that you really have to make and are so ready to do that the money is almost a minor aspect. If you can truly get to that confident state of mind, everything will fall into place much easier. Talented people will miraculously want to work with you and other people will want to give you money because they believe in you and think you are worth their time or investment."

IGNORE THE NAYSAYERS

Slacker was a very successful movie and certainly helped Richard Linklater start a long and interesting career. But during production and postproduction, no one looked upon the success of the movie as a *fait accompli*.

Linklater learned all too quickly that the world sometimes takes its sweet time recognizing the next big thing. "For every film festival it got accepted to," he recalled, "it was turned down by two, by all the major festivals across the board."

Like all filmmakers trying to break into the festival circuit, he received his share of form rejection letters. However his odd little movie also inspired some to vent their spleen with non-form letters as well.

One producer from New York who had seen the film wrote: "You are living in an entirely different world, especially when it comes to the world of movie audiences ... Your film has no potential for a release ... It is too long, there is not enough interesting dialogue to give it a special theme ... It does not hold up for anything but a quirky TV program ... And that is what you do not want to accept, your film has no theme."

That sort of letter would be enough to take the wind out of anyone's sails. But that attitude — the honking bray of the naysayer — only strengthened Linklater's resolve.

"At first, I'm a little depressed at the thought of people like him and various festival programmers out there who are no doubt against the film," he wrote in his diary.

"I suddenly get a surge of energy at the thought of this growing opposition and vow I will do everything I can humanly do to make this film a success. All future rejections will spur me on even further. I fantasize that anyone who doesn't like the film will ultimately have to answer for their cowardice or incompetence.

"A large part of me now feels 'You're either with it or against it, and if you're against it, then fuck you, out of the way!'"

PLUG THE [NOISY APPLIANCE] BACK IN!

The final lesson from *Slacker* may possibly be the most important lesson you'll read in this or any other filmmaking book.

It's a simple lesson, but one that has tripped up filmmakers ever since Al Jolson first sang "Mammy!"

That lesson is: Don't leave the set until you're sure that all the appliances you unplugged get plugged back in!

The crew forgot that while shooting *Slacker* and all the ice cream in the freezer at one location ended up melting. They refer to that day as their most expensive day of shooting.

"I always felt terrible about that," Linklater admitted, "because they were so cool to us. They were so friendly and helpful, and then we kind of boned them by leaving the freezers unplugged for sound."

The best solution I've ever heard for this problem was offered by a soundman during the production of my movie, *Grown Men*. Anytime he's on a set where he has to unplug a refrigerator or freezer ... he puts his car keys in the appliance.

That way he knows there's no way he's going home without plugging it back in.

EL MARIACHI

|||||||||||||||||||||||||||||||||||||||||||||||||||||||||||||||||||||||||||||||||||||||||||||||||||||||||

Let me get this off my chest right away: Robert Rodriguez is my hero. There, I've said it.

How can you not love a guy who put himself into the hospital for an experimental drug study to pay for his movie?

"I didn't get sick, but I wanted to," he recalled, "because if you got sick, they sent you home early, with full pay."

The result of his pharmacological sacrifice was *El Mariachi*, a fast and funny action movie about love, guns, mistaken identity and guitar playing in a small Mexican town.

Rodriguez didn't set out to make a low-budget sensation. He merely wanted to learn more about filmmaking and realized that the most efficient way to do that was to jump in and actually make a movie.

"I was inventing my own film school," he said, "where I would be the only student and where experiences, mistakes, problems, and solutions would be my teachers."

For his choice of subject matter, he didn't pander to a low-budget "arty" sensibility, but instead made the kind of movie he would enjoy watching.

"I see a lot of first-time filmmakers who make more of a personal story," he recalled. "I knew that this was going to be my first practice film, and I asked myself, 'What would I do if I didn't have to send this to festivals — if this is just for fun?' Even though we don't have a lot of money, let's just try and make a full-blown action movie."

In spite of his attitude about *El Mariachi* being merely "a practice film," Rodriguez wasn't deterred from throwing everything he had at the project. "Even though this is a throwaway movie," he wrote in his journal, "I want to give it everything I've got. If I'm going to do it, I really do have to go all the way or I'm wasting my time."

His efforts paid off handsomely. His little $7,000 "throwaway movie" won the Audience Award at Sundance and was picked up by a major studio for a theatrical release. (The DVD commentary track for *El Mariachi* begins with Rodriguez commenting wryly on the Columbia Pictures logo that opens the film: "You know, this logo probably cost more than my whole movie.")

One of the most refreshing things about Rodriguez and his *El Mariachi* fairytale success story was the integrity he demonstrated while in the midst of the whirlwind that surrounded the release of his movie.

For example, when the studio suggested some changes to the film, he said no and stood his ground, reasoning, "If they want to spruce it up, they'll have to let me reshoot first. I can't let them fix up one part and not fix up another and then say it's a $7,000 movie."

He also didn't allow himself to get caught up in the Hollywood hype. While preparing the movie for its theatrical release (he even did the spotting for subtitles himself, because he thought the bid the studio received from an outside vendor was too high), he slept in the office they gave him, showered at the studio gym and put his per diem in the bank for his brother's college expenses.

When his agent's assistant asked him where he was staying while in town, he replied, "the Sony Suites."

Rodriguez has maintained his low-budget sensibilities even after moving on to higher-budget projects. He doesn't look upon a small budget as a liability; instead, lack of funding helps to generate a creative spark that can only make the movie better. It's a challenge he enjoys.

"Low-budget movies put a wall in front of you," he reasons, "And only creativity will allow you to figure out how to get around that wall.

"With the $7,000 I had for *El Mariachi*, I could've just had two people at a dinner table, talking, but I didn't want to do that. I wanted to make an action movie. So, take a small budget and make that big movie you want to make. And you can end up with fun, cool results because you end up using more creativity, which is all a movie is, anyway.

"Instead of washing away your problems with a money hose, do it with your imagination."

WRITE TO YOUR RESOURCES

There are few movies out there that are better examples of the dictum, "Write to Your Resources," than *El Mariachi*.

While Rodriguez was in the hospital participating in the drug study, his friend Carlos Gallardo (the actor who played the title role of The Mariachi), sent him videotapes of the locations — the bars, hotels and ranches — they had available to them in the town where they planned to shoot.

Rodriguez then wrote the script based on those locations. They referred to the small section of town they ended up shooting in as "the back lot," because most of the locations for the movie were shot within that three-block radius.

"I saved money by writing the script around things I already had access to," Rodriguez explained, rattling off one of the most famous lists in independent film history: "a pit bull, a motorcycle, two bars, a ranch and a turtle.

"I don't like to write in props we don't already have access to or can't get easily," Rodriguez further explained, "because it just causes a lot of headaches trying to find things at the last minute.

"It's better to figure out all the things you own or can borrow that will add production value, and then include those in the script."

USE YOUR OWN MONEY

Unlike many filmmakers, who waste months or even years trying to raise money for the movies they want to make, Rodriquez was a firm believer in digging into his own pockets for his budgets, even if he first had to fill those pockets with money from hospital drug studies.

For an earlier short, the charming and funny *Bedhead*, he gathered his funding from a study on wound healing. That particular study required that he receive two actual wounds on his arms, scars he still has to this day.

"If you bleed for your money, I mean really bleed for it," he reasoned, "you're very careful on how you spend that money."

He applied that same thinking to the production of *El Mariachi*. "It's been my experience that you're a lot more careful where the money goes when you are using your *own* money," he said.

And, because he was able to produce the movie so economically, he didn't need to spend much of his own money to get it completed.

GO LOW-TECH

You really can't get much more low-tech than *El Mariachi*.

Consider the equipment: One (borrowed) 16mm camera. A wheelchair for dolly shots (on short-term loan from the local hospital). A cassette tape recorder. And a Radio Shack microphone.

Of course, we can't forget the lighting kit: a couple of 250-watt practical photoflood bulbs. These provided enough light in the dark bar scenes for close shots, but not for wide shots, which was fine, because he didn't have money for extras anyway.

The clip-on lamps were purchased new, because Rodriguez ran out of time to find them used or borrow them. Total price: $30. Even for that low cost, he wasn't happy with the expenditure: "I got ripped off," he lamented. "When you rush, you overspend."

Then there was the size of the crew. On a small Hollywood feature, it's not uncommon to have seventy-five to a hundred people on or around the set. On a typical low-budget feature, fifteen to twenty people. On an ultra-low-budget feature, your crew can be as small as three to five people.

On *El Mariachi*? One.

Wait, let me do the math again.

Yep. One person.

Doing everything himself was not a hardship for Rodriguez. In fact, he feels a larger crew would have made the process more complicated, which in turn would have made the shoot longer, which in turn would have made it more expensive.

"Everyone who sees it thinks it was an incredible amount of work and that it must have taken months to shoot all by myself," he said. "You'd think that it would be more work and money without a crew, but I tell them it was the complete opposite. By not having a crew I was able to get all my set-ups in fourteen days for $7,000."

One consideration that kept things moving quickly was that he wasn't shooting sync sound, so the fact that the camera he had borrowed made a lot of noise when it was running wasn't an issue.

In reality, the noise of the camera was actually helpful to him, because it acted as a constant reminder that film was running through the camera and costing him money, which in turn made him shoot faster and more economically.

This led to a fast and loose shooting style, with lots of movement and lots of edits. "I had to put so many cuts in because the shots were so erratic and leaving frame. And people go, 'Wow, that's production value!' Most of it was because of the limitations of how cheaply I was shooting."

"That's something I love about low budgets and shooting fast," he continued. "I'm not a good operator, but sometimes the shots are a little more interesting because they're not so locked down and smooth.

"A real Hollywood movie would've set up a nice dolly track. And it would be so sterile that it would probably be boring. It's nice — the less money you have, you kind of have more energy. That's something to take advantage of."

SOUND THINKING

He also received compliments for the way in which he edited the movie's dialogue scenes, which again were more influenced by economics than aesthetics.

"I was shooting with this real noisy old camera I'd borrowed," Rodriguez explained. "I'd shoot it silent, then I'd put the camera away, put the tape recorder close and say, 'Okay, repeat the lines in a natural rhythm.' Then I had to take each line and sync it by hand.

"People at film festivals would say, 'We loved the shots of the dog,' and I'm listening to them, thinking, I had to cut to the dog. Since I didn't shoot sync-sound, I was synching everything by hand. Before they go out of sync I cut to another character or to the dog or something. Then I cut back to him and he's back in sync. So all the dialogue seems to have a really fast energy."

Although the task of synching by hand was arduous, by recording the sound separate from the picture he was able to get the microphone in close to his actors, making for great sound.

This technique also speeds up your shooting time enormously, as you're not constantly stopping and re-starting every time the sound person hears an extraneous ("Wait — I hear a plane!") sound.

When it came time to record the narration, Rodriguez wanted it to sound different than the dialogue. Rather than go to the expense of renting a sound studio and then processing the finished track, he and Gallardo simply went outside and recorded it in his Datsun, which provided a nice natural reverb. And it cost nothing.

BE SCARY

Rodriguez has condensed the keys to his success down to a few simple rules: "Take advantage of your disadvantages, feature the few assets you may have, and work harder than anyone else around you," he said. "When given an opportunity, deliver excellence and never quit."

And, if you want to succeed like Rodriguez, add one more ingredient to his list: Be Scary.

What does that mean? Well, consider the fact that Rodriguez made *El Mariachi* virtually on his own. Then consider the list of titles Rodriguez has given himself on this and various other movies: Writer / Director / Producer / Director of Photography / Production Designer / Editor / Visual Effects Supervisor / Sound Designer / Re-Recording Mixer / Composer.

If you can do it yourself — literally, do everything on a movie yourself — then you don't need Hollywood. And when you don't need someone, it gives you tremendous negotiating power over them when they need you.

"Trust me, there are extreme benefits to being able to walk into this business and be completely self-sufficient," Rodriguez said.

"It scares people. Be scary."

CLERKS

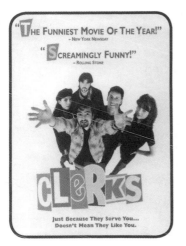

Before Kevin Smith was Kevin Smith, he was just a guy who worked in a convenience store, collected comic books and hung out. He was not your obvious choice for success.

In fact, the mother of an ex-girlfriend actually once gave him a note that read, "Kevin Smith will never be a famous writer because he lacks the drive, but I wish him well anyway."

How wrong she was. Say what you will about his films, Kevin Smith is a man with drive, and it was that drive that helped him create one of the best-known and best-loved ultra-low-budget movies of all time.

The birth of that movie, and his career, can be pinpointed at a single time and place: A midnight showing of *Slacker* at the Angelika Film Center in New York.

"It was a real eye-opening experience," he recalled, "because it was not the standard studio fare that I was used to seeing everywhere. It was kind of my first independent film. And I was really just taken aback by it, like, 'Wow, this counts as a movie? Nothing's happening, really, just people walking around.' I was fascinated by that.

"I viewed it with a mixture of awe and arrogance. I was awed by the fact that this passed for entertainment ... that people would actually sit down and enjoy it as much as I was enjoying it. And then arrogance, because I was, like, 'Well, I could do this. I mean, if this counts as a movie, count me in, I can try this.'"

From that moment grew the industry that is Kevin Smith: TV pitchman, talk show guest, movie writer, director and actor, creator of an animated

TV series, comic book writer, and proprietor of a website that shills his product to what one critic called his target demographic: undersexed, onanistic college students.

Yes, you can even buy your very own Silent Bob coat on the website (*"Licensed by Kevin Smith, Silent Bob's Coat is just like the coat used in Dogma and Jay and Silent Bob Strike Back. Kevin loaned AbbyShot his original coat, so the design is 100% accurate!! The coat features an oversized lapel, welt pockets, an inside breast pocket and your very own Silent Bob Pin of your choice!"*)

All that from a little $27,000 black-and-white movie, originally called *Inconvenience*. But, as Smith is quick to point out, "While it was a $27,000 movie, it certainly didn't *stay* a $27,000 movie."

Clerks went on to become one of the best-reviewed ultra-low-budget movies of all time, with Roger Ebert declaring, "Within the limitations of his bare-bones production, Smith shows great invention, a natural feel for human comedy, and a knack for writing weird, sometimes brilliant, dialogue."

And David Kehr in the New York Daily News called *Clerks* "a blend of Howard Stern and David Mamet."

Dollar for dollar, there are few low-budget movies that provide more important lessons on how to make a big splash with a small budget than *Clerks*.

SKIP FILM SCHOOL

To achieve his dream of becoming a filmmaker, Smith enrolled in a Vancouver film school that he found via a newspaper ad. But what the school promised and what they delivered turned out to be two different things.

"I went for hands-on, technical stuff," Smith remembered. "They were like, 'It's all practice, all practical. No theory.' And then we got there and did theory for three months. So I said, 'Fuck it, I don't need some Canadian dude telling me what Demme was trying to say with *Silence of the Lambs*.'"

Smith got a refund on the remainder of his tuition and headed home to make a movie. Looking back on the school experience, he realized that it could have been worse: "If you go to NYU or USC or UCLA," he said, "it takes you four years to realize what a total waste of time it was. [At Vancouver] all it takes is four months."

Once he had a script in place, he contacted fellow students Scott Mosier, to produce, and Dave Klein to shoot the movie.

"Dave gave us this wish list of all the things he needed at the start of production," Smith recalled. "You know, a camera, lights, lenses, filters, gels, whatever. We looked it over and said, uh, ahhhh ... you can have the camera."

Producer Mosier admits that it was a leap of faith, but feels that money not spent on film school was well-spent on *Clerks*. "It was scary, but to put it in context, how much is NYU a year? *Clerks* was a kind of school for all of us, and at the end of the day we made a product that gave us careers."

IT'S THE SCRIPT, STUPID

Smith realized early on that he couldn't put much production value on the screen, so he did something even more important: He wrote and re-wrote (and re-wrote) his script until it was perfect.

"It's all about the script," Smith still believes. "It has so very little to do with anything else.

"You know, if my career has done anything, it proves you don't need a visual style to work in film — which is ironic, because it's a visual medium — as long as you have something worthwhile to say.

"And if my first film proved anything, it's that they will forgive you so many things. *Clerks* looked shitty. Some of the performances are down-right wooden, you know, and God, for something that takes place in a visual medium, there's not much visual going on.

"But the script was there, the script was tight, the dialogue was tight, and people dug it."

IT'S NOT YOUR PROBLEM
(IT'S YOUR CHARACTER'S PROBLEM)

A key lesson that Smith discovered in the scripting process was that it makes sense, whenever possible, to turn your own production problems into the problems of your character.

A case in point: the windows that lined the front of the convenience store, which was the movie's primary location.

The story for *Clerks* takes place over a long day at the store, but the only time the movie could be shot was at night, when the store was closed

... which meant that a movie that was supposed to take place during the day would have no sunlight streaming in the front windows.

Smith's smart solution was to turn this dilemma into a problem for his main character, Dante. When Dante arrives to

Gum in the lock means no daylight for Clerks

work at the beginning of the movie, he finds that someone has jammed gum in the lock that secures the shutters that cover the front windows.

"We shot most of the movie at night," Smith recalled, "so I wrote into the screenplay that the shutters could not be opened, which made it much easier for us, because we certainly couldn't afford to rent HMIs. So in this movie the shutters are closed."

REHEARSE

In the same way that he spent a lot of time on the scriptwriting process, Smith also spent considerable time rehearsing his cast. Although the movie has an improvisational feel to it, the reality is that it was tightly scripted.

Smith estimates that only about 2% of the movie was improvised. "All the improvisation was from Jason (Mewes) because he couldn't learn his lines," Smith recalled. "He knew what he was supposed to say but couldn't remember the words to save his life.

"In his final diatribe, when he's telling Dante off and calling him a cock-smoker, that's just him goin' off. We never thought we'd use it, but it's just so outta place it's fuckin' hilarious."

Other than the leeway he granted Mewes, Smith was a taskmaster with the rest of the cast. Actor and friend Vincent Pereira remembers, "Kevin would get the actors together and go through the script until the actors were as off the book as possible.

"Kevin would work in the store until about 10:30 p.m. I have this image of driving back from a showing of Peter Jackson's *Dead Alive* in Toms River one night, and seeing Kevin at the store rehearsing. These people were just sitting on the freezers, going over the lines."

That attention to rehearsals allowed Smith to shoot quickly, and to shoot long, long takes with his cast.

BUT WE'RE JUST A STUDENT FILM, OFFICER

Although Smith and Mosier were fresh out of film school, they were no longer students. But they found a unique way to benefit from being a student, even if they, technically, weren't.

"Kodak had a program for film school students where you get 15% off your stock," Smith recalled. "We went down to the New School for Social Research and looked through their catalogue for a one-day course we could join. We found this course called 'Roasting Pig' and the fee was fifty bucks.

"I signed up for the course, put it on the credit card, got o school ID and the guy had to give us the film stock at 15% off. was still warm from the laminating machine!

"Then we went back downtown and I took my name off the So I didn't have to pay the fifty bucks because fifty bucks was money."

ALL'S WELL THAT ENDS WELL

Sometimes it's our favorite moments in what we write or shoot that are doing us the most harm. For Smith, it was his original ending for *Clerks*: Dante says goodnight to fellow clerk Randall and prepares to close the store. One final (unseen) customer enters. Dante tells him that they're closed. Suddenly the customer shoots Dante and robs the store, leaving our main character dead on the floor.

Brian O'Halloran, who played Dante, remembered his initial reaction to the idea: "I thought the script was funny, but I hated that ending. I never thought it worked. I just thought it was too quick of a twist.

"I remember going to Kevin, and I believe I told him I didn't like the ending. But we did it anyway."

Smith, however, loved the ending. "To me it was like, that's the ultimate joke," he said. "He is not even supposed to be there and he gets killed."

Cooler heads prevailed, however. "Right before we went to Sundance," Smith recalled, "John [Pierson] said, 'There is one thing you have to do with the movie: you have to cut that ending off.' And I knew that a few people who loved the movie, including Bob Hawk, John Pierson and Amy Taubin, hated the ending.

"But John was like, 'I really think you should cut the ending and if I am wrong you can put it back later on. You can talk to the distributor and ask if you can put it back.' So we cut it right before we went to Sundance."

ANTICIPATE SUCCESS

As a filmmaker, you always want to keep your focus on your current project, but it doesn't hurt to have something in your hip pocket, particularly if your current project suddenly hits it big.

That was the case with *Clerks*, and Smith and Mosier were ready when opportunity suddenly knocked.

"We met (Hollywood producer) Jim Jacks at the closing ceremonies of Sundance," Mosier recalled, "and he asked us what we wanted to do next."

"And I said, *Mallrats*," Smith remembered, "just outta nowhere — just two words — and they went with it; 'Oh yeah, that's funny!' Amazing."

"So before *Clerks* ever came out," continued Mosier, "based on our meeting with Jim Jacks, we generated our second project. By the time *Clerks* was playing in October, we were already in development on *Mallrats*."

Smith quickly and dramatically learned the value of making a successful movie like *Clerks*: "What it did more than anything financially was to put me into the next inning of the ball game," he said. "Okay, here we go, now we're going to make a bigger movie."

KEEP IT ALL IN PERSPECTIVE

The final lesson from *Clerks* is about remembering what's really important in life. In this movie, and throughout his career, Smith has always been devoted to his family and his friends, including pal Jason Mewes, who Smith refers to as "the little sonic boom with dirt on it."

"What's important is kind of the simple things: Family, survival, life," he said. "Film is just entertainment. And so I think it's weird when people tend to treat things, particularly film, so seriously. It's bizarre."

His attitude is best reflected in a story about discussing a future project with people at Miramax. "The executive said words I will never forget," Smith recalled. "'Kevin, it's not about making a movie with your friends.'

"And I was like, 'Really?' Because that's been the whole point of my career.'"

SWINGERS

||||||||||||||||||||||||||||||||||||||||||||||||||||||||||||||||||||||||||||||||||||||||||||||||||

To hear director Doug Liman tell it, he never had high expectations for *Swingers*. "I really thought that the only people who were going to see this movie were people in situations where I was going to be the one pressing 'play' on the VCR," he said.

Writer and star Jon Favreau had similar doubts about the movie's future. "When I wrote *Swingers*," Favreau has commented, "I never thought anyone would read it but my friends. It was my first screenplay, and I banged it out in less than two weeks.

"My friends read it. They got a big kick out of it. I had purposely based the characters on them, and exaggerated their most ridiculous characteristics to the point of absurdity. To be fair, I did the same to myself."

The ultimate success of Liman's and Favreau's combined vision surprised them both, and the small-budget (about $250,000) movie about struggling actors, hanging out, and swing dancing made a big splash. It also helped launch their careers, along with that of co-star Vince Vaughn. And it added the phrase "You're so money" to our film lexicon.

Ironically, it was the very fact that they didn't expect the movie to go far that allowed them to try some things that they probably wouldn't have attempted on a larger-budget venture.

The way Liman explained it, "This was meant to be a resume film, which liberated us to take chances."

For editor Stephen Mirrone, it was their very lack of experience that gave them a unique advantage. "If super-experienced people had come in and done this and it had been really polished and glossy," he said, "it wouldn't have that same feeling.

"There's no question that our incompetence at the time as filmmakers makes it a little more honest and accessible. And it also shows our heart is in it as well. A lot of time, people are afraid to show their imperfection, and as an independent filmmaker, you've got to embrace all that."

Favreau agreed. "*Swingers* was all sincerity," he said. "It was no money and no experience, it was all just pure enthusiasm and inspiration."

There's a lot of enthusiasm and inspiration on view in *Swingers,* which provides some key lessons that apply to all films.

HOLD ONTO YOUR VISION

For Favreau, holding onto his vision meant saying "no" when people offered him a lot of money to take his script and do it their way.

His agent sent the finished *Swingers* script around Hollywood, and soon Favreau found himself in a two-day session with a potential buyer, during which he received note after note from the producers, each one intended to make the movie more mainstream.

"They wanted to change everything," Favreau remembered, "I mean, everything. They wanted to set it in Vegas. They wanted a female in one of the main roles. They wanted less Trent. They wanted more violence. They wanted to cut out all the 'moneys' and 'babys.' They wanted a movie that wasn't *Swingers*."

Favreau had a better idea. "I said, 'Let me show you the script as I see it. Let me bring my friends in — who these parts are based on — and let's read it to you.'

"We staged the reading, and that reading killed. It was so funny that my agent said to me, 'You can't sell this script. We have to make this thing.' And that began the year and a half of trying to get the money together."

While trying to raise a couple million dollars to shoot the movie, Favreau encountered director Doug Liman, who liked the script but had a different approach on how to get *Swingers* made: Do it for less, not more.

"I said to them, I don't want to step on anyone's toes," Liman said, "bu̶ I think if you try to make this film for a million and a half dollar̶ think that's the kiss-of-death budget. It's not enough money to do justice to this, and it's too much money to take chances.

"We're living in Hollywood, but we need to make this film like we're kids from Pennsylvania."

Liman welcomed the difficulties that such a low budget would provide and was convinced that it would actually make the movie better. "I'm a big believer that limitations force you to be creative," he said.

As Favreau recalled, "Doug said 'Let's have a lot of money to do a *Clerks*-style movie, as opposed to not enough money to do an inexpensive, Hollywood standard indie.' And it was a stroke of genius.

"Doug had a background in making student films," Favreau continued, "so he knew that you could do it in more of a documentary style and not really obey all the laws of lighting and cinematography.

"For example, not hiring a cinematographer, because he was going to be the cinematographer himself, so there's another level of quality control that you didn't have to worry about. So there was no person who was shooting for his reel, as we say — doing a small movie and making it look good so they could get bigger jobs."

Liman's do-it-for-less approach, coupled with Favreau's vise-like grip on his vision for the movie, proved to be a powerful combination.

USE REALITY TO YOUR ADVANTAGE

Although *Swingers* is a fictional movie, it was close enough to the truth that Favreau was able to draw on his own experiences to create emotionally satisfying characters and situations.

"It wasn't a true story," Favreau explained, "but it was definitely based people and places and inspired by events that I had experienced.

When you write from that, you're incorporating a lot of things that are very real and well understood by you. And the script inherits a certain sincerity."

Besides sincerity, reality also gives you another edge as a writer. "If you stick to things that you know and understand and people that you know," he said, "you tend to come off as a better writer than you really are, because you're incorporating so much reality into your piece."

THERE'S NO SHAME IN RESHOOTING

While many filmmakers come to the decision to do some re-shooting while in postproduction, for Liman that decision formed the core of his vision for the movie.

Swingers was about taking chances, and the only way he could feel safe enough to take some of those chances was if he knew he was working with a safety net, albeit a small one.

"Part of my strategy for shooting this film," he said, "was that I left two days at the end of the schedule to re-shoot anything that didn't come out, so I could take these wild chances."

During the preproduction and production process, Liman hung onto those two days, despite the demands of the budget.

"We ended up scheduling eighteen of the days," he recalled, "and the other two days were sacred."

Liman required every second of those two days, because there were chances they took that hadn't paid off. But there were also lots of chances that had, and he feels that without that two-day safety net, he wouldn't have taken those risks.

"The movie wouldn't be the movie that it became if I hadn't done that," he said.

A PICTURE'S WORTH ...

The opening credits for *Swingers* were going to be spectacular:

helicopter shot, moving through the skies of Los Angeles at night, capturing the twinkling lights of the expansive city below.

Have you heard that old expression about best-laid plans?

"For the opening sequence," Favreau recalled, "I had written a helicopter shot, and that went out the window for budgetary reasons.

"So what happened was that Doug went out and shot some photos and created a montage in the beginning, to sort of sit you down in your seat and give you context of what was going on."

The result is an opening credit sequence of still photos that captures the feel of the movie far better than an expensive helicopter shot would have ... and for a lot, lot less. As Liman recalled, "Total cost, around $300."

Still photos also played an important emotional (and financial) role at another point in the movie.

Favreau's character, Mike, spends a good portion of the story pining away for his old girlfriend, with whom he broke up before moving to Los Angeles.

But rather than shoot flashback scenes showing the young couple in happier times, Favreau opted to tell that story with still images. That choice served two purposes, one budgetary and the other story-related.

"When you're shooting photos," Favreau explained, "you're not doing it on valuable production time. You can go out with just a few people and a still camera and put it together."

The other reason was the emotional impact created by the stills.

"Images don't have to be moving to be compelling." Favreau continued. "It gives you a lot of back story on the guy, just from those pictures that Doug took of myself and a girl we never credited in the movie, named Tiffany Kuzon, who was an assistant to one of the agents where I was represented. We just went around and shot it."

The finished scene, with Favreau looking through a stack of stills, wallowing in memories, is far stronger than any flashback would have been.

Liman agrees that the lack of money and the solution they settled upon made for a much stronger scene.

"If we'd had the money to do flashbacks," Liman said, "it would have been horrible. We were so lucky that all we could do were the stills, because at the end of the day it's so much more emotional."

CREATE AN EMOTIONAL CONNECTION

Emotion plays a key part in the final lesson in *Swingers*: If you can connect with the audience on an emotional level, they'll forgive you for almost everything else.

That point is best demonstrated in a scene late in the movie, when Heather Graham pulls Favreau out onto the dance floor. When he first tentatively starts to dance with her, the audience has been on a long,

sometimes painful, jour-ney with this character and we fear that he's going to screw up yet again.

Then, when he breaks into some reasonably assured swing dance steps, your trepidation for him starts to fade away. And then, finally, when he really starts to move, you can't help but be swept up in the fun and emotion of the scene.

"We cheated," Favreau admitted. "We cheated a little bit. If people weren't emotionally involved with the movie, they would have rejected that moment."

Emotion was the key — creating an honest, emotional connection between the character of Mike and the audience.

"We threw in some cursory explanation that I had taken some classes," Favreau explained, "but the fact is that you are so emotionally hoping that something would happen there that you gave us the permission as filmmakers to take a little artistic license."

Favreau carefully built to that moment throughout his script.

"The whole movie you're hoping that he just pulls it together," he said, "and there's so many times when you think that he will take the next step, from the trailer park in Vegas to when he gets that girl's number and leaves all those messages.

"Basically every time my character talks to a girl, you're thinking he's going to take the next step, and you just get smacked in the face with a frying pan.

"So finally when it does happen, there's such a sense of accomplishment, the audience is so hoping that it's going to happen, that they give you that permission. And it just as easily could have gone the other way."

It didn't go the other way, because Favreau had created an authentic emotional connection between his character and the audience. He recognized that emotion can be a secret weapon for low-budget filmmakers.

"It all goes to emotion," he explained. "If you're emotionally engaged, everything is going to be funnier, more satisfying, scarier, everything. It's that emotional connection that you feel with these guys. And the reason you feel that is because the story was so personal and sincere, and that's a very hard thing to maintain as you do bigger and bigger movies.

"It's the one thing that you really have going for you in a small movie, that you're doing something that's so real and usually so personal that you have a level of emotional engagement that you will not get in a high-budget, high-concept movie.

"It's that emotional engagement that's your big card to play on small movies. It's one thing that you have over the big movies, and you better not give that card up."

Chapter Seven

THE DIGITAL REALM

How much has digital technology changed the filmmaking process?

A lot ... and very little.

The benefits of digital filmmaking are plentiful (low-cost, speed, ease-of-use, availability, to name just a few). But when it comes right down to it, most of the problems a digital filmmaker faces are the same ones independent filmmakers have always faced.

What you'll find in the digital realm are some unique and not-so-unique lessons on how to overcome those problems and keep your movie (digital or otherwise) on track.

THE ANNIVERSARY PARTY

Throughout this book (and, frankly, throughout my career), I've promoted the value of getting together with your friends to make movies. It's just a flat-out, good idea.

And when your friends are the likes of Kevin Kline, Gwyneth Paltrow, Parker Posey, Jennifer Beals, Phoebe Cates and John C. Reilly, it's a *great* idea.

Plus, if you happen to be Jennifer Jason Leigh and Alan Cumming, that doesn't hurt, either. Together the pair wrote, directed and starred in the digital feature,

The Anniversary Party.

For Cumming and Leigh, the idea of working together occurred to them while they were ... well, working together.

"We were in *Cabaret* together on Broadway," Cumming explained, "but we didn't really do anything together in the show. We just got on and wanted to do something.

"We wanted to write something about how we felt about relationships at that point in our lives — something that was very current for ourselves and something that was honest and open. And also we wanted to use elements of ourselves, our experiences, and put that into a story."

The concept of going digital came from another project that Leigh had just completed.

"Jennifer had made this Dogme film in Africa," Cumming said, "and she was excited about working digitally, because you don't have to stop all the time and you just keep rolling and try out things."

"I was really intrigued by the digital video wave and how much fun it was to work like that," Leigh said. "I've worked on films that have been such great experiences, and I wanted to bring that experience to this project."

Although the world has seen lots of co-writers, the concept of co-directors doesn't pop up all that often — particularly when the co-directors are also acting in the film.

"People understand the notion that you can write together," Cumming said. "I think people have more trouble with the idea of directing together. But it wasn't divided up; it was quite smooth. We both would talk to the actors. I would do all of the shouting and general announcements."

Cumming is mindful of the fact that he and Leigh went into the project with several advantages that are outside the reach of most independent filmmakers.

"Our film was lucky to get made," he admitted. "If we weren't Alan Cumming and Jennifer Jason Leigh and if we didn't have all those people in it, we would never have gotten the money. We definitely had a lot on our side."

The making of *The Anniversary Party* provided Cumming, Leigh and company with several important lessons; however, Cumming walked away from the project with one key learning.

"Biggest lesson," he said of the experience, "Treat people respectfully. There's a sort of vogue, and there has been for decades now, that the director is God and the director is all knowing.

"But when you say to someone, 'I don't understand this and I'm asking your advice because you're better at it than me,' by doing that and involving people and making the film truly a collaborative process, you get a better film and you get happier people and an atmosphere on the set that is truly creative."

GO DIGITAL

There are many reasons to opt to go digital on a movie. For Cumming and Leigh, the reasons were a mix of sense and sensibility.

"The decision to use digital video was a very practical one that had to do with speed," Cumming explained. "We had only nineteen days to shoot the film, and with digital video, you can move faster."

In addition to the speed factor, Leigh felt that the feel of DV fit the film's aesthetic. "One of the reasons why digital video works for this film," she said, "is that there's an immediacy to it and there's an intimacy to it, and that makes you feel like you're actually in the room."

"It felt less intrusive," Cumming agreed. "That gave the film an aesthetic which was one that made all the actors more relaxed."

"There were no dressing rooms, no trailers, no barriers," explained Leigh. "Each of the actors came in every day, did their own hair and makeup and we were ready to roll. It was an incredibly liberating way to make a film."

"In the end," Cumming said, "it wasn't really a financial decision, it wasn't really an economic thing that made us go to digital, it was actually the idea that it would be more free-flowing and we could have several cameras and things like that.

"And it was great, because the eavesdropping quality of the film was helped by the fact that we could just keep rolling. Sometime actors weren't aware how many cameras were on them. It really helped the flavor; it gave the feeling that you were actually there at the party."

For Cumming, that experience is worlds away from what an actor goes through on a traditional movie set.

"You don't get that on film," he said. "On film, it's like every take is a test. There's a tension — 'We're going for a take, now. You've got to get it right.' — and you're very aware that the money's spilling through the lens.

"But on video it's much more relaxed, because you know you can keep rolling, it's not going to cost very much money.

"So I think there's more of a relaxed feeling on the set and you get more relaxed performances, too."

USE REALITY TO YOUR ADVANTAGE

When it came time to create characters for each of their friends to play, Cumming and Leigh decided that reality would make a great starting point.

"That's what was great about doing *The Anniversary Party*," Cumming admitted, "because we were able to use essences of real people and merge it all into a big script."

One example of using essences can be found in the characters played by real life husband and wife, Kevin Kline and Phoebe Cates. In the film, he plays a working actor; she plays an actress who gave up acting to raise their kids. In real life … he's a working actor and she's an actress who gave up acting to raise their kids.

And, "their kids are played by their kids," Cumming added. "That puts you a few steps ahead, because you have that real thing going on. For other characters we used little habits or idiosyncrasies that they have and put that in a bigger picture of their characters.

"I think that makes it more of an intimate experience for an audience: you're slightly on the edge of the seat, because you know there are real bits as well as fiction going on."

GIVE YOUR CHARACTERS A SECRET

Although the film was completely scripted, Cumming and Leigh did create one scene where even they — the writers, directors and lead actors in the movie — had no idea what was going to happen next.

In the scene, the married couple (Cumming and Leigh) who are throwing the anniversary party of the title are presented with gifts by each of their friends.

"For that scene," Cumming recalled, "we asked the actors to make up their own speeches or to make their own things. We guided them about what perhaps their character might say, what their character's angle might be, but we left it up to them to make up their thing. It was really fascinating."

By employing multiple cameras, the filmmakers were able to capture all the angles on this scene simultaneously.

"We shot their stuff and our reactions at the same time," Cumming explained. "We were hearing it for the first time, which was really exciting.

"And also, they were really nervous, like you would be really nervous standing up and doing that, because they were actually having to perform something that they had written for the first time, too. It was good — it worked."

BE PREPARED

Wearing so many hats, as Leigh and Cumming did, meant that little could be left to chance during production. In order to ensure that their vision for the movie made it to the screen, Cumming advocates one key step: Preparation.

"You have to be really, really, really prepared," he explained "I think any director has to be really prepared, but especially on a short shoot like that."

A big component of his preparation process involved storyboarding the movie.

"My storyboards are a little eclectic," he admitted. "Sometimes there would just be a picture and some words, and sometimes it would be more technical. I did the storyboards myself, but I don't do it frame by frame by frame, shot by shot. I did it more esoterically.

"One of the things that's good about storyboarding," he continued, "is that it makes you actually explore each scene in depth. It's a really good thing, because it makes you sit down and really concentrate on each scene."

Although preparation is important, Cumming also advocates going with the flow when the moment is right.

"I think it's really important not to be rigid with that storyboard," he explained. "It's good if you can be flexible — if something happens or something's not going to work or something better appears — then you have to be able to just go with that.

"So it's a basis, a preparation device, rather than a Bible."

KILL YOUR DARLINGS

There are literally thousands of decisions that are made during the production of a movie. Each one is important in its own way. But Cumming is firmly committed to one that he and Leigh made in postproduction.

"I think the best decision we made was cutting the last scene in the script," Cumming said.

"It was a scene where it was the next morning and she's in the hot tub and I come and join her," he explained. "We give each other our anniversary presents, and we have a big scene talking about the fact that our marriage has broken up."

Cutting such a major scene is never an easy decision. But in order to make the best movie you can, you sometimes have to think about how your story can be improved by taking things away rather than adding them.

"We weren't particularly happy with the last scene, we were having trouble editing it," Cumming said. "And then we thought, if we just cut that scene, the movie will end and we can take a shot from the beginning — the very first shot — and put that at the end and bookend the whole thing.

"I think you're always feeling that you have to be absolutely scrupulous about explaining everything and bringing everything to a conclusion," he continued. "And it was quite liberating to remove the scene. It's really interesting, you just don't need to necessarily force-feed the audience every detail.

"What it did was leave the audience having to think more about what happened in the movie, instead of being told that it was over now and this is the end."

In the filmmakers' minds, that ambiguity actually made the film stronger and more interesting.

"We don't know what will happen to them," Leigh explained. "We examine a lot of relationships in the movie and they're all kind of beautiful and funny and flawed, and yet they somehow sustain.

"And maybe they'll make it. Maybe not, but maybe they will."

TADPOLE

||||||||||||||||||||||||||||||||||||||||||||||||||||||||||||||||||||||||||||||||||

Filmmaker Gary Winick assembled an amazing cast — Sigourney Weaver, Bebe Neuwirth, Ron Rifkin, and the late, great John Ritter — for his digital feature, *Tadpole*, and was rewarded for his efforts with the Sundance Award for directing and a $5 million dollar distribution deal from Miramax.

Not bad for a little soufflé of a movie about a precocious prep school teenager, home in Manhattan for Thanksgiving, who decides to act on his attraction for his stepmother; a movie that *Rolling Stone's* Peter Travers characterized as "*Oedipus Rex* meets *The Graduate* with a stop-off at *Rushmore*."

Also in the outstanding cast was actor Adam LeFevre who got his start in the low-budget classic, *Return of the Secaucus Seven,* and who has since gone on to bigger-budgeted features, like *The Ref* and *Only You.* For him, shooting *Tadpole* was like returning to that simpler time.

"There were no trailers to go into between shots," he recalled about his time on *Tadpole*. "When I was waiting, I sat on the couch in Gary's mother's apartment and chatted with Bebe Neuwirth."

Like *The Return of the Secaucus Seven*, LeFevre felt that shooting *Tadpole* was really a team effort and a labor of love.

"There were no frills; hair and makeup were done in one of the bathrooms," he said. "When everyone is doing that, it's clear that they're there for some reason other than the paycheck, and sometimes that can be very helpful.

"I think I got paid for *Tadpole* about what I got paid for *Secaucus Seven*. In this case, everybody is basically working for peanuts and suffering the same kinds of lack of frills. You're doing it because you believe in the project, and, quite frankly, because it's fun."

FLY UNDER THE RADAR

On a low-budget shoot, you can't always play by the rules (i.e., pour tons of money into constructing sets or paying location fees). And why should you, if the perfect locations can be snagged for free — as long as no one knows you're using them?

Before he shot his scenes in *Tadpole*, which were scheduled to be shot in Winick's mother's apartment in New York, Adam LeFevre found himself in a scene right out of a Hollywood spy film.

"The day before my first day of shooting," he recalled, "I got a call from an AD saying, 'Don't come to the apartment. There's a Starbucks across the street, and someone will come meet you, because you have to be snuck up the service elevator.'"

The reason for the cloak and dagger antics was simple: The building's Condo board had refused Winick permission to shoot in the building, despite the fact that his mother lived in the apartment he wanted to shoot in.

However, since DV equipment is compact and unobtrusive, Winick decided to ignore their refusal and go ahead with the shoot.

For LeFevre, it added another layer of fun to the shoot. "It was sort of like a CIA operation; I waited at the Starbucks and an AD came over and said, 'Are you Adam?' I said, 'Yeah.' He said, "Then come with

me,' and we went up to the room."

The scenes were shot successfully, without the knowledge of the Condo board, and LeFevre thinks that the statute of limitations has probably passed on their offense.

"I guess it's safe to talk about it, because they can't come after Gary's mother now."

GO DIGITAL

The ability to sneak an entire movie crew and all their equipment under the nose of a Manhattan apartment doorman was not the primary reason that Winick opted to produce *Tadpole* digitally. Although that's a pretty solid reason.

There were, in fact, a number of compelling reasons to go digital.

"There's the economics of it, which is obviously a big deal," Winick explained. "And there's the time factor, which is actually a bigger deal."

"Another great reason for DV is that it's location friendly," he continued. "You're in there for less time, and you don't destroy the place. And there's the fact that now actors and distributors will take low-end digital filmmaking seriously. It's not discriminated against at all, in terms of getting actors or in terms of distributors wanting your film."

Winick was pleasantly surprised at just how interested actors — even name actors — were in experimenting with technology that was, at the time, relatively new.

"Not only were they open to digital, they were actually curious and looking forward to it, because digital is a performance-oriented medium," he said. "Sigourney said, 'I hear it's like a hybrid between theater and film and I want to try it.'"

Sigourney Weaver was ultimately pleased with the experience. "It's really fun to make a movie with digital," she said, "Just because there are no lengthy set-ups — or, no set-ups. Very little lighting (although I have mixed feelings about that). It's just very organic."

However, for an actress trained on single-camera film shoots, the number of DV cameras floating around the set was, at first, a bit unsettling.

"Sometimes it seemed like anybody who could hold a camera *was* holding a camera," she recalled. "I think it might be a little harder to edit (because of the number of cameras), but at the same time they're able to catch, very quickly, what's going on in the first or second take, which I always prefer.

"You know, the conventional way of covering a scene seems very out-dated now, so I loved working this way. It was just so freeing."

BE PREPARED

While some of the actors found the DV process liberating, Winick felt that preparation was the key to a successful production process, even if he deviated from that preparation once he got on the set.

"I storyboarded the film," he explained. "I believe in storyboarding, especially with DV. I feel you have to be more disciplined. And then you get more freed up to try things."

One scene in particular required intensive preparation: a thirteen-page dialogue scene at a fancy Manhattan restaurant. This sequence involved a quartet of actors — Weaver, Neuwirth, Ritter and the Tadpole of the title, Aaron Stanford — in an emotionally volatile scene, ripe with sexual tension, revelations and duplicity. All of which takes place as they're seated around a table in a crowded restaurant.

As Winick recalled, "I knew the blocking, because that's the thing about table scenes: you know the blocking. So I watched all these great table scenes that weren't subject-appropriate, but just table scenes. From *Rosemary's Baby* to *Apocalypse Now* to *Father of the Bride*, just to see how the great filmmakers did it and to see if anything applied to what I was doing, story-wise.

"Then I sat four interns down at a table and gave them the script, and I worked out all the angles. And because it was a thirteen-page scene, I knew that I had to come up with inventive ways to vary the scene and get from transition to transition."

His solution for transitions within the scene? Fast, 360-degree pans that blur the action in the restaurant to suggest the passage of time, a technique he borrowed from another great table scene, in *Citizen Kane*. Coming up with the idea wasn't all that tough, and figuring out how to shoot it turned out to be, literally, child's play.

"I went to a Toys R Us and bought a Sit-and-Spin," he revealed. "I used Susan, my editor, who weighs a lot less than me. And I went into the restaurant while it was full and said, 'Can we just sit in the restaurant for five minutes?' And I had Susan sit in the Sit-and-Spin and I spun her around."

YOU CAN FIX IT IN POST (SOMETIMES)

Interspersed throughout *Tadpole* are text screens with short quotes from Voltaire, quotes that seem to comment on the action in the movie. These title cards become an integral part of the story, because the teenage hero spends much of the movie carrying around a dog-eared Voltaire paperback.

The quotes are one of those touches that you're sure was an early idea in the script. However, the reality is that the transitional text screens were added in postproduction, in a somewhat frenzied attempt to cover up for mistakes during production.

"I had a really, really, really unfortunate experience with my cinematographer on this movie," Winick explained. "The camera wasn't on sometimes, so I'd get back to the edit room and the script supervisor had these shots that were never recorded. I had focus problems, camera operating problems.

"When I got in the editing room and found out that my DP/Operator did such a poor job, I was left with some really hard, clunky ways to get from scene to scene."

Winick realized that he needed something — anything — to help smooth out transitions between scenes, because he simply didn't have the footage that he thought he had.

"And that's when I came up with the Voltaire quotes," he said. "So it came out of necessity.

"I went to Barnes & Noble, because I'm not an Internet guy, and went through some Voltaire quotes, and I was like, 'Oh my God, this is going to work great.'"

WRITE TO YOUR RESOURCES

Before he started the project, all Winick knew for certain was that he had a budget of $150,000 and that the movie would be shot digitally. But those bits of knowledge were key factors in developing and shaping the script.

"We came up with the characters first," Winick explained, "And then thought of what sort of situation we could put them in that would support a low-budget, twelve-day shoot.

"Then you think about, how many actors, how many locations? If you do a single point-of-view movie (which are the kind of movies I like to do), then you can have two or three big locations where you have a lot of page count, but then you follow your character — which can just be you and the actor — around, getting him from one location to the next, and all of a sudden your movie appears bigger than it is.

"Another thing is you want to have as few continuity days as possible," he continued. "The less costume changes the better. So the Thanksgiving holiday gave us four days.

"And then the other thing for DV (which is kind of the opposite for film), is that you want to shoot at night and you want to shoot outside because it looks the best and it's very inexpensive.

"You want to stay away from day exteriors, and you want to shoot a lot of practical locations, because DV works well in practical light."

Although he was always considering the technical advantages and limitations of the DV technology, Winick's true focus was elsewhere.

"When you're making a low-budget film," he said, "You really only have one focus, and that focus is story. Because with costumes and lighting and design and all that stuff, you can never either afford it or have the time to do it right.

"So you really have to focus on the one thing that you know that the audience is (hopefully) going to respond to, which is the story and being engaged with those characters on screen."

Although Winick has graduated to higher budget (and higher profile) projects since *Tadpole*, he still keeps his focus on story. Even when he was in preproduction on the multi-million-dollar version of *Charlotte's Web*, story was still his primary concern.

"I have $84 million now for *Charlotte's Web*," he said, "And I have huge effects, and computer people, and Stan Winston and all this stuff ... but it all comes back to story."

DOPAMINE

||||||||||||||||||||||||||||||||||||||||||||||||||||||||||||||||||||||||||||||||||||||||||||||||||||

Sitting down and writing a screenplay is tough work. There are far too many distractions, other things you need to do, with life itself always getting in the way.

But if the Sundance Screenwriting Lab called and asked what you're working on, you'd find a way to get that script written, right? That fateful phone call was all the incentive writer/director Mark Decena needed to get moving on his script for his first feature effort, *Dopamine*.

"I'd done a couple of shorts and the first one was at Sundance in 1993," he said. "I did another one in 1996, and shortly after that Lynn Auerbach, who was an assistant in the feature film program in the Labs, gave me a call and asked if I had any feature-length scripts.

"I, of course, didn't, but I said I'll definitely start working on one. And she kept calling every three months or so ('How's the script going?') and I finally started to get afraid that she'd stop calling.

"So I really sat down with my writing partner, Tim Breitbach, and we drafted a script and then got into the Labs in 1998. So we went there not expecting anything for our first draft, and we basically got a drubbing."

"A butt kicking," added Breitbach.

"A butt kicking," agreed Decena. "In a really good way, a really supportive way. It helped us, it propelled us to really find the story and find why we needed to tell the story.

"We had a meeting with one of our advisors, Peter Hedges," continued Decena, "who wrote one of my favorite movies, *What's Eating Gilbert*

Grape?, and he basically sat us down and said, 'Why do you need to tell this story?'

"He told us we'd written a clever script, but that you can't write a movie just because you want to be a screenwriter or you want to be a director. You have to have a need to tell a story. He gave us the parable of going into a dark tunnel and not being afraid about where you're going to come out. It really pushed us to go back and find the core of the story."

The core of the story they discovered was, as Decena put it, "The conflict between two characters: one who believes that love is eternal and the other that love is conditional and physical."

For Decena, that conflict was grounded in his own personal experience. "The genesis of the story for me was when we had our first child," he recalled. "It's different for guys; when a baby's first born, mothers bond immediately, but dads sort of take a while, because the kid just cries and eats and wants their mother.

"But I remember the day I fell in love with him and the chemical rush that I felt was very similar to when I fell in love with my wife. And that triggered this dialectic that I could see in a story, with one person believing that love is magical and unexplainable, and someone else who believes that it's physiological and chemical.

"Dopamine is the natural amphetamine that we feel when we fall in love. I started to ask myself; what is 'love?' Is it this biological, physiological thing or is it really something 'magical' that just happens?" Decena used the making of *Dopamine* to try to answer that question.

After the experience of making that first feature (with all of its ups and downs, conflicts and crises), he learned the name of the chemical your body produces that makes you want to make low-budget digital movies.

"Lysergic acid diethylamide — LSD," he said, laughing, "You're definitely tripping while you're making a movie."

GO DIGITAL

For many filmmakers, the reason behind their choice to go digital has
nothing to do with aesthetics or cutting-edge technology, but instead
is more basic: simple economics. Such was Decena's situation on
Dopamine.

"I think the biggest reason for me to shoot digital," he said, "was being
a first-time director and not having to worry about burning film while
you're trying to get a performance.

"It wasn't necessarily the look. Most important to me was having time
with the actors. So I discussed the look with director of photography
Rob Humphreys and what I was going for, but ultimately I said it was
his canvas.

"I was able to run master shots and let the actors find their way,"
Decena continued, "and let me find my way, and then pick off our coverage shots from that. It just allowed me that freedom to help the actors
find the scene and let me focus on getting the performances."

REHEARSE

Before he started shooting miles and miles of tape, though, Decena made
sure that he had time in his production schedule for some thorough
rehearsals.

"We had one week of rehearsal," he recalled. "We started with a couple
table reads with the actors, to get a sense of how it was going to play.
We did some improvisations, kind of let them find the characters and
play with the scenes. We basically just had fun."

While it was fun, Decena felt the rehearsals served a greater purpose
— to ground the actors, so that they'd have resources to draw upon
during the rushed shooting schedule. The actors also found that it was
time well spent.

"Rehearsal was amazing for us," commented actress Sabrina Lloyd, speaking for herself and co-star John Livingston, "because Mark had us improvise as the characters, so we really got to understand them — not just through the words in the script, but through the emotion of working with each other.

"By the time we got on set," she continued, "John and I really had our feet under us. It was an incredible way to start. It made the first day very effortless."

Making it effortless was Decena's goal. "They say that 90% of directing is casting," he said, "and that definitely made my job easier. But the rehearsals let them get to know each other and get to know each other in character and be able to have that confidence about that character before you get on set.

"The set can be very distracting," he added, "very assaultive. I have the utmost respect for actors; I don't know how they do it."

YOU NEVER STOP WRITING

You'd think that after writing the script, and then rehearsing that script, and then shooting that script ... well, that the script would be done.

However, every step of the moviemaking process is about finding and refining the story you're trying to tell. And that doesn't stop when you pick up your script copies from Kinko's. It often continues well into postproduction.

This was the situation with *Dopamine*.

"We definitely were still writing in the editing process," Decena agreed. "After the assembly cut was done, we realized we had to go back in and find the story, which is always disheartening.

"As a first-timer you think, 'Well, I finished the script, and the script as it's shot is going to be great,' and then you realize that the story has to be brought out. We ended up moving things around: The opening scene was put into the middle of the film, which sounds really strange to have the opening move to the middle of the movie, but it worked."

Co-writer Breitbach agreed: "I think in writing a first-time script, it's hard to discern until you get in the edit bay what parts of what you wrote are subtext versus text. I think that our actors taught us a lot."

"I think we learned a lot about writing with this movie," Decena admitted. "A lot of the scenes, we over-wrote. The dialogue was much longer,

and we realized in editorial, with the looks that Sabrina gives, the acting in the scene said so much more with actions that we were able to cut out a lot of the dialogue. We found moments that we could erase. 'We don't need that line.' It was a great process."

FIND THE ANGLE/HAVE A HOOK

Just finishing the movie isn't enough. You also have to get the world at large excited about seeing your opus. That's when having a fun marketing hook comes in handy.

For *Dopamine*, the 2003 Sundance Dramatic Competition was a make-or-break event. To get festival-goers into the theater, the *Dopamine* contingent came up with a unique marketing device.

"We wanted to work the festival in a coy, playful way that represented the content of the movie and built a little buzz machine," recalled Breitbach. "We gave out these friendship bracelets that said 'Dopamine' in block letters.

"The physical act of handing out the bracelets was an intimate, one-on-one gesture that connected us with a lot of people, chatting with them while we slipped it onto their svelte, delicate wrists. And yes, we focused on women."

As clever as this approach was, it was also a repetitive activity, which like any repetitive activity eventually drove the participants a little wacko.

"After about three days," Breitbach admitted, "the group of us that were spreading the *Dopamine* love started to play games to save ourselves from boredom on Park City's frozen streets.

"We started doing stuff like, 'Only give the bracelet to someone you would like to have a threesome with, while naming the starlet who would be included,' etc.

"Needless to say, the giving was more selective, but the results more encouraging. I mean, hey, we got distribution, right?"

MELVIN GOES TO DINNER

||||||||||||||||||||||||||||||||||||||||||||||||||||||||||||||||||||||||||||||||||||||||||||||

I had the pleasure of meeting writer/actor Michael Blieden at the Waterfront Film Festival in Saugatuck, Michigan. We were on a boat, taking part in a filmmakers' cruise, a special event for the filmmakers who were exhibiting their movies at the festival.

Michael's movie was *Melvin Goes to Dinner*, a digital feature about a bunch of friends hanging out at a restaurant, telling stories about their lives. It's an alternately funny and sad movie that used the device of inter-cutting between the restaurant scenes and flashbacks of the stories they're telling.

I was there with my movie, *Grown Men*, a digital feature about a bunch of friends hanging out at a restaurant, telling stories about their lives. It's an alternately funny and sad movie that used the device of inter-cutting between the restaurant scenes and flashbacks of the stories they're telling.

Needless to say, we had a lot to talk about.

In reality, despite their superficial similarities, the movies are quite different. *Melvin Goes to Dinner* was based on Blieden's play, *Phyro-Giants!,* a five-character, one-set play that he produced (and starred in) at a small theater in Los Angeles.

It likely wouldn't have gone much farther than that theatrical production if director Bob Odenkirk hadn't been in the audience one night. This was a rare occurrence, because Odenkirk — co-creator of the cult classic, *Mr. Show*, with David Cross — is an infrequent visitor to Los Angeles' theater scene.

"My wife went to see the play and said it was really great, funny, sad, entertaining and amazing," Odenkirk recalled, "and I said 'I don't believe you.' Because most plays suck.

"Most small plays in New York or L.A. that are by friends or people you know are terrible. Going to one of them is like having someone in the room with you who will not stop embarrassing themselves for hours."

However, this was not the reaction Odenkirk had to *Phyro-Giants!* He immediately recognized its big-screen potential.

"I saw the play a couple times," he said, "and I felt that if all I do is shoot this play in some form, then that would be worthy of the effort. It was so well played, so well written, and the cast was so perfect. It was just worth shooting.

"And," he continued, "I thought I had an idea of how to shoot it and keep it lively, which was multiple, handheld cameras."

That use of multiple cameras enabled him to shoot the bulk of the movie — the restaurant scenes among the four friends (and the occasional visits to their table by a waitress) — in one long night during which they covered a staggering sixty-five pages of dialogue.

"We used five cameras, so everybody is on camera at all times," Odenkirk explained. "And we tried to layer it so that you can follow everyone's performance throughout the movie. When a person's talking and telling a story, we cut from them to watch the people listening, because the way that any one of that person's stories is affecting the other people is the depth of the piece.

"When one person tells a story about infidelity, clearly there is an issue there with some of the other people, and you can read that, I think, subconsciously. And, if you watch the movie a second time, you can read it consciously. You can see people getting uncomfortable at certain topics, and now you know why."

Odenkirk requested only two changes to the script: That some of the stories recounted in the restaurant be visualized as flashbacks, and that the script be re-worked so that it's all told from one character's point of view.

"I felt we needed to commit to one person's story," Odenkirk said, "and see them go at least in some way on a journey.

"In the play, it's like the audience goes on a journey; they discover something they didn't know at the beginning. So we decided to concentrate on Melvin, who is the one character who is as clueless as the audience is to the true relationship of all these people. He's the last person in the group to learn what is really going on."

Making those changes was no problem for Blieden. "When I sat down to write the screenplay," he said, "we'd been performing the play for so long and the characters were so vivid to me, it felt like I was writing the sequel, because I got to write more words for these same characters in this same world."

Blieden also felt he had an understanding of how to shape the material so that it didn't seem like a movie that took place entirely in a restaurant.

"I'd been working as an editor for a while," he explained, "and I felt that I could see how the movie could — and couldn't — cut together.

"I knew that I didn't want to keep us at the table for more than seven or eight minutes at a time, so I tried to make it modular, where each restaurant passage had its own little arc, and then you'd leave, do something else, and then come back."

With the script in place, the next question was a big one: who would play the four friends at the table?

AVOID NAME TALENT

For Odenkirk, there were just two possible and radically divergent choices: Keep the cast of the play, or get well-known actors.

"The disadvantage of using the original cast is that they're not name actors," he said. He knew that distributors would find the finished movie more appealing, for marketing and promotional purposes, if they had a name cast.

But there was also a downside to using well-known talent. "The negative is that there's no way you could have rehearsed it as much as this cast had rehearsed," Odenkirk said. "This movie is all dialogue, it's all about feeling real, like you're really eavesdropping."

And, he reasoned, the inclusion of stars would have meant changes to a script that didn't need to be changed.

"There would have been a re-write of the piece," he explained "Every moment would have had to have been injected with a little more concept, a little more direction, instead of this quieter, more realistic feeling to it.

"More importantly, I think, the performances could never have been this good, because there's no way you could get a group of name actors to rehearse the piece sixty times."

In the end, he decided to keep the play's cast intact, a decision he still feels was correct.

"Ultimately, you're going to live with your film for a long, long time," he said. "And if it's well performed and everyone is aptly cast, that's all that's going to matter in the long run."

CONSIDER CAMEOS

Although he shied away from casting name actors in the lead roles, Odenkirk realized that the addition of flashbacks in the script had created a handful of opportunities for some fun cameos in the film.

"Of course one of the goals for any production is to have names, but we sacrificed that for quality," Odenkirk recalled. "So we said 'We've got these cameos and they're smaller roles, so let's try to use that to get some names to attract distributors.'"

With that goal in mind, they were able to secure a handful of known

performers — David Cross, Jack Black, Maura Tierney, and Melora Walters — to appear in the brief but important away-from-the-restaurant stories.

"I thought having a few name people would help the movie," Odenkirk said. "Now, some of the people, like Jack Black and Melora Walters, wouldn't let us put their name or their image on the poster, which is fine and understandable. The last thing I would want would be for the movie to be released as 'The Jack Black Movie.' People would hate me, Jack, and the asshole who made the poster.

"I do think the cameos help. They're little boosts to the movie," he added. "It helps people to consider the movie legitimate."

Now, before you begin to think that it's a piece of cake to get name talent for small roles, understand that Odenkirk cast most of the cameos by simply pressing the speed dial on his cell phone.

"Jack, David, and Maura were all friends of mine who did it because I was their friend and because they liked the script," Odenkirk explained. "But I doubt any of them would have done it if they didn't know me. The parts just weren't big enough or juicy enough to motivate them, even if they did respect the work. So … it helps to know people. Especially if you aren't paying anything."

However, before you lose all hope, read on:

"Melora Walters was the only cameo who I didn't have a personal relationship with before the filming," Odenkirk added. "We sent the script to her agent, she read it, we met with her, she liked it a lot and was willing to do it. She was perfect and she nailed it great. We were very lucky."

Let's do the math: Four cameos. Four name actors. Three are friends of the director. One is a stranger who takes the part because she likes it.

I'm not sure this means you have a one-in-four chance of snagging a name for a small part in your movie, but if it's an interesting movie and a well-written part, it can't hurt to try.

"The thing I'm most happy about is that those people were right for their parts," Odenkirk said. "They were funny and good in their parts, and they don't overshadow the movie.

"When the movie's over, you don't go, 'Wow, that was about Jack Black's scene.' Instead, you totally go, 'That was about this couple who are lying and this friend who's in a bad relationship and this girl's story about ghosts,' and about the ninth thing you mention is that Jack Black's in it. And that's perfect. Perfect."

A PICTURE'S WORTH ...

In order to draw a distinction between the flashbacks and the restaurant scenes, Odenkirk devised a smart visual plan for the movie.

"One of the things that I settled on quickly was that I would like everything that happens that day to be shot on the digital camera," he explained. "And then I would like everything that happened a year before or ten years before to be shot in some other medium.

"It can be still film, it can be 16mm, it can be a different kind of video — in the case of the David Cross scene, we just put a very strong look on the video. And then everything that happens that day — where people are meeting and getting ready for the dinner and leaving the dinner — all happens in this same media. That was our core concept."

For a key flashback — one character's memory of a possibly-adulterous trip to Houston — Odenkirk left motion media behind and shot the sequence on 35mm slide film.

His reasoning for shooting slides was simple: "It feels like a memory, it feels like just pieces that you remember, that you feel when you remember something. And it's beautiful, too."

That experience made Odenkirk an advocate for being willing to explore different media in making a movie. "You can tell stories with stills," he said, "and I think it should be done a little more often. It can be beautiful and evocative."

DON'T HESITATE TO HESITATE

Making a movie is all about, well ... *moving*. Hustling, setting up, getting the pages shot, moving onto the next thing, moving, moving, moving.

While that's all true, Odenkirk suggests fighting against this whirlwind to ensure that you're getting the most out of your time on the set.

"You've got to be patient once you hit the set," he recommended. "You spend so much time preparing and hoping and working toward making a film. You can't get on the set and then hurry up and leave.

"You're there, the actors are there, the lights are there, the cameras are there, the set is there. It's all there. It's not going to be there again tomorrow.

"Every time you approach a scene," he continued, "get it the way you originally planned it. Go ahead and do all that stuff. But don't hesitate to hesitate and go, 'Okay, what else could happen here? What else is really going on?'

"And if there's anything that strikes you as needing to be there, see if you can get it.

"You're there. There's not going to be a better time to do it. So make use of that opportunity."

OPEN WATER

||||||||||||||||||||||||||||||||||||||||||||||||||||||||||||||||||||||||||||||||||||||||||||||||

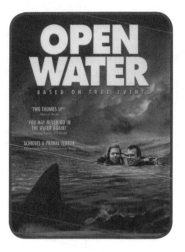

Independent filmmakers are always looking for that Holy Grail of low-budget filmmaking: The simple, brilliant, yet unique premise — the idea that will allow them to shoot a great movie for little or no money. Conventional wisdom tells us to keep the cast small and stick to one location.

Director and writer (and cinematographer and editor) Chris Kentis found his simple premise by tweaking conventional wisdom and placing his two-person cast in one of the largest single locations possible: the ocean.

A scuba diver himself, the idea for *Open Water* came to Kentis when he happened across a cautionary tale in a scuba publication.

"We read this story about this couple that were on vacation," Kentis recalled, "and boarded a dive boat and due to some mix-ups in headcount, they were accidentally left in the water. The script just poured out of me quickly; I wrote the first draft in about six days.

"What attracted us to this story was the simplicity of it and the challenge of it," Kentis continued. "We're taking two people that are used to having control of their lives and putting them in a situation where they have little or no control whatsoever and watching what unfolds."

With his simple premise established, Kentis worked hard to maintain that simplicity and not over-complicate his story.

"I wanted to do this in a very linear way," he explained. "You're just out there on the water with the two characters and you're experiencing what they're experiencing. There was going to be no cutting away, no back stories, no side stories, no little intrigue, no confessions, no 'I found out you were sleeping with my sister' crap."

Although Kentis was pleased with the success and acclaim that *Open Water* ultimately achieved, success and acclaim were not his focus while making the movie. "We were really anxious to try to make a movie in a different way," he said, "to try to stretch and challenge ourselves creatively.

"This project was about the process," he continued. "When the film was first done, before we got to any festivals — and we got rejected from plenty of festivals — I remember screening the film for the actors.

"They were thrilled with the film, and I said, 'Let's remember this feeling. We're done, we're successful. This movie might not ever make it anywhere, no one might ever see it but us and our parents. But we did what we set out to do.' We were really proud, and it felt really good, and none of us had any regrets."

Ultimately, Kentis was glad that he made the movie he wanted to make, without trying to second-guess distributors and audiences, which he feels is a waste of time anyway.

"No one can ever really predict what's going to hit and what's not," Kentis said. "If you find that at the expense of your own ideas you're trying so desperately hard to please someone else, then you could end up with a film that doesn't please anybody ... including yourself."

AVOID NAME TALENT

One of the first choices Kentis made was to eschew the idea of using name actors to play the roles of the ill-fated Daniel Kinter and Susan Watkins. (Pop Quiz: What other famous shark movie had two characters named Kinter and Watkins? Here's a hint: It was *Jaws*.)

"We knew purposefully that we wanted to cast unknown actors," Kentis explained. "It supported the whole style and the approach we wanted to take to the film.

"This goes back to the idea of working in digital video: I think one of the advantages is you get a certain sense of immediacy and realism, and that dictated working with unknown actors.

"So much of the film was trying to take perceived disadvantages and turn them to our advantage," he continued. "The use of unknowns was dictated by the fact that we wanted to be as realistic as possible. And certainly if we enlisted recognizable actors, let alone movie stars, I think that would have shattered that illusion."

Although he advocated using unknown actors for the two primary roles, the part of the villains in the piece — the sharks — were played by the closest thing you can get to trained professionals.

Working with shark experts who have wrangled sharks for other films, Kentis got the shots he needed, while keeping his actors as (relatively) safe as possible.

For the actors, it was an unnerving experience, surrounded by potential killers. Not unlike a typical audition, really.

"These sharks have actually been in a lot of films," agreed actor Daniel Travis. "I think they have a longer resume than I do."

USE YOUR OWN MONEY

Before making *Open Water*, Kentis and his producer wife, Laura Lau, had made a more traditional low-budget movie, *Grind*, with name actors and outside investors. For this new project, they chose to use their own money, which provided them some fresh options.

"We could really experiment and play," explained Lau. "And that was one really fun thing about making this movie and the way in which we made it.

"Since we were spending our own money, we could do whatever we wanted. We could take as long as we wanted, shoot whatever we wanted, we could do whatever we wanted. No one else was telling us what we had to do. We didn't just have to execute something that had already been storyboarded."

"Or get approval or worry about test audiences," added Kentis.

"We wanted total control," Lau continued. "We didn't even want to take money from family. We thought we could do the whole thing very modestly, although for us the budget was huge. We had to buy all the equipment, camera, sound housings, filters and computers for the edit.

"Then of course we had to shoulder the cost of shooting in the Bahamas because that's where the shark experts are. Being in the Bahamas is expensive, the food is expensive, the hotels are expensive, renting a boat is expensive."

For Kentis and Lau, it wasn't about not being able to raise money; it was about the sacrifices you have to make when you're using money that isn't your own.

"It's always difficult to get financing," Kentis explained, "but we had places to go for financing, because our first film was successful enough. It was more because we wanted the freedom to experiment and be in creative control."

TIME IS ON YOUR SIDE

One of the key benefits of using your own money is that you can move at your own speed, which Kentis feels has several advantages.

"The first advantage of taking our time was that I was able to work full time and help finance the film," Kentis explained. "Another is that movies tend to be rushed, especially if you look at the things coming out of Hollywood today.

"I think there's a lot to be said for taking the time to get it right, and I think most films don't really have that advantage. It's a process of refinement.

"You write the script, and you're going to write at least ten drafts of a script," he continued, "and just when you think you can't possibly have it more concise and more economical, then you shoot the thing and you can't believe how much fat there was on it. And it's the same thing when you go through the editing process.

"When you're making a film like this, without a crew, lack of objectivity can be a real problem, so having the time to step back and get some distance is really critical."

Kentis was given more than enough time to get some distance when actor Daniel Travis had an accident just before they were scheduled to head out for some final shooting.

"We were three days away from going back to finish shooting the film," Travis explained, "and I was trying to get physically ready to get back down there and kick under water for ten hours a day. I blew out my knee playing volleyball.

"People keep talking about how scary it must have been for us to shoot this film," Travis continued, "but it was nothing compared to the phone call that I had to make to Chris from the hospital, refusing any drugs until I'd spoken to him to tell him that not only was I going into surgery but that I was going to go through months of physical rehab before we could go back and shoot again."

For his part, Kentis was philosophical about the long delay the accident caused.

"If you're working alone," he said, "it's very easy to let a project slip away. You need to have the discipline of maintaining a certain kind of forward motion.

"Having something happen like what happened to Daniel certainly threatens this — you've got to keep it alive and going for a whole year, but your shooting has just been shut down.

"You try again to refine your script, you edit the footage you can, you keep in touch with the actors."

TAKE STOCK

One of the appeals of the movie for Kentis was the visual challenge he had created for himself.

"We were going to take two unknown actors," he explained, "and without even the benefit of their bodies for three-quarters of the movie, we're going to have to carry the film in one location.

"Two actors, from the shoulders up, in one location, for well over an hour. Can we do it, can we keep this interesting? Not only can we hold an audience's attention, but hopefully make it an engaging experience?"

Because nature was a big theme for the film, Kentis determined that one approach would be to cut away from the actors between sequences with various shots of nature.

He needed shots of water, clouds, and underwater animals, among other things, to create this unique pacing element. However, this required shooting a virtual stock library of these nature images, in addition to shooting the film's dramatic scenes. And Kentis refused the concept of buying stock images.

"There was no way in the film we were ever going to use any stock footage or go to somebody else's library," he declared. "It was key that we shoot every shot in the film.

"The only way to get that," Kentis continued, "on our comfortable, relaxed pace but still know that we'd have what we need, was to build these libraries.

"Whenever we went on location, whether it was on weekends or even at home, we were just always shooting. So when I found myself in the cutting room, as every editor does, you go, 'Jeez I could really use a shot of such and such,' well, I knew I would have at least ten to choose from."

HOLD ONTO YOUR VISION

It's no secret that Hollywood loves a happy ending. However, despite its success, *Open Water* was never intended to be a Hollywood movie, and Kentis never intended to provide a requisite happy ending. He knew what he wanted from the beginning, and he stuck to his guns.

"The whole impetus behind this story," Kentis explained, "was when I read about the true incident, it deeply affected me, and so it was to try to capture that. To have the audience have the same kind of emotional response that I had when I read the story.

"Our hope was that when people watch the movie, they'll ask themselves, 'What if that were me? What would I do in that situation?' and experience it that way."

"People have asked us a lot about the ending," Travis added, "and whether there was ever a discussion or an intent to shoot a different ending. And we did, we had a discussion that lasted probably about four minutes.

"I think Chris realized that if we ever did shoot a different ending and this movie did ever make it to a studio purchase, they would try to change it. And so we never did, we never shot another ending."

"Ending-wise," Kentis said, "we always knew the audience was pretty much counting on Ending A, rescue or Ending B, eaten by sharks, and we wanted to come up with a C, and wanted it to fit one of the themes of the movie. It seems to work pretty well.

"Because the film was based on a true story," Kentis continued, "that was going to be the ending from the get-go, from day one. To the credit of Lions Gate, and all the distributors that were interested in the film at Sundance, it was never questioned."

For Kentis, the topic of the ending of *Open Water* is a perfect microcosm of his process for the entire movie.

"That was the whole point of the project: To not have to answer to anyone. None of the choices were made because they were the most commercial choices; they were made because this was the film we wanted to make."

Chapter Eight

THE LESSONS REDUX

The sixty-nine lessons derived from the thirty-three movies profiled in this book provide a comprehensive overview of many of the obstacles (practical, artistic and philosophical) you're likely to encounter while making your own low-budget classic.

Those lessons are re-stated here in alphabetical order to help you quickly compare and contrast how different filmmakers approached similar problems.

ALL'S WELL THAT ENDS WELL

Your ending is the last thing your audience is going to experience when they're watching your movie. A great ending can't save a bad movie, but a bad ending can hurt an otherwise good movie. Choose your ending with care, while staying true to your overall vision.
(Clerks, The Last Broadcast, In the Company of Men)

ANTICIPATE SUCCESS

Before you finish your movie, your hip pocket should be bulging with new ideas and scripts for your next project. Then, when someone with the power to finance your next movie says, "What else are you working on?" you'll be ready to go.
(Clerks, sex, lies and videotape)

AVOID NAME TALENT

Often, an unknown face can provide more impact and a performance with more zest than a well-known face, and at a fraction of the cost.
(In the Company of Men, Melvin Goes to Dinner, Open Water)

BE DIFFERENT

Why make a movie that's like a thousand movies that have already been made? Take the road less traveled, and bring your camera along.
(Caged Heat, The Last Broadcast, Slacker, Symbiopsychotaxiplasm: Take One)

BE PREPARED

Thorough preparation can save you tons of money while shooting. You literally can't afford not to be prepared.
(The Anniversary Party, Grand Theft Auto, In the Company of Men, The Little Shop of Horrors, Tadpole)

BE SCARY

Robert Rodriguez said it better than I ever could: "Trust me, there are extreme benefits to being able to walk into this business and be completely self-sufficient. It scares people. Be scary."
(El Mariachi)

BEWARE THE CUTTING EDGE

There is often a downside to being a pioneer, particularly with new technology. Factor that in before you proceed, and tread cautiously.
(Lisa Picard Is Famous)

BUT WE'RE JUST A STUDENT FILM, OFFICER

Make your project look *smaller*, rather than *bigger*, and you can get away with murder.
(Clerks, The Little Shop of Horrors)

CAST WITH CARE

Don't be cavalier about the actors (and the crew) that you assemble for your movie. They will make or break you.
(The Blair Witch Project, Grand Theft Auto, Night of the Living Dead, Patti Rocks)

CONSIDER CAMEOS

Even if your budget can't support a star for the length of your shoot, a well-written smaller part may attract some name talent at a fraction of their normal rate.
(Caged Heat, Melvin Goes to Dinner)

CREATE AN EMOTIONAL CONNECTION

If you can connect with the audience on an honest, emotional level, they'll forgive you on almost everything else.
(Swingers)

CREATE CONFLICT

If you don't have conflict, you don't have drama. Put obstacles in front of your characters and make them work to get what they want.
(Symbiopsychotaxiplasm: Take One)

DON'T BE PREPARED

Remember when we said "Be Prepared"? Well, for some unique situations, non-preparation may provide some on-camera surprises that would be impossible to create any other way.
(Lisa Picard Is Famous)

DON'T HESITATE TO HESITATE

After putting all that effort into getting a location, setting up lights and sound, and shooting the scene, don't hesitate to hesitate. Spend some time thinking about *what else* you can do with the scene and the set-up before you tear down and move on.
(Melvin Goes to Dinner)

DO OR DO NOT ... THERE IS NO TRY

Get past the notion that you're trying to make a movie. There is no try. You either do it or you don't. So do it.
(What Happened Was...)

DUMPSTERS ARE YOUR FRIENDS

One man's garbage is another man's set, costumes, equipment and props.
(Eraserhead, π)

EXPLOIT THE UNIQUE

If you're lucky enough to have access to something that people don't see everyday, find a way to make it part of your movie.
(Carnival of Souls, Targets)

FAKE IT 'TIL YOU MAKE IT

The difference between being a confident director and a quivering mass of jelly is one of perception. Behave confidently and confidence will be yours.
(Judy Berlin)

THE FAMILY AND FRIENDS PLAN

There are a myriad reasons to employ your friends and family in your filmmaking ambitions: emotional and financial support, dependability, and shorthand communication are just a few. But recognize that manipulation and help in building a career can also be factors.
(Grand Theft Auto, Judy Berlin, π, Patti Rocks, Someone to Love)

FEWER TAKES, MORE SHOTS

You'll be better served in the editing room by shooting a greater variety of camera set-ups rather than endless repetitions of the same take.
(Judy Berlin)

FIND THE ANGLE/HAVE A HOOK

Figure out early on what sort of unique marketing hook you can create to promote your movie.
(Dopamine, In the Company of Men, π, Patti Rocks)

FIRST IMPRESSIONS/SECOND CHANCES

In the rush of the moviemaking process, you can't always trust your first impressions. Take the time to give (ideas, actors, music) a second chance.
(Carnival of Souls, sex, lies and videotape)

FIX PROBLEMS QUICKLY

Don't assume that problems will go away on their own. They probably won't. Fix it now. It will be more difficult later.
(Judy Berlin)

FLY UNDER THE RADAR

Some people don't want you and your crew around. Be circumspect. Just get what you need, quietly, and then slip away.
(Tadpole)

GIVE YOUR CHARACTERS A SECRET

A wise man once said, "Don't spill all your candy in the lobby," which means you should keep some secrets for the audience to learn about your characters throughout the course of your story.
(The Anniversary Party)

GO DIGITAL

There are a lot of excellent reasons (speed, cost, ease-of-use) to consider using digital technology.
(The Anniversary Party, Dopamine, Lisa Picard Is Famous, Tadpole)

GOD IS IN THE DETAILS

The secret to persuading the audience that you've captured reality is often found by judiciously faking just a few key details.
(The Last Broadcast)

GO LOW-TECH

High-tech and low-budget don't usually go hand-in-hand. So employ classic low-tech techniques that can make an impact without emptying your wallet.
(Carnival of Souls, Dark Star, El Mariachi, π)

GOT THEME?

Having a stated theme for your movie will help guide your decision-making process and keep your movie on track.
(Grand Theft Auto, π, Someone To Love)

HOLD ONTO YOUR VISION

By sticking to your guns on key issues, you'll make your movie stronger and better.
(Night of the Living Dead, Open Water, Swingers)

HONESTY IS THE BEST POLICY

You can put fiction on the screen, but tell the truth at every step of the process.
(The Blair Witch Project)

IGNORE THE NAYSAYERS

The world is full of people just dying to tell you how you're going to fail. Shun the bastards.
(Eraserhead, The Last Broadcast, Slacker, What Happened Was...)

IMPROVISE THE EMOTIONS, WRITE THE WORDS

Improvisation can be a great tool for generating ideas while writing and rehearsing, but it's not particularly helpful (or cost-effective) as an on-camera approach.
(David Holzman's Diary, Patti Rocks, Shadows)

IT'S NOT YOUR PROBLEM (IT'S YOUR CHARACTER'S PROBLEM)

Use production problems to your advantage by making them obstacles for your characters instead of for your crew.
(Clerks, Monty Python and the Holy Grail, Night of the Living Dead, Patti Rocks)

IT'S THE SCRIPT, STUPID

Your movie will never be any better than your script. Or, to put it another way, the more work you put into the script, the better your movie will be.
(Clerks, π)

JUST DO IT

You'll be able to find a million reasons *not* to make your movie. Ignore them and just do it.
(In the Company of Men)

KEEP IT ALL IN PERSPECTIVE

It's just a movie; it's not brain surgery. Have some fun.
(Clerks, sex, lies and videotape)

KEEP MOVING

Precious moments wasted between shots add up to wasted minutes and wasted hours. Keep moving.
(The Little Shop of Horrors)

KEEP SOME SECRETS

The world will find your movie more interesting if you don't give away all the secrets of how you created it.
(Eraserhead)

KILL YOUR DARLINGS

Sometimes it's your favorite scenes that are slowing down your movie. Be ruthless. (You can always put them in the Deleted Scenes portion of the DVD.)
(The Anniversary Party, The Blair Witch Project, Eraserhead)

KNOW WHAT YOU'RE SIGNING

Everyone you meet throughout the moviemaking process does *not* have your best interests at heart. Sign contracts with care.
(The Blair Witch Project, Carnival of Souls, What Happened Was...)

LEAVE NO STONE UNTURNED

Look everywhere — I mean, EVERYWHERE — when trying to find money to make your movie.
(In the Company of Men)

LET THEM DO THEIR JOBS

Micro-managing is not managing. Your movie will be made better by the contributions of others only if you actually let them make a contribution.
(Caged Heat)

LONG TAKES

Long takes have an upside and a downside. Recognize the impact of both sides before shooting long takes with no coverage.
(In the Company of Men, Targets)

MAKE THE BEST DAMNED [FILL IN THE BLANK] MOVIE YOU CAN

Be 100% committed to the movie you're making.
(Caged Heat, Night of the Living Dead)

MAKE YOUR OWN OPPORTUNITIES

It's very unlikely that anyone is going to knock on your door and ask you to make a movie. You need to make it happen.
(Dark Star, Dementia 13, Grand Theft Auto, Return of the Secaucus Seven)

MORE TAKES/LESS STOPPING

Don't get so caught up in technical aspects that you ignore the needs of your actors. Give them the opportunity to give you their best work.
(Monty Python and the Holy Grail)

A MOVING PHILOSOPHY

To keep your movie from feeling static (unless static is what you're after), either move the camera or shoot enough footage to keeps things moving via the editing.
(Caged Heat)

NEVER NEED HOLLYWOOD

The less you need them, the happier you're gonna be.
(Someone to Love)

NO MONEY = MORE CONTROL

Oddly enough, the less money you have to work with, the more control you can exert over your work. Go figure.
(Dark Star, Judy Berlin, sex, lies and videotape)

A PICTURE'S WORTH...

Even though you're making a moving picture, sometimes stills (or other visual formats) can provide a greater impact at a very low cost.
(Swingers, Melvin Goes to Dinner)

PLUG THE [NOISY APPLIANCE] BACK IN!

Put your car keys in the refrigerator when you unplug it. There's no way you're going home without plugging it back in.
(Slacker)

POVERTY BREEDS CREATIVITY

Having no resources forces you to be more creative. It's a good thing. Really, it is.
(π, Shadows, Slacker, Someone to Love, Targets)

PREVIEWS

There's real value in putting your unfinished movie in front of a real audience before you really finish it. Really.
(The Blair Witch Project, Grand Theft Auto, The Last Broadcast, Monty Python and the Holy Grail)

REHEARSE

Rehearse before you shoot. You'll save time (and money) on the set and get stronger performances to boot!
(Clerks, Dopamine, The Little Shop of Horrors, sex, lies and videotape, What Happened Was...)

REHEARSE? NEVER!

Magical things can happen in front of the camera when actors surprise each other (and you). Rehearsing kills that.
(Someone to Love)

SHARE THE WEALTH

People are working hard to make your movie happen. They deserve to share in the rewards (if any).
(Eraserhead, π)

SKIP FILM SCHOOL

We'll let Quentin Tarantino cover this one: "When people ask me if I went to film school, I tell them, 'No, I went to films.'" Thanks, Q.
(Clerks)

SOUND THINKING

Shoot first, add sound later. Save time, save money.
(El Mariachi, Targets)

TAKE A BREAK

Get away from your word processor or the set or the editing room and have some fun from time to time. All work and no play makes Jack a dull boy.
(sex, lies and videotape, π)

TAKE STOCK

While in production, grab a lot of shots that may prove helpful in editing.
(Open Water)

THERE'S NO SHAME IN RESHOOTING

There really isn't, and if it makes your movie better, why not do it?
(David Holzman's Diary, Shadows, Swingers)

TIME IS ON YOUR SIDE

Big-budget movies are like speeding trains. One of the benefits to working at the low-budget level is that you can take your time during the process. And your movie may be better because of it.
(Dark Star, Eraserhead, Judy Berlin, Open Water, What Happened Was...)

USE REALITY TO YOUR ADVANTAGE

Reality is free. Why wouldn't you use it when it helps your movie?
(The Anniversary Party, The Blair Witch Project, Judy Berlin, Swingers)

USE YOUR OWN MONEY

Do you want to be a truly independent filmmaker? Use only your own money.
(El Mariachi, Open Water)

YOU CAN FIX IT IN POST (SOMETIMES)

But not always. Be grateful when you can, but don't count on it.
(Tadpole)

YOU NEVER STOP WRITING

The storytelling process doesn't end when you take the script to Kinko's.
Be open to refining your story at every step in the process.
(Dopamine)

WHAT'S YOUR CLEARANCE, CLARENCE?

If you don't have clearance on copyrighted items (words, music, images, people), then don't use them. End of story.
(The Last Broadcast, Lisa Picard Is Famous, Symbiopsychotaxiplasm: Take One)

WRITE TO YOUR RESOURCES

Write your script based on what you own or can borrow for free.
(The Blair Witch Project, El Mariachi, Judy Berlin, The Little Shop of Horrors, Return of the Secaucus Seven, Tadpole)

AFTERWORD

This is, reluctantly, the conclusion of the lessons.

I've run out of space — and time — so we'll have to leave it to these thirty-three movies to get you jump-started.

However, this is far from the end. We've really only scratched the surface. There are so many other movies, of all budget levels, from which you can learn.

And, sadly, there are so many other great films and filmmakers we didn't get to. Stuart Gordon's *Re-Animator* ... David Cronenberg's *Shivers* (Barbara Steele told me some wonderful stories that have to land somewhere) ... Jim Jarmusch's *Stranger Than Paradise* ... Martin Scorsese's *Who's That Knocking On My Door* ... Rob Reiner's *This Is Spinal Tap* ... Tom Laughlin's *Billy Jack* ... the Coens' *Blood Simple* ... the work of Hal Hartley, Whit Stillman, Lodge Kerrigan, Atom Egoyan, Wes Craven, Peter Jackson, early Brian DePalma (*Sisters*, anyone? How about *Greetings*?) ... not to mention all the foreign films.

And what about other films from the filmmakers we did cover? Soderbergh and *Schizopolis*? Romero and *Martin*? Carpenter and *Halloween* or O'Bannon and *Return of the Living Dead*? *Symbiopsychotaxiplasm: Take 2 1/2*? *Faces*? *Go*? *Venice/Venice*? *Chasing Amy*?

I'm sure you have your own favorites, movies that have both taught and inspired you. Drop me a line and let me know what they are ... and what you learned from them. Perhaps they'll make it into the next book.

The truth is, you can learn something valuable from just about any movie you watch. With the low-budget ones, at least you know it's a level playing field. They dealt with the same resources (and obstacles) that you face.

If you take only one idea away from this book, let it be this: Don't repeat the mistakes of others. Make your own unique mistakes.

John Gaspard
www.graniteproductions.org

NOTES

CHAPTER ONE: CORMAN & COMPANY

"You work with Roger…" Beverly Gray, *Roger Corman: An Unauthorized Biography of the Godfather of Indie Filmmaking*, page 129

Little Shop of Horrors
"The title was changed …" Ed Naha, *The Films of Roger Corman: Brilliance on a Budget*

"One of the Viking girls…" Roger Corman, *How I Made a Hundred Movies in Hollywood and Never Lost a Dime*, page 47

"I think it's a worthwhile thing to…" Bob Thomas, *Directors in Action*, page 33

"It was done partially as an experiment…" author interview

"I sacrificed too much by shooting that fast…" author interview

"Because it was a comedy-horror film…" author interview

"I did it almost as a joke…" Andrew J. Rausch, "An Interview with Roger Corman," *www.imagesjournal.com*

"You can hire an actor by the day…" Andrew Hamlin, "It Came from Roger Corman," *Moviemaker*, Issue No. 42, Vol. 8, page 45

"I'm a strong believer in pre-production …" author interview

"On a ten-day shoot…" author interview

"Be flexible…" author interview

"I'm a believer in both instinct and preparation…" Joseph Gelmis, *The Film Director as Superstar*, page 173

"If you're young and starting…" Eric Sherman, *Directing the Film*, page 67

"When I was young…" author interview

"You waste a lot of time after you get a shot…" author interview

"I've been quoted as saying..." *AFI: The Directors*, DVD

"I feel that any script can be made for any budget..." Eric Sherman, *Directing the Film*, page 66

"I'd like to have unlimited time, unlimited budget..." Eric Sherman, *Directing the Film*, page 56

Dementia 13

"You're stepping off a cliff..." Gene D. Phillips, *Godfather: The Intimate Francis Ford Coppola*, page 313

"Francis came to me as a film editor..." Andrew J. Rausch, "An Interview With Roger Corman," *www.imagesjournal.com*

"I had bought the American rights..." author interview

"Francis and our key grip built racks..." author interview

"When the picture was finished..." author interview

"The secret of all my getting things off the..." Joseph Gelmis, *The Film Director as Superstar*, page 180

"Essentially, I sold the English rights..." Joseph Gelmis, *The Film Director as Superstar*, page 180

"He came up with a very interesting idea..." author interview

"The film was meant to be an exploitation film..." Joseph Gelmis, *The Film Director as Superstar*, page 180

"I think it showed promise..." Joseph Gelmis, *The Film Director as Superstar*, page 180

"I meet a lot of young filmmakers..." Joseph Gelmis, *The Film Director as Superstar*, page 181

"Roger was always straight with you..." Roger Corman, *How I Made a Hundred Movies in Hollywood and Never Lost a Dime*, page 91

Targets

"Peter had a great knowledge of film..." author interview

"As a result of various complications in a contract..." author interview

"One of the best debut films..." Andrew J. Rausch, "An Interview With Roger Corman," *www.imagesjournal.com*

"*Targets* isn't a very good film..." Roger Ebert, *Chicago Sun-Times*, August 15, 1968

"The one thing you can't replace is the image..." author interview

"It goes a little bit against my rules..." author interview

"There was a merchant in Bagdad..." W. Somerset Maugham, *Sheppey: A Play in Three Acts*, Methuen Drama-Random House, The Royal Literary Fund

"I think there's nothing better than being told..." Eric Sherman, *Directing the Film*, pages 65-66

Caged Heat

"There was a male sexual fantasy to be exploited..." Michael Bliss and
   Christina Banks, *What Goes Around Comes Around: The Films of
   Jonathan Demme*, page 15
"After I did publicity..." Michael Bliss and Christina Banks, *What Goes
   Around Comes Around: The Films of Jonathan Demme*, page 2
"I've always liked the idea of a new..." author interview
"We had done *The Big Doll House*..." *Caged Heat* DVD, Roger Corman
   interview
"Ever since my days working with Roger Corman..." Michael Bliss and
   Christina Banks, *What Goes Around Comes Around: The Films of
   Jonathan Demme*, page 5
"Roger is a real, sincere bleeding heart..." Dan Persons, "The Corman
   Connection," *Cinefantastique*, February, 1992
"The Lunch..." *AFI: The Directors*, DVD
"Having made sure that you accepted the rules..." David Thompson, *Demme
   on Demme, Part 2: Caged Heat to Fighting Mad*
"Jonathan learned from us..." Dan Persons, "The Corman Connection,"
   Cinefantastique, February, 1992
"I'd always felt a little uneasy..." *Caged Heat* DVD, Roger Corman interview
"He made a really good picture ..." *Caged Heat* DVD, Roger Corman
   interview
"Another thing Corman had said was..." David Thompson, *Demme on
   Demme, Part 2: Caged Heat to Fighting Mad*
"He changed the evil warden into a crazy woman..." *Caged Heat* DVD, Roger
   Corman interview
"She had grown a couple of years too old..." *Caged Heat* DVD, Roger
   Corman interview
"That was just an amazing, bizarre moment in time..." author interview
"I'd done so many low-budget movies..." author interview
"Everybody is in it together..." author interview
"I think the most important thing..." author interview
"Jonathan was lovely to work with..." Christopher S. Dietric with Peter
   Beckman, "Barbara Steele: Queen of Horror," *Imagi-Movies*, Spring 1994,
   page 45
"I think he's a fantastic director..." Christopher S. Dietric with Peter Beckman,
   "Barbara Steele: Queen of Horror," *Imagi-Movies*, Spring 1994, page 45
"I tried very hard to get people..." David Thompson, *Demme on Demme, Part
   2: Caged Heat to Fighting Mad*
"I'll never tell the editor how to cut a scene..." Michael Bliss and Christina
   Banks, *What Goes Around Comes Around: The Films of Jonathan
   Demme*, page 145

"I never discuss the lighting with Tak at all..." David Thompson, *Demme on Demme, Part 2: Caged Heat to Fighting Mad*

"I had a long discussion with Jonathan..." Gary Morris, "Fun in the New World," *www.brightlightsfilm.com*

"The directors who say..." *Grand Theft Auto*, DVD Commentary

"Jonathan told me..." *Grand Theft Auto*, DVD Commentary

Grand Theft Auto

"Nobody who has ever wanted to see a Rolls-Royce..." Lawrence Van Gelder, *"Demolition Derby," The New York Times*, September 29, 1977, page C19

"You should do something with that, boy." Ellen Pfeifer, "Opie Grows Up," *Herald American* (Boston), July 30, 1982

"I was 21 years old and I was itching to direct a film..." *Grand Theft Auto* DVD, A Conversation between Roger Corman and Ron Howard

"I hated *Eat My Dust*, hated the script..." Todd McCarthy, "Auteur Opie," *Film Comment*, May/June 1984, page 41

"One of the problems in this business..." *Grand Theft Auto* DVD, A Conversation between Roger Corman and Ron Howard

"I wouldn't let my agent accompany me..." *Grand Theft Auto* DVD, A Conversation between Roger Corman and Ron Howard

"Ron said, 'I will do another movie for you...'" author interview

"They had to come up with an idea for a script..." *Grand Theft Auto* DVD, Roger Corman interviewed by Leonard Maltin

"The whole thing was inspired by..." *Grand Theft Auto*, DVD Commentary

"When Ron said that the climax..." *Grand Theft Auto*, DVD Commentary

"We thought the Rolls Royce..." author interview

"The beauty of the idea was that..." *Grand Theft Auto* DVD, Roger Corman interviewed by Leonard Maltin

"Ron told me, during the shoot..." author interview

"The thing I learned on that movie is that..." author interview

"I think any director likes to use people..." author interview

"We had been feeding the crew Kentucky Fried Chicken..." author interview

"There was no partying for them..." author interview

"No matter how silly a movie..." *Grand Theft Auto*, DVD Commentary

"So much of directing is managing your compromises..." *Grand Theft Auto*, DVD Commentary

"You need to be tenacious..." author interview

"Back then I used to say to myself..." author interview

"Ron later said to me..." author interview

"I think Alan and I set a record..." *Grand Theft Auto*, DVD Commentary

"I always knew that preparation and rehearsal..." author interview

"You can do it better with more time..." *Grand Theft Auto*, DVD
  Commentary
"When you finish directing a movie for Roger..." *The Directors: Roger
  Corman* DVD (AFI)
"You can't really know what your film is saying..." *Grand Theft Auto*, DVD
  Commentary
"I'm a firm believer in putting the film..." author interview
"Funny is funny..." *Grand Theft Auto*, DVD Commentary
"When in doubt, hit somebody in the groin." *Grand Theft Auto*, DVD
  Commentary

CHAPTER TWO: FIERCELY INDEPENDENT

Return of the Secaucus Seven

"I was catapulted from total obscurity..." Gavin Smith, *Sayles on Sayles*, page
  50
"I wrote three movies..." Vittorio Carli, *Sayles Has Learned Film Success
  Without Selling Out, www.artinterviews.com*
"Basically, the more you get paid..." Gavin Smith, *Sayles on Sayles*, page 42
"The nice thing about Roger Corman..." Gavin Smith, *Sayles on Sayles*, pages
  34 – 35
"John wanted to direct..." author interview
"The only way you get to direct in Hollywood..." David Rosen, with Pete
  Hamilton, *Off-Hollywood*, page 182
"If I'd known how hard it is to make a movie..." Gavin Smith, *Sayles on
  Sayles*, page 62
"There weren't many film schools or film books at the time..." Vittorio Carli,
  *Sayles Has Learned Film Success Without Selling Out, www.artinterviews.
  com*
"The fact that it really took off and did so well..." author interview
"John had very specifically tailored the script..." author interview
"A lot of that movie came out of my experiences..." *Return of the Secaucus
  Seven*, DVD Commentary
"Everybody knew everybody..." author interview
"After *Return of the Secaucus Seven*, sometimes you arrive..." author interview
"When you have a lot of characters in a movie..." *Return of the Secaucus
  Seven*, DVD Commentary
"Take advantage of art direction that's been done for you..." *Return of the
  Secaucus Seven*, DVD Commentary
"People have said that a lot of it sounded improvised..." author interview
"Sometimes your budget can become an aesthetic..." *Return of the Secaucus
  Seven*, DVD Commentary

Patti Rocks

"I saw *Memories of Underdevelopment*…" author interview
"I was thinking about getting out of the business…" author interview
"I thought, two guys in a car…" author interview
"In theory, David was right…" author interview
"The camera got so cold most of the time…" author interview
"I had a lot of fun making the film…" author interview
"It started with some general conversations…" author interview
"I did a draft…" author interview
"So the script really came out of those improvisations…" author interview
"It's a funny thing…" author interview
"I had to do all the actorly stuff…" author interview
"He had very few notes…" author interview
"We got the money in November…" author interview
"It actually turned into a more interesting film…" author interview
"The lesson from *Patti Rocks*…" author interview
"I cast well, including the crew…" author interview
"We set out to do that…" author interview
"Sam Grogg felt the language was its strong point…" author interview
"You watch HBO…" author interview
"Film is a collaborative art, there's no question…" author interview
"There was a level of trust in the sex scene…" author interview
"It was difficult to do…" author interview
"A lot of these small films…" author interview
"You have your own calling card…" author interview

What Happened Was…

"You're not here very long…" author interview
"Because I'd never acted in something I'd directed…" author interview
"I went to dinner at a friend's house…" Tom Noonan, *www.tomnoonan.com*
"When the woman told him…" Tom Noonan, *www.tomnoonan.com*
"I got up from the table…" Tom Noonan, *www.tomnoonan.com*
"When we performed…" Tom Noonan, *www.tomnoonan.com*
"Part of what I would try to do during the play…" author interview
"There were times when I was doing the play…" author interview
"Most people who read the script…" author interview
"I'd written scripts for many years…" author interview
"My general rule is that either you rehearse a lot…" author interview
"The last night of the play…" author interview
"Most of the people on the crew were all involved…" author interview
"When I finally shot the film…" author interview
"One thing I learned making the film…" author interview

"I was not thrilled about the photo..." author interview

"When you sell a film to a distributor..." author interview

"Distribution is the creepiest part of making a movie..." author interview

"To 'try' is to struggle..." Tom Noonan, *www.tomnoonan.com*

"If you're interested in becoming..." Tom Noonan, *www.tomnoonan.com*

"You make the movie because you want to make..." author interview

In the Company of Men

"That line of dialogue was the first idea..." *In the Company of Men*, Sony Classics Pictures, *www.sonypictures.com/classics*

"I was interested in making something that was familiar..." Nicholas Jarecki, *Breaking In*, page 207

"The film is not a soap-box lecture..." *In the Company of Men*, Sony Classics Pictures, *www.sonypictures.com/classics*

"We've had some really nasty reviews..." Matthew Hayes, *Montreal Mirror*, September 4, 1997

"A selling point was the controversy." *In the Company of Men*, DVD Commentary

"In the Company of Men — it's funny that it became successful..." John Anderson, *Sundancing: Hanging Out and Listening In at America's Most Important Film Festival*, page 32

"When we were filming this..." *In the Company of Men*, DVD Commentary

"There's been a lot of women not wanting to see it..." *London Student*, Vol. 18, Issue 10

"The film pulls you in and makes you an accomplice." *In the Company of Men*, DVD Commentary

"What's great about the film..." *In the Company of Men*, DVD Commentary

"There are bits of me in all of those characters..." *London Student*, Vol. 18, Issue 10

"I'm happy having people think about it..." *London Student*, Vol. 18, Issue 10

"The first to get hit on were of course friends..." Nicholas Jarecki, *Breaking In*, page 208

"I had heard that some former students of mine..." Nicholas Jarecki, *Breaking In*, page 208

"I couldn't have asked for better actors..." *London Student*, Vol. 18, Issue 10

"The nice thing about shooting in long takes..." *In the Company of Men*, DVD Commentary

"That was a problem we ran into all the time..." *In the Company of Men*, DVD Commentary

"Lack of preparation can kill..." Nicholas Jarecki, *Breaking In*, page 211

"I felt that it was truer to the story that Chad..." *London Student*, Vol. 18, Issue 10

"I think that perhaps my unfamiliarity..." Nicholas Jarecki, *Breaking In*, page 207

"I think that everyone I came into contact with..." Nicholas Jarecki, *Breaking In*, page 211

Judy Berlin

"I don't consider myself either one of them..." Daniel Lee, "A Talk with Eric Mendelsohn, Director of *Judy Berlin*," *www.reel.com,*

"I edited the film on his flatbed..." *SplicedWire.com, /www.splicedonline.com*

"The original idea was..." *Judy Berlin*, DVD Commentary

"So I wrote a script with seventeen actors..." *Judy Berlin*, DVD Commentary

"I had been collecting ideas..." author interview

"I'm a big collector, in real life..." Cynthia Fuchs, "Alone Inside Our Own Skins, Interview with Eric Mendelsohn," *www.popmatters.com*

"...a kind of cinematic haiku." Mick LaSalle, "Judy Berlin Finds the Poetry in Suburban Lives," *San Francisco Chronicle*, Friday, February 25, 2000

"David Lynch directing an Arthur Miller script." Joshua Klein, *The Onion, www.theonion.com*

"I'm an idiot." author interview

"Multiple-character, ensemble pieces are not simple..." author interview

"It's really hard to do upper-middle..." *Judy Berlin*, DVD Commentary

"The problem was..." author interview

"I realize why independent films always revolve..." author interview

"People were offering us a lot of money..." author interview

"They wanted to make the film at a higher budget..." author interview

"There are so many advantages..." author interview

"I worked on films my whole life..." author interview

"It's sort of unheard of, but I knew that..." author interview

"The problem that you have two weeks..." author interview

"You think, 'Well, it's two weeks before the shoot...'" author interview

"Do fewer takes and shoot more shots..." author interview

"You get a lot of directors who are nervous..." author interview

"I had this crazy idea at the beginning of my short..." author interview

"It was a terrible decision..." author interview

"If you use your friends..." author interview

"A lot of the films I've done..." author interview

"I didn't want them to become comfortable..." author interview

"I thought it was just a matter of scheduling..." author interview

"I think in retrospect it did help..." author interview

"It was nice to find that it worked..." author interview

"If you do not naturally have the kind of personality..." author interview

CHAPTER THREE: OUT OF THIS WORLD

Carnival of Souls

"It's a heck of a note when a film..." *Carnival of Souls* DVD: *The Movie That Wouldn't Die*

"We didn't set out to make a classic..." Dan Lybarger, "Digital Souls: An Interview with Maurice Prather on *Carnival of Souls*," February 3, 2000. Originally appeared in the February 3-9, 2000 issue of *Pitch Weekly*

"It never occurred to me that *Carnival of Souls*..." Mitch Persons, *Cinefantastique*, Vol. 31, No. 5

"Robert Altman, also an industrial filmmaker..." *Carnival of Souls* DVD Commentary

"I talked to a couple of local investors..." *Carnival of Souls* DVD: *The Movie That Wouldn't Die*

"There were no dressing room facilities..." *Carnival of Souls* DVD Commentary

"People have asked why *Carnival of Souls* is still around..." *Carnival of Souls* DVD Commentary

"From the writer's angle I was freed..." *Carnival of Souls* DVD Commentary

"It was night and I was driving back..." *Carnival of Souls* DVD Commentary

"When I got back to Kansas I discussed Saltair..." *Carnival of Souls* DVD Commentary

"Herk described to me a straight indoor ballroom..." *Carnival of Souls* DVD Commentary

"While thinking about a character and a story..." *Carnival of Souls* DVD Commentary

"I liked the weirdness of the atmosphere..." David Zinman, *Fifty Grand Movies of the 1960s and 1970s*, page 187

"The definitive study of a nerd in lust." Roger Ebert, *Chicago Sun-Times*, July 27, 1989

"I wanted a girl who had an ethereal quality..." David Zinman, *Fifty Grand Movies of the 1960s and 1970s*, page 189

"When Candace got off the plane in Kansas City..." *Carnival of Souls* DVD Commentary

"The next morning she was to read for us..." *Carnival of Souls* DVD Commentary

"We decided the film would feature someone being chased..." *Carnival of Souls* DVD Commentary

"We had basically no special effects whatsoever..." Dan Lybarger, "Digital Souls: An Interview with Maurice Prather on *Carnival of Souls*," February 3, 2000. Originally appeared in the February 3-9, 2000 issue of *Pitch Weekly*

"We created that in the studio ourselves…" Dan Lybarger, "Digital Souls: An Interview with Maurice Prather on *Carnival of Souls*," February 3, 2000. Originally appeared in the February 3–9, 2000 issue of *Pitch Weekly*

"In the early days of independent productions…" Dan Lybarger, *Digital Souls: An Interview with Maurice Prather on Carnival of Souls*, February 3, 2000. Originally appeared in the February 3–9, 2000 issue of *Pitch Weekly*

"We finally ended up with a distributor in California…" *Carnival of Souls* DVD Commentary

"When I returned, I contacted the distributor…" *Carnival of Souls* DVD Commentary

"The deal with the laboratories is if you don't…" Dan Lybarger, "Digital Souls: An Interview with Maurice Prather on *Carnival of Souls*," February 3, 2000. Originally appeared in the February 3-9, 2000 issue of *Pitch Weekly*

"It was a big mistake…" Jeffrey Frentzen, "Herk Harvey's *Carnival of Souls*," *Cinefantastique*, Vol. 13 No. 6 / Vol. 14 No. 1

"Making the film had been very exciting…" *Carnival of Souls* DVD Commentary

"Looking back I was surprised that we even had the guts…" Daniel Schweiger, "*Carnival of Souls*," *Cinefantastique*, May 1990, Vol. 20, No. 5

Night of the Living Dead

"Romero's groundbreaking film…" *Night of the Living Dead*, DVD Liner Notes

"The hero of *Night of the Living Dead*…" *Night of the Living Dead*, DVD Liner Notes

"'We're going to make a movie…" John Russo, *The Complete Night of the Living Dead Filmbook*, page 17

"Ten of us formed a corporation…" John Russo, *The Complete Night of the Living Dead Filmbook*, pages 6-7

"I had written a short story…" John Russo, *The Complete Night of the Living Dead Filmbook*, pages 6-7

"We found this old farmhouse…" *Night of the Living Dead*, DVD Commentary

"Our first finished 35mm print…" John Russo, *The Complete Night of the Living Dead Filmbook*, page 21

"The only problem…" *Night of the Living Dead*, DVD Commentary

"The truth of the matter is that Duane…" *Night of the Living Dead*, DVD Commentary

"We cast a black man not because he was black…" John Russo, *The Complete Night of the Living Dead Filmbook*, page 7

"He just turned out to be the best person for the part…" Gary Anthony Surmacz, "Anatomy of a Horror Film," *Cinefantastique*, Vol. 4, page 17

"Between the first day of shooting…" *Night of the Living Dead*, DVD
   Commentary

"We made it look as though this had happened…" John Russo, *The Complete
   Night of the Living Dead Filmbook*, page 53

"We showed the film to distributors…" David Zinman, *Fifty Grand Movies of
   the 1960s and 1970s*, page 198

"We had talked for some time…" *Night of the Living Dead*, DVD
   Commentary

"At its best, *Night of the Living Dead*…" *Night of the Living Dead*, DVD
   Liner Notes

"We were dealing with a fantasy premise…" John Russo, *The Complete Night
   of the Living Dead Filmbook*, page 73

"The philosophy of our movie-making group…" John Russo, *The Complete
   Night of the Living Dead Filmbook*, page 39

"And I think that's one of the reasons the film…" *Night of the Living Dead*,
   DVD Commentary

Dark Star

"At the start, Dan O'Bannon…" Dale Winogura, *Cinefantastique*, Vol. 3, No. 4

"When we took it to the USC Cinema…" author interview

"John and I were pretty upset about that…" author interview

"The only thing that made it possible with the small…" author interview

"I believe that I am the inventor of the used future,…" author interview

"I was getting more dissatisfied with high-tech stuff …" author interview

"When we looked at footage, the actors…" author interview

"When *Alien* came along and Ridley Scott…" author interview

"What we would do with this giant beach ball…" Gilles Boulenger, *John
   Carpenter — The Prince of Darkness*, page 76

"When I did a few little special effects on the first *Star Wars*…" *Return of the
   Living Dead*, DVD Commentary

"The first thing we thought…" author interview

"The elevator shaft was built on a sound stage…" Dale Winogura,
   Cinefantastique, Vol. 3, No. 4

"I ended up having an appendectomy…" author interview

"I was twenty-six years old, and you really don't think…" author interview

"The most talented directors that I knew in my class…" Nicholas Jarecki,
   Breaking In, page 94

"You gotta go out and make it happen for yourself…" Nicholas Jarecki,
   Breaking In, page 96

"That's really the answer that every director…" Nicholas Jarecki, *Breaking In*,
   page 96

"One of the advantages to having no money…" author interview

π

"I have a single image of Sean Gullette..." Darren Aronofsky, π — *The Guerilla Diaries*, pages 3–4

"The core of the film is a thriller..." Andrew L. Urban, Interview with Darren Aronofsky, *www.UrbanCinefile.com*

"If you fly too high to the sun, you get burnt..." Andrea Chase, *www.chitchatmagazinecom*

"It's Prometheus: if you steal fire from the gods..." Andrea Chase, *www.chitchatmagazinecom*

"Personally, I don't believe there are that many original ideas..." David Geffner, DGA Interview with Darren Aronofsky, *www.dga.org*

"I want to call the movie π." Darren Aronofsky, π — *The Guerilla Diaries*, page 8

"1. Always move forward. If you have a problem..." Darren Aronofsky, π — *The Guerilla Diaries*, page 10

"Basically what we try to discipline ourselves..." JaxomLOTUS, Interview with Darren Aronofsky, *www.worth1000.com*, October 19, 2000

"You start with your theme and your story..." JaxomLOTUS, Interview with Darren Aronofsky, *www.worth1000.com*, October 19, 2000

"While working on this movie on paranoia..." Jeffrey M. Anderson, "Darren Aronofsky: Easy as 3.14," *www.combustiblecelluloid.com*, June, 1998

"I know all this may sound soft..." Darren Aronofsky, π — *The Guerilla Diaries*, page 6

"I believe the three of us will make a firm base..." Darren Aronofsky, π — *The Guerilla Diaries*, page 6

"Eric and I have decided to put our commie leanings to the test..." Darren Aronofsky, π — *The Guerilla Diaries*, page 27

"That's the only way to get it done..." Anthony Kaufman, An Interview with Darren Aronofsky and Sean Gullette, *www.indiewire.com*, January 21, 1998

"The entire crew and cast joined hands..." Darren Aronofsky, π — *The Guerilla Diaries*, page 27

"I gave the editing crew the weekend off..." Darren Aronofsky, π — *The Guerilla Diaries*, page 50

"When you watch any of the old sci-fi films..." Dan Persons, *Pi — Searching for the Mathematical Secrets of the Universe, Cinefantastique*, Vol. 30, No. 4, August, 1998, page 13

"We tried to learn from a master..." π DVD Commentary

"The whole idea was we took Terry Gilliam's..." Andrea Chase, *www.chitchatmagazinecom*

"When I was picking up my last check from the Evil Petroleum Empire..." Darren Aronofsky, π — *The Guerilla Diaries*, page 20

"People normally perceive science fiction as effects-laden...." Dan Persons, *Pi — Searching for the Mathematical Secrets of the Universe, Cinefantastique*, Vol. 30, No. 4, August, 1998, page 12

CHAPTER FOUR: IN A LEAGUE OF THEIR OWN

Shadows

"As an actor you don't get the freedom..." Ray Carney, *Cassavetes on Cassavetes*, page 47.

"*Shadows* began as a dream..." Ray Carney, *Cassavetes on Cassavetes*, page 55.

"I went on a radio show..." Eric Sherman for The American Film Institute, *Directing the Film*, page 58

"Over a period of three years we worked..." Eric Sherman for The American Film Institute, *Directing the Film*, page 59

"Fitfully dynamic, endowed with a raw but vibrant strength," Diane Jacobs, *Hollywood Renaissance*, page 35

"I don't even think of myself as a director..." *A Constant Forge*, produced, written and directed by Charles Kiselyak

"The emotion was improvisation. The lines were written." Joseph Gelmis, *The Film Director as Superstar*, page 83

"I believe in improvising on the basis of the written...' Ray Carney, *Cassavetes on Cassavetes*, page 217

"The only way a director can create an environment...' *A Constant Forge*, produced, written and directed by Charles Kiselyak.

"I felt totally safe..." *A Constant Forge*, produced, written and directed by Charles Kiselyak

"He never got his nose out of joint..." *A Constant Forge*, produced, written and directed by Charles Kiselyak

"John was more interested in the surprised moment..." *A Constant Forge*, produced, written and directed by Charles Kiselyak

"For each scene I give the basic idea of the scene..." Ray Carney, *Cassavetes on Cassavetes*, page 68)

"I could see the flaws in *Shadows* myself..." Ray Carney, *Cassavetes on Cassavetes*, page 80

"The one thing that came at all alive to me..." Ray Carney, *Cassavetes on Cassavetes*, page 80

"We started again, and I tried to shoot it..." Ray Carney, *Cassavetes on Cassavetes*, page 82

"The second version is completely different..." Ray Carney, *Cassavetes on Cassavetes*, page 82

"Money has nothing to do with film..." *I'm Almost Not Crazy ... John Cassavetes: The Man and His Work*, written and directed by Michael Ventura

"John wanted to be in a struggle to make his films..." *A Constant Forge*, produced, written and directed by Charles Kiselyak

Symbiopsychotaxiplasm: Take One

"I first heard about it through my colleague..." author interview

"It's the ultimate reality show..." author interview

"The title comes from symbiotaxiplasm..." *All Things Considered*, National Public Radio, Sunday, January 23, 2005

"I taught acting for quite a while in Canada..." author interview

"The Heisenberg Principle of Uncertainty..." Scott MacDonald, "Sunday in the Park with Bill," *The Independent*, May, 1992

"Another scientific theory that interested me..." Scott MacDonald, "Sunday in the Park With Bill," *The Independent*, May, 1992

"I said to myself, 'What would happen..." author interview

"This film was an attempt to look..." Scott MacDonald, "Sunday in the Park With Bill," *The Independent*, May, 1992

"*Symbiopsychotaxiplasm: Take One* is about revolution..." *Symbiopsychotaxiplasm: Take One*, Press Kit

"One of the elements of my characterization..." author interview

"I set up a series of situations..." *All Things Considered*, National Public Radio, Sunday, January 23, 2005

"He was looking for some form of rebellion..." author interview

"I was hoping to have any conflict..." author interview

"If you ask him what is the film about..." *Symbiopsychotaxiplasm: Take One*, DVD

"Bill, we have a little present for you." Scott MacDonald, "Sunday in the Park With Bill," *The Independent*, May, 1992

"When I saw this material..." author interview

"Luckily for Bill, they took it to 11..." author interview

"I think that one of the things that happened..." author interview

"It's a movie? So who's moving who?" *Symbiopsychotaxiplasm: Take One*, DVD

"Here once again is that division..." author interview

"I was very happy with the fact that there was confusion..." Scott MacDonald, "Sunday in the Park With Bill," *The Independent*, May, 1992

"That's the way life is..." author interview

Monty Python and the Holy Grail

"We were learning as it went along..." *Monty Python and the Holy Grail*, DVD Commentary

"The coconut gag was the original gag..." The Pythons (with Bob McCabe), *The Pythons Autobiography*, page 236

"This device was funny ," *Monty Python and the Holy Grail*, DVD Commentary

"If we'd had the money..." The Pythons (with Bob McCabe), *The Pythons Autobiography*, page 239

"It's funny how you get used to them not having horses..." *Monty Python and the Holy Grail*, DVD Commentary

"It makes a wonderful leap because with that opening shot... ' The Pythons (with Bob McCabe), *The Pythons Autobiography*, page 239

"In movies everybody concentrates on the fucking technical aspects..." David Morgan, *Monty Python Speaks!*, page 165

"In filmmaking you can find yourself being made completely..." David Morgan, *Monty Python Speaks!*, page 165

"I remember doing one of the best takes in my life..." The Pythons (with Bob McCabe), *The Pythons Autobiography*, page 255

"Now this is for me the perfect example of the tail wagging the dog..." The Pythons (with Bob McCabe), *The Pythons Autobiography*, page 256

"When I'm working, I will sometimes say..." David Morgan, *Monty Python Speaks!*, pages 164–165

"A take can vary tremendously..." David Morgan, *Monty Python Speaks!*, page 165

"The first showing of *Holy Grail* was a total disaster..." The Pythons (with Bob McCabe), *The Pythons Autobiography*, page 263

"It was a disaster, an absolute disaster.. " Dave Eggers, "Sixteen Tons of Fun: Eric Idle brings the *Holy* Grail to Broadway," *The New Yorker*, December 20 & 27, 2004, page 171

"It was one of those evenings when Python flopped..." The Pythons (with Bob McCabe), *The Pythons Autobiography*, page 263

"What had happened was, Terry Gilliam and Terry Jones decided..." David Morgan, *Monty Python Speaks!*, page 175

"That's the good thing about Python..." The Pythons (with Bob McCabe), *The Pythons Autobiography*, page 264

"I don't think I realized in those days how late..." The Pythons (with Bob McCabe), *The Pythons Autobiography*, page 264

"There were 13 screenings of *The Holy Grail*..." The Pythons (with Bob McCabe), *The Pythons Autobiography*, page 264

"I was sitting there thinking, it can't be that unfunny..." The Pythons (with Bob McCabe), *The Pythons Autobiography*, page 236

"There was the realization that you can just pull the soundtrack off..." The Pythons (with Bob McCabe), *The Pythons Autobiography*, page 264

"When I look back at *Grail*..." *Monty Python and the Holy Grail*, DVD Commentary

Eraserhead

"My original image was of a man's…" David Hughes, *The Complete Lynch*, page 19

"It is a personal film…" *Eraserhead*, DVD Commentary

"*Eraserhead* is the real *Philadelphia Story…*" K. George Godwin, "*Eraserhead*: The Story behind the Strangest Film Ever Made, and the Cinematic Genius Who Directed It," *Cinefantastique*, September, 1984, Vol. 14 No. 4 / Vol. 14 No. 5, page 47

"I think it's going to be a bit longer than that." K. George Godwin, "*Eraserhead*: The Story behind the Strangest Film Ever Made, and the Cinematic Genius Who Directed It," *Cinefantastique*, September, 1984, Vol. 14 No. 4 / Vol. 14 No. 5, page 46

"We had about five or six rooms…" K. George Godwin, "*Eraserhead*: The Story behind the Strangest Film Ever Made, and the Cinematic Genius Who Directed It," *Cinefantastique*, September, 1984, Vol. 14 No. 4 / Vol. 14 No. 5, page 49)

"I started living in the stables in 1972…" *Eraserhead*, DVD Commentary

"I got this paper route…" Chris Rodley, *Lynch on Lynch*, pages 60-61

"David was always in charge…" *Eraserhead*, DVD Commentary

"It was a real artist's film…" K. George Godwin, " "*Eraserhead*: The Story behind the Strangest Film Ever Made, and the Cinematic Genius Who Directed It," *Cinefantastique*, September, 1984, Vol. 14 No. 4 / Vol. 14 No. 5, page 57

"I once said it was…" David Hughes, *The Complete Lynch*, page 33

"We didn't have any money…" *Eraserhead*, DVD Commentary

"One day Jack Fisk and I found…" *Eraserhead*, DVD Commentary

"We showed it to one guy…" Chris Rodley, *Lynch on Lynch*, page 82

"It was supposed to take a few weeks to shoot…" K. George Godwin, "*Eraserhead*: The Story behind the Strangest Film Ever Made, and the Cinematic Genius Who Directed It," *Cinefantastique*, September, 1984, Vol. 14 No. 4 / Vol. 14 No. 5, page 50

"After a film's going for a couple of years…" David Hughes, *The Complete Lynch*, page 21

"What we lacked in monetary resources, we had in time…" K. George Godwin, "*Eraserhead*: The Story behind the Strangest Film Ever Made, and the Cinematic Genius Who Directed It," *Cinefantastique*, September, 1984, Vol. 14 No. 4 / Vol. 14 No. 5, page 66

"There's one particular shot…" *Eraserhead*, DVD Commentary

"Those things can be extremely frightening…" Chris Rodley, *Lynch on Lynch*, page 74

"There were some dark moments…" John Alexander, *The Films of David Lynch*, page 43

"It just turned into this monster we couldn't finish..." David Hughes, *The Complete Lynch*, page 21

"I feel now that I shouldn't have spent so much time..." Chris Rodley, *Lynch on Lynch*, page 75

"The thing is, the film isn't done until it's done." K. George Godwin, "*Eraserhead*: The Story behind the Strangest Film Ever Made, and the Cinematic Genius Who Directed It," *Cinefantastique*, September, 1984, Vol. 14 No. 4 / Vol. 14 No. 5, page 55)

"My parents came to the first screening of *Eraserhead*..." *Eraserhead*, DVD Commentary

"At the end of the screening..." K. George Godwin, "*Eraserhead*: The Story behind the Strangest Film Ever Made, and the Cinematic Genius Who Directed It," *Cinefantastique*, September, 1984, Vol. 14 No. 4 / Vol. 14 No. 5, page 68

"The pacing is slow in *Eraserhead*, and that's great..." K. George Godwin, "*Eraserhead*: The Story behind the Strangest Film Ever Made, and the Cinematic Genius Who Directed It," *Cinefantastique*, September, 1984, Vol. 14 No. 4 / Vol. 14 No. 5, pages 67-68

"After that screening I drove over to Fred Elmes's house..." Chris Rodley, *Lynch on Lynch*, page 83

"Magicians keep their secrets to themselves..." Chris Rodley, *Lynch on Lynch*, page 78

"Because he couldn't pay us..." K. George Godwin, "*Eraserhead*: The Story behind the Strangest Film Ever Made, and the Cinematic Genius Who Directed It," *Cinefantastique*, September, 1984, Vol. 14 No. 4 / Vol. 14 No. 5, page 63

"There was a sense of collaboration..." K. George Godwin, "*Eraserhead*: The Story behind the Strangest Film Ever Made, and the Cinematic Genius Who Directed It," *Cinefantastique*, September, 1984, Vol. 14 No. 4 / Vol. 14 No. 5, page 63

Someone to Love

"You have a different way of making movies..." *Someone to Love*

"I was alone, and I didn't understand why..." author interview

"There will never be an action sequence..." Marianne Cotter, "The Life & Times of Henry Jaglom," *Moviemaker*, May, 1994

"Most people spend their time..." Prairie Miller, "Deja Vu: Interview with Henry Jaglom," *www.minireviews.com/interviews/jaglom.htm*

"There's no such thing as too personal..." West 57th Interview, *www.goingshopping-themovie.com/*

"I figured out once that I made one of my movies..." West 57th Interview, *www.goingshopping-themovie.com/*

"He allowed me, finally and for the first time..." West 57th Interview, *www. goingshopping-themovie.com/*

"I thought it was fitting, somehow..." West 57th Interview, *www. goingshopping-themovie.com/*

"I hate rehearsal." author interview

"In the case of *Someone to Love*..." author interview

"The most truthful moments..." author interview

"If you surprise yourself..." "The Independent's Independent," *Moviemaker*, Issue No. 14, July/August 1995, page 30

"The best stuff in the world can happen the first time..." *Who Is Henry Jaglom*, directed by Henry Alex Rubin and Jeremy Workman

"I had a plan, a super structure..." author interview

"I didn't set out to work this way..." author interview

"Orson always said that the difference between me..." Clive Johnson, *www. londonstudent.org.uk/7issue/film/jaglom.htm*

"I knew all the people in *Someone to Love* ..." author interview

"If I had had Henry as a father or a husband..." *Who Is Henry Jaglom*, directed by Henry Alex Rubin and Jeremy Workman

"I keep the economics down..." "The Independent's Independent," *Moviemaker*, Issue No. 14, July/August 1995, page 30

"I was complaining about not having more time..." author interview

"If you don't have any limitations..." "The Independent's Independent," *Moviemaker*, Issue No. 14, July/August 1995, page 30

"For me the most valuable lesson from Orson..." author interview

"Never depend on it for your financing..." Henry Jaglom, "Lessons From Orson," *Moviemaker*, Issue No. 10, November 1994

"This is a great time to be an independent filmmaker..." "The Independent's Independent," *Moviemaker*, Issue No. 14, July/August 1995, page 45

"I really am the only person I know in this town that's happy..." West 57th Interview, *www.goingshopping-themovie.com/*

"From watching Orson deal with Hollywood..." West 57th Interview, *www. goingshopping-themovie.com/*

"You may love my films, you may hate my films..." Marianne Cotter, "The Life & Times of Henry Jaglom," *Moviemaker*, May, 1994

CHAPTER FIVE: FAKE OUT!

David Holzman's Diary

"I was very interested in Cinema Verité" author interview

"People were really passionate about this idea..." author interview

"We set about doing this book..." author interview

"There was always in my mind an image..." Joseph Gelmis, *The Film Director as Superstar*, pages 14-15

"Jim had conceived of this..." author interview

"On my Easter break from college in Texas..." author interview

"Over a period of three months..." Joseph Gelmis, *The Film Director as Superstar*, page 12

"I came back from Texas..." author interview

"I know that this film is an important..." author interview

"You don't understand the basic principle..." *David Holzman's Diary*, written by Jim McBride and L.M. Kit Carson

"In 1966 I was working at a company... author interview

"So all of a sudden, two events happen..." author interview

"For those parts of the film that took..." author interview

"He would do it again and together we refined..." Joseph Gelmis, *The Film Director as Superstar*, page 15

"We were satisfied that we had the shape of the scene..." author interview

"I like the idea of not filtering the moment..." author interview

"It's a lot simpler when it's just one person...." author interview

The Last Broadcast

"Stefan and I got excited about..." author interview

"I remember the shock when..." author interview

"We had wanted to make a movie for no money..." author interview

"Not having any money made us..." author interview

"Having no money gave us a..." author interview

"We had no shortage of people..." author interview

"Throughout the process..." *The Last Broadcast*, DVD Commentary

"We called it Theater of the Minimal..." author interview

"We knew that if we cast..." author interview

"We joked that the first thing we tried..." author interview

"I would hope that a filmmaker has figured out..." author interview

"Having good legal representation..." author interview

"A lot of times when people are..." author interview

"Sometimes people get caught up in their vision..." author interview

"I think when you know a story..." author interview

"*The Last Broadcast*. Worst ending ever? Maybe." James Berardinelli, *http://movie-reviews.colossus.net/movies/l/last_broadcast.html*

"The ending was one of the first things..." author interview

"I was hoping people would be as pissed off..." author interview

"The movie really takes you on this ride..." author interview

"Because the movie didn't cost anything to make..." author interview

"We started thinking, 'we've been digital this long...'" author interview

The Blair Witch Project
"When we did the film..." Richard Corliss, *"Blair Witch* Craft,*" Time*, August 16, 1999
"Ed and I were both fans of the *In Search of...*" author interview
"We just wanted to make a scary movie..." *Fortean Times*, November 1999, FT 128, *www.forteantimes.com*
"For most of that ride, we were on the outside..." author interview
"I definitely think it was a convergence..." author interview
"I think *The Blair Witch Project* is an exceptionally well-conceived..." Andrew J. Rausch, "An Interview with Roger Corman," *www.imagesjournal.com*
"I think Hitchcock once said that 90%..." author interview
"Start of with a good idea..." Cliff Stephenson, "Scaring Up the Blair Witch with Eduardo Sanchez," *www.dvdfile.com*
"I read an ad in *Backstage* in New York..." "Interview with Heather Donahue of *The Blair Witch Project*," *KAOS Magazine*, *www.kaos2000.net*
"When we signed on to do the project..." Brett Mannes, "Something Wicked," *www.salon.com*, July 13, 1999
"We hated a lot of traditional fake documentaries..." author interview
"We took the Method approach..." Richard Corliss, *"Blair Witch* Craft," *Time*, August 16, 1999
"Our theory was, let's shoot this like a documentary..." Richard Corliss, *"Blair Witch* Craft," *Time*, August 16, 1999
"Pretty much everything you see being done to the actors..." *Fortean Times*, November 1999, FT 128, *www.forteantimes.com*
"We'd go out on our raids and scare them..." Richard Corliss, *"Blair Witch* Craft," *Time*, August 16, 1999
"I think we came away with what looked very natural..." Richard Corliss, *"Blair Witch* Craft," *Time*, August 16, 1999
"We initially shot two phases of *Blair Witch...*" author interview
"We knew it was different, and a risk..." Richard Corliss, *"Blair Witch* Craft," *Time*, August 16, 1999
"It was a very tough decision for us to jettison..." author interview
"Once you get so close to the editing process..." *Fortean Times*, November 1999, FT 128, *www.forteantimes.com*
"We screened a very long cut of the student's footage..." author interview
"We had this three-picture deal, post-*Blair Witch...*" author interview

Lisa Picard Is Famous
"Truth is really, really small..." L.M. Kit Carson as David Holzman in *Lisa Picard Is Famous*
"It started with just some monologues..." author interview
"About fifty pages later..." author interview

"When I first read what Nat and Laura wrote..." author interview
"Did you know that Fame..." Buck Henry in *Lisa Picard Is Famous*
"I just thought it needed a bigger perspective..." author interview
"A lot of the criticism that we faced..." author interview
"They did the first cut, or maybe the second cut..." author interview
"Afterwards I said, 'Griffin, you have to implicate...'" author interview
"The digital video thing had just begun..." author interview
"The exciting thing for me..." "Griffin Dunne's Famous," *DGA Magazine,*
    www.dga.org
"A director's job is to be the most prepared..." author interview
"It struck me that working digitally..." "Griffin Dunne's Famous," *DGA*
    Magazine,www.dga.org
"With movies I'd done before..." author interview
"I remember that we changed it to yogurt..." author interview
"How did we get clearance..." author interview
"Like most real documentaries..." "Griffin Dunne's Famous," *DGA Magazine,*
    www.dga.org
"Everything that could go wrong..." Andy Rose, "What They Really Want to
    Do Is Direct," *www.moviemaker.com*
"It was complicated..." Anthony Kaufman, "Griffin Dunne Is 'Famous',"
    www.indiewire.com
"So, because of all the footage I shot..." author interview
"We were the soldiers who other..." Andy Rose, "What They Really Want to
    Do Is Direct," *www.moviemaker.com*

CHAPTER SIX: THE NEW ESTABLISHMENT

sex, lies and videotape

"If I had a nickel for every prospectus..." John Pierson, *Spike, Mike, Slackers*
    & Dykes, page 131
"After *sex, lies and videotape*, the festival..." John Anderson, *Sundancing:*
    Hanging Out And Listening In At America's Most Important Film
    Festival, page 5
"Having made only one feature film..." Steven Soderbergh, *sex, lies and*
    videotape, page 6
"I think you have an idea..." author interview
"In the case of Andie..." author interview
"I was ambivalent when his name was first brought up..." Steven Soderbergh,
    sex, lies and videotape, page 50
"Jimmy gave me the best compliment an actor could give me..." Steven
    Soderbergh, *sex, lies and videotape*, page 235

"From now on, I'll assume an actor can do anything..." Steven Soderbergh, *sex, lies and videotape*, page 50
"It happened to me the other day..." author interview
"So you have to keep your prejudices in check..." author interview
"Rehearsals for me are not about exploring the piece..." *sex, lies and videotape*, DVD Commentary
"This quartet was a classic example of how each actor..." *sex, lies and videotape*, DVD Commentary
"If you drift off compass a couple of degrees..." *sex, lies and videotape*, DVD Commentary
"A feature-length resume piece..." *sex, lies and videotape*, DVD Commentary
"The great thing about that was that all of us felt pretty free..." *sex, lies and videotape*, DVD Commentary
"On that movie..." author interview
"*Out of Sight* cost $49 million..." sex, lies and videotape, DVD Commentary
"Day off felt good. Saw *Tucker: The Man and His Dream*..." Steven Soderbergh, *sex, lies and videotape*, page 185
"I'm more and more finding ways..." author interview
"The benefit of having several projects..." author interview
"It's all very personal..." author interview
"As my career has gone on..." author interview
"For those aspiring to a career in the film business..." Steven Soderbergh, *sex, lies and videotape*, page 7
"I think the reason a lot of suddenly successful people..." Steven Soderbergh, *sex, lies and videotape*, page 249
"My definition of success..." author interview

Slacker
"I was awed by *Slacker*..." Stephen Lowenstein, *My First Movie: 20 Celebrated Directors Talk About Their First Film*, page 74
"I remember I was driving to Houston..." *Slacker*, DVD Commentary
"I sat down and went through my notebooks..." *Slacker*, DVD Commentary
"That's one thing about the movie..." *Slacker*, DVD Commentary
"What *Bullit* is to San Francisco..." *Slacker*, DVD Commentary
"People are crazy everywhere..." *Slacker*, DVD Commentary
"I always felt regular life was worthy of a movie..." Richard Linklater, *Slacker*, page 17
"If you are going to do a low-budget film..." Richard Linklater, *Slacker*, page 120
"It was a total experiment that could very well..." Richard Linklater, *Slacker*, page 20
"*Slacker* was made exactly opposite of the way..." Richard Linklater, *Slacker*, pages 117-118

"My favorite review was in *Playboy*..." *Slacker*, DVD Commentary
"I remember watching Siskel and Ebert..." *Slacker*, DVD Commentary
"We pulled off stuff with this movie..." *Slacker*, DVD Commentary
"Your limitations dictate everything." *Slacker*, DVD Commentary
"Make your liabilities into your assets..." *Slacker*, DVD Commentary
"Filmmaking is an unfolding..." Richard Linklater, *Slacker*, page 129
"The biggest obstacle..." Richard Linklater, *Slacker*, pages 125-126
"For every film festival it got accepted to..." David Walsh, "You Can't Hold Back the Human Spirit," *www.wsws.org/art*, March 27, 1998
"You are living in an entirely different world..." Richard Linklater, *Slacker*, page 20
"At first, I'm a little depressed..." Richard Linklater, *Slacker*, page 20
"I always felt terrible about that..." *Slacker*, DVD Commentary

El Mariachi

"I didn't get sick, but I wanted to..." Roger Ebert, "The Learning Curve of a Novice Director," *Chicago Sun-Times*, March 14, 1993
"I was inventing my own film school..." Robert Rodriguez, *Rebel without a Crew*, page xvi
"I see a lot of first-time filmmakers..." Rustin Thompson, "The Reformation of a Rebel without a Crew," *Moviemaker Magazine*, Issue No. 15 Sept./Oct. 1995
"Even though this is a throwaway movie..." Robert Rodriguez, *Rebel without a Crew*, page 58
"You know, this logo probably cost more..." *El Mariachi*, DVD Commentary
"If they want to spruce it up..." Robert Rodriguez, *Rebel without a Crew*, page 135
"The Sony Suites." Robert Rodriguez, *Rebel without a Crew*, page 165
"Low-budget movies put a wall in front of you..." Robert Rodriguez, *Rebel without a Crew*, page 175
"With the $7,000 I had for *El Mariachi*..." Rustin Thompson, "The Reformation of a Rebel without a Crew," *Moviemaker Magazine*, Issue No. 15 Sept/Oct. 1995
"I saved money by writing the script around..." Robert Rodriguez, *Rebel without a Crew*, page 173
"I don't like to write in props we don't already have access..." Robert Rodriguez, *Rebel without a Crew*, page 31
"If you bleed for your money..." Robert Rodriguez, *Rebel without a Crew*, page 11
"It's been my experience that you're a lot more careful..." Robert Rodriguez, *Rebel without a Crew*, page 9
"I got ripped off..." Robert Rodriguez, *Rebel without a Crew*, page 37

"Everyone who sees it thinks..." Robert Rodriguez, *Rebel without a Crew*, page 140

"By not having a crew..." Robert Rodriguez, *Rebel without a Crew*, page 144

"I had to put so many cuts..." Rustin Thompson, "The Reformation of a Rebel without a Crew," *Moviemaker Magazine*, Issue No. 15 Sept./Oct. 1995

"I was shooting with this real noisy old camera..." Rustin Thompson, "The Reformation of a Rebel without a Crew," *Moviemaker Magazine*, Issue No. 15 Sept/Oct. 1995

"Take advantage of your disadvantages..." Robert Rodriguez, *Rebel without a Crew*, pages 203 – 204

"Trust me, there are extreme benefits to being able to walk..." Robert Rodriguez, *Rebel without a Crew*, page 198

Clerks

"Kevin Smith will never be a famous writer..." John Pierson, *Spike, Mike, Slackers & Dykes*, page 123

"It was a real eye-opening experience..." PBS Frontline, *The Monster that Ate Hollywood*, Interviews: Kevin Smith, www.pbs.org

"Licensed by Kevin Smith, Silent Bob's Coat..." www.viewaskew.com

"While it was a $27,000 movie, it certainly..." John Pierson, *Spike, Mike, Slackers & Dykes*, page 231

"Within the limitations of his bare-bones production..." Roger Ebert, November 4, 1994, www.rogerebert.com

"A blend of Howard Stern and David Mamet." John Pierson, *Spike, Mike, Slackers & Dykes*, page 293

"I went for hands-on, technical stuff...'" *An Evening with Kevin Smith*, DVD

"If you go to NYU or USC or UCLA..." *"Clerks* Prove Ignorance Is Bliss," *Moviemaker Magazine*, Issue No. 10, November 1994

"Dave gave us this wish list of all the..." *"Clerks* Prove Ignorance Is Bliss," *Moviemaker Magazine*, Issue No. 10, November 1994

"It was scary, but to put it in context..." John Kenneth Muir, *An Askew View*, page 45

"It's all about the script..." Keith Phillips, *The Onion AV Club*, www.theonion.om

"We shot most of the movie at night..." *Clerks*, DVD Commentary

"All the improvisation was from Jason..." *"Clerks* Prove Ignorance Is Bliss," *Moviemaker Magazine*, Issue No. 10, November 1994

"Kevin would get the actors..." John Kenneth Muir, *An Askew View*, page 35

"Kodak had a program for film school students..." Stephen Lowenstein, *My First Movie 20 Celebrated Directors Talk About Their First Film*, page 83

"I thought the script was funny..." John Kenneth Muir, *An Askew View*, page 39

"To me it was like, that's the ultimate joke..." Stephen Lowenstein, *My First Movie 20 Celebrated Directors Talk About Their First Film*, page 96

"Right before we went to Sundance..." Stephen Lowenstein, *My First Movie 20 Celebrated Directors Talk About Their First Film*, page 96

"We met (Hollywood producer) Jim..." John Kenneth Muir, *An Askew View*, pages 62-63

"And I said, *Mallrats*..." *"Clerks* Prove Ignorance Is Bliss,*" Moviemaker Magazine*, Issue No. 10, November 1994

"So before *Clerks* ever came out..." John Kenneth Muir, *An Askew View*, pages 62-63

"What it did more than anything financially..." John Pierson, *Spike, Mike, Slackers & Dykes*, page 233

"The little sonic boom with dirt on it." *Clerks*, DVD Commentary

"What's important is kind of the simple things..." *PBS Frontline, The Monster that Ate Hollywood, Interviews: Kevin Smith, www.pbs.org*

"The executive said words I will never forget..." *An Evening with Kevin Smith*, DVD

Swingers

"I really thought that the only people..." *Swingers* DVD: *"Making It in Hollywood" Documentary*

"When I wrote *Swingers*..." Jon Favreau, *Swingers Screenplay* (Preface)

"This was meant to be a resume film..." *Swingers*, DVD Commentary

"If super-experienced people..." *Swingers*, DVD Commentary

"*Swingers* was all sincerity..." author interview

"They wanted to change everything..." *Swingers* Screenplay, By Jon Favreau (Preface)

"I said, 'Let me show you the script ...'" *Swingers* DVD: *"Making It in Hollywood" Documentary*

"I said to them, I don't want to step..." *Swingers* DVD: *"Making It in Hollywood" Documentary*

"I'm a big believer that limitations..." *Swingers* DVD: *"Making It in Hollywood" Documentary*

"Doug said 'Let's have a lot of money..." *Swingers* DVD: *"Making It in Hollywood" Documentary*

"Doug had a background in making student films..." author interview

"It wasn't a true story..." author interview

"If you stick to things that you know..." author interview

"Part of my strategy for shooting this film..." *Swingers*, DVD Commentary

"We ended up scheduling 18 of the days..." *Swingers* DVD: *"Making It in Hollywood" Documentary*

"The movie wouldn't be the movie..." *Swingers* DVD: *"Making It in*

Hollywood" Documentary
"For the opening sequence..." author interview
"Total cost, around $300..." *Swingers*, DVD Commentary
"When you're shooting photos..." author interview
"Images don't have to be moving..." author interview
"If we'd had the money to do..." *Swingers*, DVD Commentary
"We cheated. We cheated a little bit..." author interview
"We threw in some cursory explanation..." author interview
"The whole movie you're hoping..." author interview
"It all goes to emotion..." author interview

CHAPTER SEVEN: THE DIGITAL REALM

The Anniversary Party
"We were in *Cabaret* together on Broadway..." author interview
"Jennifer had made this Dogme film in Africa..." author interview
"I was really intrigued by the digital video wave..." Andy Rose, "What They
     Really Want To Do Is Direct," *www.moviemaker.com*
"I've worked on films..." Holly Willis, "Party Crashers," *Res*, Vol. 4, No. 3,
     May/June 2001, page 40
"People understand the notion..." author interview
"Our film was lucky to get made..." Holly Willis, "Party Crashers," *Res*, Vol.
     4, No. 3, May/June 2001, page 41
"Biggest lesson..." author interview
"The decision to use digital video..." Holly Willis, "Party Crashers," *Res*, Vol.
     4, No. 3, May/June 2001, page 39
"One of the reasons why digital video works..." *The Anniversary Party*, DVD
     — *Anatomy of a Scene*
"It felt less intrusive..." *The Anniversary Party*, DVD — *Anatomy of a Scene*
"There were no dressing rooms..." Andy Rose, *"What They Really Want To
     Do Is Direct," www.moviemaker.com*
"In the end..." author interview
"You don't get that on film..." author interview
"That's what was great about doing *The Anniversary Party*..." *The
     Anniversary Party*, DVD Commentary
"Their kids are played by their kids..." *The Anniversary Party*, DVD
     Commentary
"For that scene..." author interview
"We shot their stuff and our reactions..." author interview
"You have to be really, really, really prepared..." author interview
"My storyboards are a little eclectic..." author interview
"I think it's really important not to be rigid..." author interview

"I think the best decision we made..." author interview
"We weren't particularly happy with the last scene..." author interview
"We don't know what will happen to them..." *The Anniversary Party*, DVD Commentary

Tadpole

"*Oedipus Rex* meets *The Graduate*..." Peter Travers, *Rolling Stone*, August 1, 2002
"There were no trailers to go into between shots..." author interview
"There were no frills; hair and make-up..." author interview
"The day before my first day of shooting..." author interview
"It was sort of like a CIA operation..." author interview
"I guess it's safe to talk about it..." author interview
"There's the economics of it..." author interview
"Not only were they open to digital..." author interview
"It's really fun to make a movie with digital..." *Tadpole*, video press kit
"Sometimes it seemed like anybody..." *Tadpole*, video press kit
"I storyboarded the film..." *Tadpole*, DVD commentary
"I knew the blocking..." author interview
"I went to a Toys R Us and bought a Sit-And-Spin..." author interview
"I had a really, really, really unfortunate experience..." author interview
"And that's when I came up with the Voltaire quotes..." author interview
"We came up with the characters first..." author interview
"When you're making a low budget film..." author interview
"I have $84 million now for *Charlotte's*..." author interview

Dopamine

"I'd done a couple of shorts..." author interview
"So we went there not expecting anything..." *Dopamine*, DVD Commentary
"We had a meeting with one of our advisors..." author interview
"The conflict between two characters..." author interview
"The genesis of the story for me..." author interview
"Dopamine is the natural amphetamine..."Michelle Talks LOVE with Director Marc Decena, and "Slider's" Sabrina Lloyd!!!," *Eclipsemagazine.com*, posted 2003/10/21
"Lysergic acid diethylamide..." author interview
"I think the biggest reason for me to shoot digital..."author interview
"It wasn't necessarily the look..." Jennifer M. Wood, "Digital by Design: A Conversation with *Dopamine* Writer-Director Mark Decena," *Moviemaker.com*
"I was able to run master shots..." author interview
"We had one week of rehearsal..." author interview

"Rehearsal was amazing for us..." *Dopamine*, DVD Commentary
"They say that 90% of directing is casting..." author interview
"We definitely were still writing..." *Dopamine*, DVD Commentary
"After the assembly cut was done..." author interview
"I think in writing a first time script..." *Dopamine*, DVD Commentary
"We wanted to work the festival..." Brian O'Hare, "Schmooze Like a
    Champion," *Moviemaker*, Issue No. 56, Vol. 11, Fall 2004, page 19
"After about three days..." Brian O'Hare, "Schmooze Like a Champion,"
    Moviemaker, Issue No. 56, Vol. 11, Fall 2004, page 19

Melvin Goes to Dinner
"My wife went to see the play..." Matt Mulcahey, Interview with Bob
    Odenkirk, *Hollywood Bitchslap.com*, March 31, 2003
"I saw the play a couple times..." author interview
"We used five cameras, so everybody is on camera..." author interview
"I felt we needed to commit to one person's story..." author interview
"When I sat down to write the screenplay..." author interview
"I'd been working as an editor for a while..." author interview
"The disadvantage of using the original cast..." author interview
"The negative is that there's no way..." author interview
"There would have been a re-write of the piece..." *Melvin Goes to Dinner*,
    DVD Commentary
"Ultimately, you're going to live with your film..." author interview
"Of course one of the goals for any production..." Matt Mulcahey, Interview
    with Bob Odenkirk, *Hollywood Bitchslap.com*, March 31, 2003
"I thought having a few name people would help..." author interview
"I do think the cameos help." author interview
"They're little boosts..." *Melvin Goes to Dinner*, DVD Commentary
"It helps people to consider the movie legitimate." author interview
"Jack, David, and Maura were all friends of mine..." author interview
"Melora Walters was the only cameo..." author interview
"The thing I'm most happy about is that those people..." author interview
"One of the things that I settled on quickly was that..." author interview
"It feels like a memory, it feels like just pieces..." author interview
"You can tell stories with stills..." author interview
"You've got to be patient once you hit the set..." author interview

Open Water
"We read this story about this couple..." *Open Water*, DVD, *Calm Before the
    Storm: Making Open Water* documentary
"What attracted us to this story..." Chris Kentis interview, *www.
    horrorchannel.com*

"I wanted to do this in a very linear way..." Edward Boyce, "The Last Bite,"
   Filmmaker, Vol. 12, #4, Summer 2004, page 51
"We were really anxious to try to make a movie..." author interview
"No one can ever really predict..." *Open Water*, DVD, *The Indie Essentials:*
   Gearing Up for a Marketable Movie documentary
"We knew purposefully..." *Open Water*, DVD, *Calm Before the Storm:*
   Making Open Water documentary
"So much of the film was trying to take..." author interview
"These sharks have actually..." *Open Water*, DVD Commentary
"We could really experiment and play..." *Open Water*, DVD Commentary
"We wanted total control..." Edward Boyce, "The Last Bite," *Filmmaker*, Vol.
   12, #4, Summer 2004, page 51
"It's always difficult to get financing..." author interview
"The first advantage of taking our time..." author interview
"We were three days away..." *Open Water*, DVD Commentary
"If you're working alone..." author interview
"We were going to take two unknown actors..." author interview
"There was no way in the film we were ever..." author interview
"The whole impetus behind this story..." author interview
"People have asked us a lot about..." *Open Water*, DVD Commentary
"Ending-wise, we always knew..." *Open Water*, DVD Commentary
"Because the film was based on a true story..." author interview
"That was the whole point of the project..." author interview

CHAPTER EIGHT: THE LESSONS REDUX

"When people ask me if I went to film school..." Phillip Williams, "A Singular
   Vision," *Moviemaker*, Issue No. 58, Vol. 12, Spring 2005, page 68

THE MOVIES

The majority of the movies in the book are available on DVD; the rest can be found on VHS, either new or for sale used somewhere on-line. All are worth a look.

The Anniversary Party — © 2001, Fine Line Features, © 2002 New Line Home Entertainment, Inc.

The Blair Witch Project — © 1999, Blair Witch Film Partners, Ltd., Artisan Home Entertainment

Caged Heat — © 1974, Artists Entertainment Complex, Inc., © 2001 Concorde-New Horizon Corp.

Carnival of Souls — © 1987, Harold Harvey and John Clifford, © 2000, The Criterion Collection

Clerks — © 1994, Buena Vista Home Entertainment

Dark Star — © 1974, Jack H. Harris Enterprises, © 2001 Blair & Associates, Ltd.

David Holzman's Diary — © 1967, 1993, Fox Lorber Video

Dementia 13 (1963) — © 2002, Navarre Video

Dopamine — © 2004, Sundance Channel LLC

El Mariachi — © 1993, Columbia Pictures

Eraserhead — © 2002, Absurda

Grand Theft Auto — © 1977 New World Pictures, Inc., ™ 2002 Concorde-New Horizon Corp.

In the Company of Men — © 1997 Company One Productions, © 1997 Columbia TriStar Home Video

Judy Berlin — © 2000, Shooting Gallery

The Last Broadcast — © 1999, Wavelength Releasing

The Little Shop of Horrors — © MMII Passion Productions

Lisa Picard Is Famous — © 2001, Greenstreet Films, First Look Media Inc.

Melvin Goes to Dinner — © 2003, Sundance Channel L.L.C.

Monty Python and the Holy Grail — © National Film Trustee Company, Python (Monty) Pictures, Ltd., Columbia Home Video

Night of the Living Dead — © 1968, Elite Entertainment

Open Water — © 2004, MMIV Plunge Pictures, LLC, MMIV Lions Gate Entertainment

Patti Rocks — © 1987, FilmDallas Pictures, Virgin Vision

π — © 1998, Protozoa Pictures, Artisan Entertainment

Return of the Secaucus Seven — © 2003 Anarchists' Convention and IFC Films

sex, lies and videotape — ©1989, Outlaw Productions, Columbia Home Video

Shadows — © 1960, Gena Enterprises, Castle Hill Productions

Slacker — © 1991, Detour, Inc., © 2004 The Criterion Collection

Someone to Love — © 1987 International Rainbow Pictures, Paramount Home Video

Swingers — © 1996, Buena Vista Home Entertainment

Symbiopsychotaxiplasm: Take One — ©, 1971, William Greaves Productions, Inc.

Tadpole — © 2002, Buena Vista Home Entertainment

Targets — ©1967, Saticoy Productions, © 2003 Paramount Pictures

What Happened Was... — © 1994, The Samuel Goldwyn Company

The author acknowledges the copyright owners of the preceding home video releases from which images have been used in this book for purposes of commentary, criticism and scholarship under the Fair Use Doctrine.

No endorsement or sponsorship of this book by the copyright owners is claimed or implied. Images have been reproduced as a guide to readers who may wish to buy or rent films analyzed by the author.

BIBLIOGRAPHY

Books

Alexander, John, *The Films of David Lynch*. London: Charles Letts & Co., 1993

Anderson, John, *Sundancing: Hanging Out and Listening In at America's Most Important Film Festival*. New York: Avon Books, 2000

Aronofsky, Darren, *π — The Guerilla Diaries*. New York: Faber and Faber, 1998

Bliss, Michael and Christina Banks, *What Goes Around Comes Around: The Films of Jonathan Demme*. Carbondale and Edwardsville: Southern Illinois University Press, 1996

Boulenger, Gilles, *John Carpenter — The Prince of Darkness*. Los Angeles: Silman-James Press, 2003

Carney, Ray, *Cassavetes on Cassavetes*. New York: Faber and Faber, 2001

Corman, Roger, *How I Made a Hundred Movies in Hollywood and Never Lost a Dime*. New York: Dell Publishing, 1991

Favreau, Jon, *Swingers Screenplay*. New York: Hyperion, 1996

Gelmis, Joseph, *The Film Director as Superstar*. New York: Doubleday, 1970

Gray, Beverly, *Roger Corman: An Unauthorized Biography of the Godfather of Indie Filmmaking*. Los Angeles: Renaissance Books, 2000

Hughes, David, *The Complete Lynch*. London: Virgin Books, 2003

Jacobs, Diane, *Hollywood Renaissance*. New York: Dell Publishing, 1977

Jarecki, Nicholas, *Breaking In*. New York: Broadway Books, 2001

Linklater, Richard, *Slacker*. New York: St. Martin's Press, 1992

Lowenstein, Stephen, *My First Movie: 20 Celebrated Directors Talk About Their First Film*. New York: Penguin Books, 2000

Maugham, W. Somerset, *Sheppey: A Play in Three Acts*, Methuen Drama-Random House, The Royal Literary Fund

Morgan, David, *Monty Python Speaks!* New York: Avon Books, 1999

Muir, John Kenneth, *An Askew View*. New York: Applause Theatre & Cinema, 2002

Naha, Ed, *The Films of Roger Corman: Brilliance on a Budget*. New York: Arco Publishing, 1982

Pierson, John, *Spike, Mike, Slackers & Dykes*. New York: Hyperion, 1995

Phillips, Gene D., *Godfather: The Intimate Francis Ford Coppola*. Lexington: The University Press of Kentucky, 2004

Pythons, The (with Bob McCabe), *The Pythons Autobiography*. New York: Thomas Dunner Books, St. Martin's Press, 2003

Rodley, Chris, *Lynch on Lynch*. London: Faber and Faber, 1997

Rodriguez, Robert, *Rebel without a Crew*. New York: Plume/Penguin Group, 1996

Rosen, David, with Hamilton, Pete, *Off-Hollywood*. New York: Grove Weidenfeld, 1987

Russo, John, *The Complete Night of the Living Dead Filmbook*. New York: Harmony Books, 1985

Sherman, Eric, *Directing the Film*. Boston: Little, Brown and Company, 1976

Smith, Gavin, *Sayles on Sayles*. London: Faber and Faber, 1998

Soderbergh, Steven, *sex, lies and videotape*. New York: Harper & Row, 1990

Thomas, Bob, *Directors in Action*. Indianapolis, New York: Bobbs-Merrill, 1968

Zinman, David, *Fifty Grand Movies of the 1960s and 1970s*. New York: Crown, 1986

Periodicals

Boyce, Edward, "The Last Bite," *Filmmaker*, Vol. 12, No. 4, Summer 2004

"*Clerks* Prove Ignorance Is Bliss," *Moviemaker Magazine*, Issue No. 10, November 1994

Corliss, Richard, "*Blair Witch* Craft," *Time*, August 16, 1999

Cotter, Marianne, "The Life & Times of Henry Jaglom," *Moviemaker*, May, 1994

Dietric, Christopher S. with Beckman, Peter, "Barbara Steele: Queen of Horror," *Imagi-Movies*, Spring 1994

Ebert, Roger, *Chicago Sun-Times*, August 15, 1968

Ebert, Roger, *Chicago Sun-Times*, Oct. 27, 1989

Ebert, Roger, "The Learning Curve of a Novice Director," *Chicago Sun-Times*, March 14, 1993

Eggers, Dave, "Sixteen Tons of Fun: Eric Idle Brings the Holy Grail to Broadway," *The New Yorker*, December 20 & 27, 2004

Frentzen, Jeffrey, "Herk Harvey's *Carnival of Souls*," *Cinefantastique*, Vol 13 No 6 / Vol 14 No 1

Godwin, K. George, "*Eraserhead*: The Story behind the Strangest Film Ever Made, and the Cinematic Genius Who Directed It," *Cinefantastique*, September, 1984, Vol 14 No 4 / Vol 14 No 5

Hamlin, Andrew, "It Came from Roger Corman," *Moviemaker*, Issue No. 42, Vol. 8

Hayes, Matthew, *Montreal Mirror*, September 4, 1997

"The Independent's Independent," *Moviemaker*, Issue No. 14, July/August 1995

Jaglom, Henry, "Lessons from Orson," *Moviemaker*, Issue No. 10, November 1994

Johnson, Clive, *www.londonstudent.org.uk/7issue/film/jaglom.htm*

LaSalle, Mick, "Judy Berlin Finds the Poetry in Suburban Lives," *San Francisco Chronicle*, Friday, February 25, 2000

London Student, Vol. 18, Issue 10

Lybarger, Dan, "Digital Souls: An Interview with Maurice Prather on *Carnival of Souls*," February 3, 2000. Originally appeared in the February 3–9, 2000 issue of *Pitch Weekly*

McCarthy, Todd, "Auteur Opie," *Film Comment*, May/June 1984

MacDonald, Scott, "Sunday in the Park with Bill," *The Independent,* May, 1992

O'Hare, Brian, "Schmooze Like a Champion," *Moviemaker*, Issue No. 56, Vol. 11, Fall 2004

Persons, Dan, "Pi — Searching For The Mathematical Secrets of the Universe," *Cinefantastique*, Vol. 30, No. 4, August, 1998

Persons, Dan, "The Corman Connection," *Cinefantastique*, February, 1992

Persons, Mitch, *Cinefantastique*, Vol. 31, No. 5

Pfeifer, Ellen, "Opie Grows Up," *Herald American* (Boston), July 30, 1982

Rose, Andy, "What They Really Want to Do Is Direct," *www.moviemaker.com*

Schweiger, Daniel, *"Carnival of Souls,"* *Cinefantastique*, May 1990, Vol. 20, No. 5

Surmacz, Gary Anthony, "Anatomy of a Horror Film," *Cinefantastique*, Vol. 4

Thompson, Rustin, "The Reformation of a Rebel without a Crew," *Moviemaker Magazine*, Issue No. 15 Sept/Oct. 1995

Travers, Peter, *Rolling Stone*, August 1, 2002

Van Gelder, Lawrence, "Demolition Derby," *The New York Times*, September 29, 1977

Williams Phillip, "A Singular Vision," *Moviemaker*, Issue No. 58, Vol. 12, Spring 2005

Willis, Holly, "Party Crashers," *Res*, Vol. 4, No. 3, May/June 2001

Winogura, Dale, *Cinefantastique*, Vol. 3, No. 4

Videos/DVDs
AFI: The Directors: Roger Corman
The Anniversary Party
Caged Heat
Carnival of Souls

A Constant Forge
David Holzman's Diary
Dopamine
El Mariachi
Eraserhead
An Evening with Kevin Smith
Grand Theft Auto
I'm Almost Not Crazy ... John Cassavetes: The Man and His Work
In the Company of Men
Judy Berlin
The Last Broadcast
Lisa Picard Is Famous
Melvin Goes to Dinner
Monty Python and the Holy Grail
Night of the Living Dead
Open Water
Return of the Living Dead
Return of the Secaucus Seven
sex, lies and videotape
Slacker
Someone to Love
Swingers
Symbiopsychotaxiplasm: Take One
Tadpole
Who Is Henry Jaglom?

Radio
All Things Considered, National Public Radio, Sunday, January 23, 2005

Websites
Anderson, Jeffrey M., Darren Aronofsky: Easy as 3.14, *www. combustiblecelluloid.com*, June, 1998
Berardinelli, James, *http://movie-reviews.colossus.net/movies/l/last_broadcast. html*
Carli, Vittorio, Sayles Has Learned Film Success Without Selling Out, *www. artinterviews.com*
Chase, Andrea, *www.chitchatmagazinecom*
Chris Kentis interview, www.horrorchannel.com
Ebert, Roger, November 4, 1994, *www.rogerebert.com*
Fortean Times, November 1999, FT 128, *www.forteantimes.com*
Fuchs, Cynthia, Alone Inside Our Own Skins, Interview with Eric Mendelsohn, *www.popmatters.com*

Geffner, David, DGA Interview with Darren Aronofsky, *www.dga.org*

"Griffin Dunne's Famous," *DGA Magazine, www.dga.org*

"Interview with Heather Donahue of *The Blair Witch Project*," *KAOS Magazine, www.kaos2000.net*

JaxomLOTUS, Interview with Darren Aronofsky, *www.worth1000.com*, October 19, 2000

Kaufman, Anthony, "Griffin Dunne Is 'Famous'," *www.indiewire.com*

Kaufman, Anthony, An Interview with Darren Aronofsky and Sean Gullette, *www.indiewire.com*, January 21, 1998

Klein, Joshua, *The Onion, www.theonion.com*

Lee, Daniel, A Talk with Eric Mendelsohn, Director of *Judy Berlin, www.reel.com*

Mannes, Brett, "Something Wicked," *www.salon.com*, July 13, 1999

"Michelle Talks LOVE with Director Marc Decena, and Slider's Sabrina Lloyd!!!," *Eclipsemagazine.com*, Posted 2003/10/21

Miller, Prairie, "Deja Vu: Interview With Henry Jaglom," *www.minireviews.com/interviews/jaglom.htm*

Morris, Gary, "Fun in the New World," *www.brightlightsfilm.com*

Mulcahey, Matt, Interview with Bob Odenkirk, *Hollywood Bitchslap.com*, March 31, 2003

Noonan, Tom, *www.tomnoonan.com*

PBS Frontline, *The Monster that Ate Hollywood, Interviews: Kevin Smith www.pbs.org*

Phillips, Keith, *The Onion AV Club, www.theonion.om*

Rausch, Andrew J., "An Interview with Roger Corman," *www.imagesjournal.com*

Rose, Andy, "What They Really Want to Do Is Direct," *www.moviemaker.com*

Sony Classics Pictures, *In the Company of Men, (www.sonypictures.com/classics/)*

www.splicedonline.com

Stephenson, Cliff, "Scaring Up the Blair Witch with Eduardo Sanchez," *www.dvdfile.com*

Thompson, David, "Demme on Demme, Part 2: *Caged Heat* to *Fighting Mad,* Projections," *www.storefrontdemme.com*

Urban, Andrew L., Interview with Darren Aronofsky, *www.UrbanCinefile.com*

www.viewaskew.com

Walsh, David, "You Can't Hold Back the Human Spirit," *www.wsws.org/art*, March 27, 1998

West 57th interview, *www.goingshopping-themovie.com/*

Wood, Jennifer M., "Digital by Design: A Conversation with *Dopamine* Writer-Director Mark Decena," *www.moviemaker.com*

ABOUT
THE
AUTHOR

John Gaspard has directed and/or produced six low-budget features, including
the digital feature, *Grown Men*, which
premiered at the Ashland International
Film Festival and won the "Best of Fest/
Best Screenplay" award at the Black
Point Film Festival.

He directed and co-wrote the award-
winning feature film, *Beyond Bob*, and
directed the science-fiction comedy feature film, *Resident Alien*. He was also a
writer and story editor for the international television comedy/western
series, *Lucky Luke*, starring Terence Hill.

His screenplay, *The Sword and Mr. Stone* (co-written with Michael Levin)
was the first winner of the Barry Morrow Screenwriting Fellowship,
as well as a finalist at the Austin Heart of the Film Screenwriting
Competition.

John co-authored, with Dale Newton, the books *Digital Filmmaking 101:
An Essential Guide to Producing Low-Budget Movies* and *Persistence
of Vision: An Impractical Guide to Producing A Feature Film For Under
$30,000*, both published by Michael Wiese Productions.

He can be contacted via his website, *www.graniteproductions.org*.

FILM DIRECTING: SHOT BY SHOT
VISUALIZING FROM CONCEPT TO SCREEN

STEVEN D. KATZ

BEST SELLER
OVER 161,000 UNITS SOLD!

Film Directing: Shot by Shot — with its famous blue cover —
is the best-known book on directing and a favorite of
professional directors as an on-set quick reference guide.

This international bestseller is a complete catalog of visual
techniques and their stylistic implications, enabling working
filmmakers to expand their knowledge.

Contains in-depth information on shot composition, staging sequences, visualization tools,
framing and composition techniques, camera movement, blocking tracking shots, script
analysis, and much more.

Includes over 750 storyboards and illustrations, with never-before-published storyboards
from Steven Spielberg's *Empire of the Sun*, Orson Welles' *Citizen Kane*, and Alfred Hitchcock's
The Birds.

*"(To become a director) you have to teach yourself what makes movies good and what
makes them bad. John Singleton has been my mentor... he's the one who told me what
movies to watch and to read* Shot by Shot.*"*
> — *Ice Cube*, New York Times

*"A generous number of photos and superb illustrations accompany each concept, many of the
graphics being from Katz' own pen...* Film Directing: Shot by Shot *is a feast for the eyes."*
> — Videomaker Magazine

*"... demonstrates the visual techniques of filmmaking by defining the process whereby the
director converts storyboards into photographed scenes."*
> — Back Stage Shoot

"Contains an encyclopedic wealth of information."
> — Millimeter Magazine

STEVEN D. KATZ is also the author of *Film Directing: Cinematic Motion*.

$27.95 | 366 PAGES | ORDER # 7RLS | ISBN: 0-941188-10-8

24 HOURS | 1.800.833.5738 | WWW.MWP.COM

THE WRITER'S JOURNEY
2ND EDITION
MYTHIC STRUCTURE FOR WRITERS

CHRISTOPHER VOGLER

BEST SELLER
OVER 116,500 UNITS SOLD!

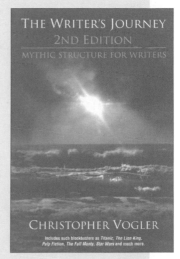

See why this book has become an international bestseller and a true classic. *The Writer's Journey* explores the powerful relationship between mythology and storytelling in a clear, concise style that's made it required reading for movie executives, screenwriters, playwrights, scholars, and fans of pop culture all over the world.

Both fiction and nonfiction writers will discover a set of useful myth-inspired storytelling paradigms (i.e., "The Hero's Journey") and step-by-step guidelines to plot and character development. Based on the work of Joseph Campbell, *The Writer's Journey* is a must for all writers interested in further developing their craft.

The updated and revised second edition provides new insights and observations from Vogler's ongoing work on mythology's influence on stories, movies, and man himself.

"This book is like having the smartest person in the story meeting come home with you and whisper what to do in your ear as you write a screenplay. Insight for insight, step for step, Chris Vogler takes us through the process of connecting theme to story and making a script come alive."
> — Lynda Obst, Producer
> Sleepless in Seattle, How to Lose a Guy in 10 Days
> *Author*, Hello, He Lied

"This is a book about the stories we write, and perhaps more importantly, the stories we live. It is the most influential work I have yet encountered on the art, nature, and the very purpose of storytelling."
> — Bruce Joel Rubin, Screenwriter
> Stuart Little 2, Deep Impact, Ghost, Jacob's Ladder

CHRISTOPHER VOGLER, a top Hollywood story consultant and development executive, has worked on such high-grossing feature films as *The Lion King, The Thin Red Line, Fight Club,* and *Beauty and the Beast.* He conducts writing workshops around the globe.

$24.95 | 325 PAGES | ORDER # 98RLS | ISBN: 0-941188-70-1

24 HOURS | 1.800.833.5738 | WWW.MWP.COM

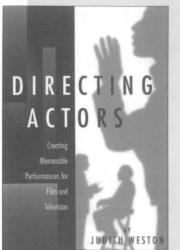

DIRECTING ACTORS
CREATING MEMORABLE PERFORMANCES FOR FILM AND TELEVISION

JUDITH WESTON

BEST SELLER
OVER 32,300 UNITS SOLD!

Directing film or television is a high-stakes occupation. It captures your full attention at every moment, calling on you to commit every resource and stretch yourself to the limit. It's the white-water rafting of entertainment jobs. But for many directors, the excitement they feel about a new project tightens into anxiety when it comes to working with actors.

This book provides a method for establishing creative, collaborative relationships with actors, getting the most out of rehearsals, troubleshooting poor performances, giving briefer directions, and much more. It addresses what actors want from a director, what directors do wrong, and constructively analyzes the director-actor relationship.

"Judith Weston is an extraordinarily gifted teacher."
> — David Chase, Emmy Award-Winning Writer,
> Director, and Producer
> The Sopranos, Northern Exposure, I'll Fly Away

"I believe that working with Judith's ideas and principles has been the most useful time I've spent preparing for my work. I think that if Judith's book were mandatory reading for all directors, the quality of the director-actor process would be transformed, and better drama would result."
> — John Patterson, Director
> Six Feet Under, CSI: Crime Scene Investigation,
> The Practice, Law and Order

"I know a great teacher when I find one! Everything in this book is brilliant and original and true."
> — Polly Platt, Producer, Bottle Rocket
> Executive Producer, Broadcast News, The War of the Roses

JUDITH WESTON was a professional actor for 20 years and has taught Acting for Directors for over a decade.

$26.95 | 314 PAGES | ORDER # 4RLS | ISBN: 0-941188-24-8

24 HOURS | 1.800.833.5738 | WWW.MWP.COM

SETTING UP YOUR SHOTS

SETTING UP YOUR SHOTS
GREAT CAMERA MOVES
EVERY FILMMAKER
SHOULD KNOW

JEREMY VINEYARD

Great Camera Moves Every Filmmaker Should Know
By Jeremy Vineyard   Illustrated by Jose Cruz

BEST SELLER
OVER 27,300 UNITS SOLD!

Written in straightforward, non-technical language and laid out in a nonlinear format with self-contained chapters for quick, on-the-set reference, *Setting Up Your Shots* is like a Swiss army knife for filmmakers! Using examples from over 140 popular films, this book provides detailed descriptions of more than 100 camera setups, angles, and techniques — in an easy-to-use horizontal "wide-screen" format.

Setting Up Your Shots is an excellent primer for beginning filmmakers and students of film theory, as well as a handy guide for working filmmakers. If you are a director, a storyboard artist, or an animator, use this book. It is the culmination of hundreds of hours of research.

Contains 150 references to the great shots from your favorite films, including *2001: A Space Odyssey*, *Blue Velvet*, *The Matrix*, *The Usual Suspects*, and *Vertigo*.

"Perfect for any film enthusiast looking for the secrets behind creating film. Because of its simplicity of design and straightforward storyboards, Setting Up Your Shots *is destined to be mandatory reading at film schools throughout the world."*
— Ross Otterman, Directed By Magazine

"Setting Up Your Shots is a great book for defining the shots of today. The storyboard examples on every page make it a valuable reference book for directors and DPs alike! This great learning tool should be a boon for writers who want to choose the most effective shot and clearly show it in their boards for the maximum impact."*
— Paul Clatworthy, Creator, StoryBoard Artist and StoryBoard Quick Software

"This book is for both beginning and experienced filmmakers. It's a great reference tool, a quick reminder of the most commonly used shots by the greatest filmmakers of all time."
— Cory Williams, President, Alternative Productions

JEREMY VINEYARD is a filmmaker, internationally published author, and screenwriter. He is currently assembling a cast and crew for a crime feature to be shot in 2005.

$19.95 | 132 PAGES | ORDER # 8RLS | ISBN: 0-941188-73-6

DIGITAL FILMMAKING 101

AN ESSENTIAL GUIDE
TO PRODUCING LOW-BUDGET MOVIES
2ND EDITION

DALE NEWTON & JOHN GASPARD

Available January 2007

America's top two gurus of low-budget independent filmmaking are back with the second edition of their popular bestseller.

From script to screen, every aspect of low-budget digital feature production is covered in this updated classic. This second edition provides additional detail on new business structures for the independent filmmaker, looks at camera and editing system options that are available for budgets as low as $8,000, examines new trends in film festivals and distribution, and provides a wealth of information for anyone who has the passion and the zeal to bring their cinematic dreams to life.

"These guys don't seem to have missed a thing when it comes to how to make a digital movie for peanuts. It's a helpful and funny guide for beginners and professionals alike."
        – Jonathan Demme, Academy-Award®-Winning Director, *Silence of the Lambs*

"Gaspard and Newton are the undisputed champs of straight talk when it comes to moviemaking."
        – Timothy Rhys, Publisher and Editor, *MovieMaker* Magazine and *MovieMaker.com*

"Simply put, this is the best book on digital moviemaking I've yet read."
        – *Screentalk* Magazine

"Strong, smart, funny advice for independent filmmakers from people who've gone through the process more than once – and lived to tell about it."
        – Peter Tolan, Co-Creator and Producer, *Rescue Me*;
          Screenwriter, *The Larry Sanders Show*, *Analyze This*, *My Fellow Americans*

"The book is a vast storehouse of ideas of acquiring capital, preproduction, casting, finding a crew, the production process, special effects, post and distribution. *Digital Filmmaking 101* will almost certainly change your perception of getting your project off the ground."
        – *Videomaker* Magazine

When it comes to producing successful movies on a shoestring, JOHN GASPARD and DALE NEWTON, both residents of Minneapolis, MN, know of what they speak. Together they created the award-winning digital feature, *Grown Men*, as well as *Resident Alien* and *Beyond Bob*, two critically acclaimed ultra-low-budget feature films. The first edition of *Digital Filmmaking 101* has been a bestseller, racking up sales of over 15,000 units worldwide.

$26.95 · 309 PAGES · ORDER NUMBER 124RLS · ISBN: 1-932907-23-0

24 HOURS | 1.800.833.5738 | WWW.MWP.COM

MICHAEL WIESE PRODUCTIONS

Since 1981, Michael Wiese Productions has been dedicated to providing both novice and seasoned filmmakers with vital information on all aspects of filmmaking. We have published more than 70 books, used in over 500 film schools and countless universities, and by hundreds of thousands of filmmakers worldwide.

Our authors are successful industry professionals who spend innumerable hours writing about the hard stuff: budgeting, financing, directing, marketing, and distribution. They believe that if they share their knowledge and experience with others, more high quality films will be produced.

And that has been our mission, now complemented through our new web-based resources. We invite all readers to visit www.mwp.com to receive free tipsheets and sample chapters, participate in forum discussions, obtain product discounts — and even get the opportunity to receive free books, project consulting, and other services offered by our company.

Our goal is, quite simply, to help you reach your goals. That's why we give our readers the most complete portal for filmmaking knowledge available — in the most convenient manner.

We truly hope that our books and web-based resources will empower you to create enduring films that will last for generations to come.

Let us hear from you at anytime.

Sincerely,

Michael Wiese

Publisher, Filmmaker

www.mwp.com

FILM & VIDEO BOOKS

Cinematic Storytelling: The 100 Most Powerful Film Conventions Every Filmmaker Must Know / Jennifer Van Sijll / $24.95

Complete DVD Book, The: Designing, Producing, and Marketing Your Independent Film on DVD / Chris Gore and Paul J. Salamoff / $26.95

Complete Independent Movie Marketing Handbook, The: Promote, Distribute & Sell Your Film or Video / Mark Steven Bosko / $39.95

Costume Design 101: The Business and Art of Creating Costumes for Film and Television / Richard La Motte / $19.95

Could It Be a Movie?: How to Get Your Ideas Out of Your Head and Up on the Screen / Christina Hamlett / $26.95

Creating Characters: Let Them Whisper Their Secrets
Marisa D'Vari / $26.95

Crime Writer's Reference Guide, The: 1001 Tips for Writing the Perfect Crime
Martin Roth / $20.95

Cut by Cut: Editing Your Film or Video
Gael Chandler / $35.95

Digital Filmmaking 101: An Essential Guide to Producing Low-Budget Movies
Dale Newton and John Gaspard / $24.95

Digital Moviemaking, 2nd Edition: All the Skills, Techniques, and Moxie You'll Need to Turn Your Passion into a Career / Scott Billups / $26.95

Directing Actors: Creating Memorable Performances for Film and Television
Judith Weston / $26.95

Directing Feature Films: The Creative Collaboration Between Directors, Writers, and Actors / Mark Travis / $26.95

Eye is Quicker, The: Film Editing; Making a Good Film Better
Richard D. Pepperman / $27.95

Fast, Cheap & Under Control: Lessons Learned from the Greatest Low-Budget Movies of All Time / John Gaspard / $26.95

Film & Video Budgets, 4th Updated Edition
Deke Simon and Michael Wiese / $26.95

Film Directing: Cinematic Motion, 2nd Edition
Steven D. Katz / $27.95

Film Directing: Shot by Shot, Visualizing from Concept to Screen
Steven D. Katz / $27.95

Film Director's Intuition, The: Script Analysis and Rehearsal Techniques
Judith Weston / $26.95

Film Production Management 101: The Ultimate Guide for Film and Television Production Management and Coordination / Deborah S. Patz / $39.95

Filmmaking for Teens: Pulling Off Your Shorts
Troy Lanier and Clay Nichols / $18.95

First Time Director: How to Make Your Breakthrough Movie
Gil Bettman / $27.95

From Word to Image: Storyboarding and the Filmmaking Process
Marcie Begleiter / $26.95

Hitting Your Mark, 2nd Edition: Making a Life - and a Living - as a Film Director
Steve Carlson / $22.95

Hollywood Standard, The: The Complete and Authoritative Guide to Script Format and Style / Christopher Riley / $18.95

I Could've Written a Better Movie Than That!: How to Make Six Figures as a Script Consultant even if You're not a Screenwriter / Derek Rydall / $26.95

Independent Film Distribution: How to Make a Successful End Run Around the Big Guys / Phil Hall / $24.95

Independent Film and Videomakers Guide - 2nd Edition, The: Expanded and Updated / Michael Wiese / $29.95

Inner Drives: How to Write and Create Characters Using the Eight Classic Centers of Motivation / Pamela Jaye Smith / $26.95

I'll Be in My Trailer!: The Creative Wars Between Directors & Actors
John Badham and Craig Modderno / $26.95

Moral Premise, The: Harnessing Virtue & Vice for Box Office Success
Stanley D. Williams, Ph.D. / $24.95

Myth and the Movies: Discovering the Mythic Structure of 50 Unforgettable Films / Stuart Voytilla / $26.95

On the Edge of a Dream: Magic and Madness in Bali
Michael Wiese / $16.95

Perfect Pitch, The: How to Sell Yourself and Your Movie Idea to Hollywood
Ken Rotcop / $16.95

Power of Film, The
Howard Suber / $27.95

Psychology for Screenwriters: Building Conflict in your Script
William Indick, Ph.D. / $26.95

Save the Cat!: The Last Book on Screenwriting You'll Ever Need
Blake Snyder / $19.95

Screenwriting 101: The Essential Craft of Feature Film Writing
Neill D. Hicks / $16.95

Screenwriting for Teens: The 100 Principles of Screenwriting Every Budding Writer Must Know / Christina Hamlett / $18.95

Script-Selling Game, The: A Hollywood Insider's Look at Getting Your Script Sold and Produced / Kathie Fong Yoneda / $16.95

Selling Your Story in 60 Seconds: The Guaranteed Way to get Your Screenplay or Novel Read / Michael Hauge / $12.95

Setting Up Your Scenes: The Inner Workings of Great Films
Richard D. Pepperman / $24.95

Setting Up Your Shots: Great Camera Moves Every Filmmaker Should Know
Jeremy Vineyard / $19.95

Shaking the Money Tree, 2nd Edition: The Art of Getting Grants and Donations for Film and Video Projects / Morrie Warshawski / $26.95

Sound Design: The Expressive Power of Music, Voice, and Sound Effects in Cinema / David Sonnenschein / $19.95

Stealing Fire From the Gods, 2nd Edition: The Complete Guide to Story for Writers & Filmmakers / James Bonnet / $26.95

Storyboarding 101: A Crash Course in Professional Storyboarding
James Fraioli / $19.95

Ultimate Filmmaker's Guide to Short Films, The: Making It Big in Shorts
Kim Adelman / $16.95

What Are You Laughing At?: How to Write Funny Screenplays, Stories, and More / Brad Schreiber / $19.95

Working Director, The: How to Arrive, Thrive & Survive in the Director's Chair
Charles Wilkinson / $22.95

Writer's Journey, - 2nd Edition, The: Mythic Structure for Writers
Christopher Vogler / $24.95

Writer's Partner, The: 1001 Breakthrough Ideas to Stimulate Your Imagination
Martin Roth / $24.95

Writing the Action Adventure: The Moment of Truth
Neill D. Hicks / $14.95

Writing the Comedy Film: Make 'Em Laugh
Stuart Voytilla and Scott Petri / $14.95

Writing the Killer Treatment: Selling Your Story Without a Script
Michael Halperin / $14.95

Writing the Second Act: Building Conflict and Tension in Your Film Script
Michael Halperin / $19.95

Writing the Thriller Film: The Terror Within
Neill D. Hicks / $14.95

Writing the TV Drama Series: How to Succeed as a Professional Writer in TV
Pamela Douglas / $24.95

DVD & VIDEOS

Field of Fish: VHS Video
Directed by Steve Tanner and Michael Wiese, Written by Annamaria Murphy / $9.95

Hardware Wars: DVD / Written and Directed by Ernie Fosselius / $14.95

Sacred Sites of the Dalai Lamas- DVD, The: A Pilgrimage to Oracle Lake
A Documentary by Michael Wiese / $22.95